Circle and Oval in
the Square of Saint Peter's

Bernini's Art of Planning

The publication of this monograph
has been aided by a grant from the
Samuel H. Kress Foundation

Frontispiece: Rome, Piazza Obliqua, view, Piranesi's engraving

TIMOTHY K. KITAO

Circle and Oval in
the Square of Saint Peter's

Bernini's Art of Planning

PUBLISHED BY

NEW YORK UNIVERSITY PRESS

for the College Art Association of America

NEW YORK 1974

Monographs on Archaeology and the Fine Arts
sponsored by
THE ARCHAEOLOGICAL INSTITUTE OF AMERICA
AND
THE COLLEGE ART ASSOCIATION OF AMERICA
XXIX
Editor: Lucy Freeman Sandler

SOURCES OF PHOTOGRAPHS

Grateful acknowledgment is made to all those sources who granted the author
permission to reproduce the photographs they have supplied.

Arte cristiana, Figs. 93, 94
Atti della Pontificia Accademia Romana di Archeologia, Fig. 8
Busiri-Vici, *La Piazza di San Pietro,* Figs. 39, 40
Falda, *Il nuovo teatro delle fabriche,* Fig. 36
Cambridge, Mass., Harvard University, Fogg Art Museum, Frontispiece, Fig. 83
Falda, *Il nuovo teatro delle fabriche,* Fig. 36
Ferabosco, *Architettura della basilica di S. Pietro,* Fig. 10
Florence, Alinari, Figs. 2, 3, 31, 78, 81, 82, 84, 85, 95
Florence, Uffizi, Gabinetto Disegni e Stampe, Figs. 44, 47, 80
Fontana, *Templum Vaticanum,* Figs. 13, 54, 62, 86, 87, 88, 89, 90
Frutaz, *Le piante di Roma,* Fig. 64
Letarouilly, Le Vatican, Fig. 63
London, British Museum, Fig. 60
London, Royal Institute of British Architects, Fig. 33
Palladio, *Quattro libri dell'architettura,* Fig. 77
Pozzo, *Perspectiva architectorum et pictorum,* Fig. 38
Rome, Archivio di Stato di Roma, Fig. 76
Rome, Biblioteca Apostolica Vaticana, Figs. 6, 11, 14, 15, 17, 19, 24, 25, 26,
34, 50, 57, 61, 65, 67, 68, 69, 71, 72, 73, 74, 79, 91, 92
Rome, Fototeca Unione, Figs. 20, 21, 22, 23, 66
Rome, Bibliotheca Hertziana, Figs. 7, 12
Rome, Gabinetto Nazionale delle Stampe, Fig. 32
Serlio, *Libro Quinto dell'architettura,* Fig. 48
Swarthmore, Pa., Private Collection, Fig. 27
Vienna, Graphische Sammlung Albertina, Fig. 49
Vignola, *Le due regole della prospettiva pratica,* Fig. 75

TO MY MOTHER AND FATHER

Preface

Gian Lorenzo Bernini is best known as a sculptor. The brilliance of his sculpture is no longer contested. His architecture, by contrast, is not yet as well understood. The number of outstanding studies on Bernini *scultore* that have appeared in the past decade is astounding; all put together, the number of publications on Bernini *architetto* is not as great. My effort in this study is to make a contribution toward the better understanding of this neglected side of the great Baroque artist. More specifically, my aim is to elucidate the nature of Bernini's architecture—its style, principles, and method—more precisely than has hitherto been done.

The Square of Saint Peter's, needless to say, is one of the best known monuments in Rome; it is a work of vast conception and scale and vies with the Colosseum on the map of Rome. For this reason alone, it deserves a monograph, but yet another reason justifies the effort.

Architecture clearly constitutes a significant part of Bernini's artistic production. But in studying Bernini's architecture, one immediately encounters the difficulty of isolating architecture from the artist's *oeuvre*. For architecture and sculpture are inseparably combined in many of his works; and they include not only altars, tombs, and fountains, but also chapels and churches. A great many of these works are certainly better characterized as decorative than architectural, but judgment as to exactly which works of Bernini constitute his architecture is often arbitrary.

The Square of Saint Peter's nevertheless stands apart in Bernini's *oeuvre* as a work that is generally considered strictly architectural; and it is a work from the artist's mature period and of major importance in his career. It is, moreover, especially well documented. In these respects, the Square of Saint Peter's serves my aim particularly well; and this should also explain the special orientation of this study toward the problem of ideation in the process of artistic design. My chief concern is to understand what Bernini understood architecture to be, and I hoped to arrive at this understanding by examining very closely how he developed his architectural ideas—forms and meanings.

Emphasis is accordingly placed on the internal history, as it evolved in the artist's mind, extrapolated from the external history. In this respect, therefore, the study is self-limiting, if also old-fashioned (to some) in method; it relies heavily on visual documentation—rigorous reading of visual forms. No social history, at this time, was attempted.

The kernel of the study began in 1960 as a master's thesis at the University of California, Berkeley; it was subsequently incorporated in a substantially altered form in my doctoral dissertation on Bernini's architecture, which was accepted by the faculty of Harvard University in 1966. The material has since then been further modified, expanded, and rewritten. Research in Rome was made possible in 1969 and 1970 by a fellowship grant from the Old Dominion Foundation Fund of Swarthmore College. I was further aided by grants from the Research Funds of Swarthmore College in purchasing photographs and preparing the manuscript; the Ford Foundation Fund and Mellon Fund also assisted me in making possible the indispensable trip to Rome in the summer of 1972.

Like all writers on Bernini, I am first of all indebted to the late Professor Rudolf Wittkower for many scholarly contributions to the subject, without which this work could not have been started. To James S. Ackerman, *il miglior fabbro,* I owe my profoundest gratitude; he introduced me to art history, guided me through my apprenticeship, and has generously given me assistance, counsel, and encouragement through all these years. I also want to thank John W. Williams, friend and former colleague, who read the manuscript in an earlier form with impeccable care, and Linda Rabben and Mrs. Teresa Klinger, who patiently typed it in its final form. Charles E. Gilbert, as provost of Swarthmore College, graciously helped me obtain research grants. Lucy Freeman Sandler, as editor of this monograph series, was most sympathetic, and I am very grateful to her.

Thanks are also due to the following teachers, friends, and colleagues, who directly or indirectly gave me support through the preparation of my work: Don Cipriano, Maria Cipriano, John Coolidge, Marcello and Maurizio Fagiolo dell'Arco, Howard Hibbard, Irving Lavin, Signora Eniz Longobardi, Naomi Miller, Henry Millon, Charles W. Moore, Ted Musho, Ernest Nash, Hedley H. Rhys, Juergen Schulz, and Eduard S. Sekler. Last but not least, I must thank my wife, Tokiko, who unfailingly gave me her loving support by wisely and artfully leaving me alone through many hours when I had to think alone.

Contents

List of Illustrations

Frontispiece: Rome, Piazza Obliqua, view, Piranesi's engraving

Chronology

July 31, 1656	Bernini appointed.
August 19, 1656	Bernini's first submission, trapezoidal plan, two porticos with offices and dwellings; Congregazione recommends a rectangular plan.
September 8, 1656	False Bernini design, rectangular plan (with an alternative circular plan), a third portico closing the Borgo side.
September 29, 1656	Site clearance started.
End of 1656	Bernini's sketch plan, pseudo-oval; *in situ* demonstration, allegedly put up by the Pope, for determining visibility.
March 17, 1657	Bernini's second submission, oval plan (probably pseudo-oval), single-aisled arcades.
August 28, 1657	Medal I and II, three-aisled colonnades of paired columns, Piazza Retta with corridors, straight *terzo braccio*.
Fall 1657	Medal III, colonnades of single columns.
1658	Colonnade terminations established (tetrastyle drawing); elaborations—cross-passages, twin-pilasters, and graded column diameters.
End of 1658	Vatican Plan (colonnades but not corridors); Bonacina Engraving and Medal IV in preparation; Bernini's *giustificazione* submitted to the Pope.
Early 1659	Counterproject of 1659.
Spring-Summer 1659	Bonacina Engraving in circulation; construction of northern colonnade in progress.
July 30, 1659	Forty-seven columns standing.
August 1661	Northern colonnade completed; Medal V/VI; southern Colonnade begun.

November 18, 1662	Northern half, colonnade and corridor, completed.
April 1663	Scala Regia begun.
April 17, 1666	Southern colonnade completed; Scala Regia completed.
January 22, 1667	Southern corridor and the stairs to the Basilica begun.
February 19, 1667	Revision, clock tower and propylaeum, proposed.
March 19, 1667	The Priorato block demolished.
May 22, 1667	Death of Pope Alexander VII.

Introduction: Oval and Circle

THE SQUARE OF SAINT PETER'S, Bernini's masterpiece, is a composite of three urban spaces (Figs. 1 and 2).[1] Adjoining the Basilica, there is the trapezoid-shaped Piazza Retta; framed laterally by corridors, it is dominated by monumental stairs that lead up to Maderno's facade of Saint Peter's. On the east side, at the terminus of the Via della Conciliazione, there opens another trapezoidal area, the Piazza Rusticucci (now Piazza Pio XII); this is where a propylaeum would have stood, had Bernini's last known revision of February 1667 been brought to completion.

The third piazza, which stretches between these two, is the Piazza Obliqua; we owe the designation to Carlo Fontana.[2] The piazza is oval in plan; it is enframed by two free-standing circular colonnades, each with a fountain within its arc, and a soaring obelisk marks the center of the piazza.[3]

Needless to say, one cannot in reality experience the Piazza Obliqua in isolation; it is only a component of an ensemble, which in turn is a part of a larger urban fabric. It is nevertheless not only the largest of the three components but also the central and most outstanding feature in the ensemble. The oval, moreover, is a unique form in itself; it is striking, engaging, and highly suggestive. Having a strong identity, the oval piazza is in its visual form not only highly legible but also memorable; or it is, in current expression, imageable.[4] We therefore *read* the oval piazza independently even though we may experience it in its total context; and we read in it an image, variously, of the amphitheater, the globe, and the embracing arms of the Church. Furthermore, in planning the general area of the piazza, Bernini, as we shall see, developed this middle part first, and initially as an entity by itself. Obviously, then, the oval of the Piazza Obliqua is central in Bernini's design.

But with regard to this very oval, what we see—and, for that matter, even what we know—contains no little measure of ambiguity.

The Piazza Obliqua, we take for granted, is an oval space. But it does not take us long to realize that the oval of the Piazza Obliqua is only a two-dimensional reality; its outline is complete only in the pavement design. The oval, for this reason, is more manifest in bird's-eye view (Fig. 2); and this is the best remembered view, too, owing to its more frequent appearance in publications. But, even then, what strikes us first is not its oval plan but the two circular colonnades. The image is that of a single, perfectly circular colonnade split in two and pulled apart.

From a more normal, pedestrian's point of view, the colonnades also dominate the scene; framing the facade of Saint Peter's, they swing out powerfully toward us (Fig. 1). Once we are well within the piazza, the colonnades sweep around us, and their circular form is all the more vivid (Fig. 3). Because the oval is so enormous, it is not apparent; its sheer magnitude dissipates its effect. Notwithstanding its oval plan, the space of the piazza thus owes its sense of form to the outline of the two free-standing colonnades.

At this immense scale, the colonnades might well *appear* circular even if the piazza had been truly elliptical in outline. But they *are* circular (Fig. 4). It is today common knowledge that the oval of the Piazza Obliqua is not a true ellipse but an approximate form constructed from two interlocking circles; it is a construction known to us from Serlio's manual (Fig. 5).[5] The large plan of the piazza and colonnades from Bernini's workshop and now in the Vatican (hereafter, the Vatican Plan) confirms this observation (Fig. 6.)[6]

Moreover, the circular form of the colonnades is borne out visually in the layout of the quadruple columns.[7] In each colonnade, they are arranged fanlike on the radii of the arcs they describe. Consequently, when we reach a point halfway across the piazza, we see the columns are aligned, one row behind another in perfect order, presenting to our view a single row of alternating solids and voids (Fig. 4). This effect is obviously so planned that no visitor, alert to architectural forms, should fail to experience it in his normal course across the piazza; for the obelisk blocks the passage in the middle and channels us between it and one or the other of the two fountains, and we inevitably pass very near, if not through the center of the radial system, and this point, as tourists in Rome well know, is actually marked out on the pavement. It is true that the two hemicycles can be experienced only one at a time. The split halves do not realize a circle. The radial unity comes nevertheless as a climax, and the circular form of the colonnade is immediate, tangible, and dramatic.

The oval of the Piazza Obliqua was at one time more frequently taken for the true ellipse which it approximates; contrasted with the circle, the ellipse was regarded as fluid and "dynamic," and characteristically Baroque for that.[8] This view carries little conviction in this instance; it is oversimplifying. We do know that Bernini himself professed predilection for the circle and for regular polygons; we know, too, of his deep reverence for the Pantheon, the paradigm of circular buildings, which he regarded as faultless.[9] It would not be surprising, then, if the oval was for Bernini more a circle than an ellipse. But it is equally simplistic for that to characterize Bernini as being more classicist than Baroque.

The study that follows focuses on this issue and tries to demonstrate that, while the oval was the central element of Bernini's design, the circle rather than the oval was the generative idea in (1) the genesis of the design, (2) its iconography, (3) the layout of the colonnades, and (4) the architect's own revision of 1667.

I   Square into Circle: The Genesis

APPOINTMENT, COURSE OF EVENTS, TOPOGRAPHY

POPE ALEXANDER VII announced his proposal for developing the Square of Saint Peter's in 1656, the second year of his pontificate. The Congregazione della Fabbrica di San Pietro, the committee of cardinals responsible for administering the project, received the announcement at its meeting of July 31 and immediately instructed Gian Lorenzo Bernini to prepare a preliminary study for further discussion.[10] The events of the next several months are fairly clear and can be rapidly summarized.

Bernini was ready with his design in three weeks. He presented it to the Congregazione on August 19. It was probably only a schematic plan; for the architect read an explanation. The committee was generally favorable to it but recommended that the piazza might be lengthened rather than shortened and, if possible, kept uniform in width rather than widened toward the Basilica.[11] On the very same day, the papal *avviso* reported that clearance of the site should soon begin.[12] But this work was actually delayed, probably by the emergence in September of a certain design that falsely claimed Bernini's name; finally, late in September, demolition began near the Campo Santo.[13] In December the Pope authorized the purchase of private houses for demolition.[14] Then, the following spring—on March 17, 1657—Bernini returned to the Congregazione with his second submission: this was an oval plan. This time, the committee found no objection and passed it on to the Pope for his approval.[15]

4

The existing piazza at this time had an awkward, bootlike shape on account of the Vatican premises that wedged into this area from the northwest (Fig. 5).[16] The palaces surrounding the Cortile di San Damaso, built on a higher terrain with a sharp drop on the south side, restricted the usable space immediately in front of the Basilica (Fig. 2). In addition, the stone wall of Nicholas V extended southward from the east corner of the Palace of Sixtus V and joined another wall which ran westward toward the Basilica along the outside of the lower half of the present northern corridor up to a corner of the Cortile. These were, as they still are, the retaining walls establishing the boundaries of the Vatican premises, that rose higher against the low-lying piazza; for this reason, they could not conceivably be disturbed without endangering some of the Vatican palaces.[17]

Other salient features of the site appear on the Map of Rome of 1640 (Figs. 7 and 8), which was an updated version of the Map of 1577 by Du Pérac and Lafréry.[18] On the south side of the piazza, there was a continuous row of buildings, constituting a part of the block called the *isola grande,* most of which housed various offices connected with the Chapter of Saint Peter's; it continued the line of buildings on the Borgo Vecchio, the older of the two main thoroughfares leading into the piazza.[19] Toward the Borgo, the piazza was considerably lower, as indicated by the monumental stairs–Maderno's work–in front of the Basilica.[20] The obelisk, transferred to this location in 1586 under Sixtus V from what was believed to be the site of the Circus of Caligula and Nero, south of the Basilica (Fig. 90), unalterably fixed the grade of this area as well as the axes of the future development.[21] The newest construction on the site was the Tower of Paul V of 1617–18 (Fig. 8), which, together with the adjoining corridor, was a contribution of Ferabosco and Vasanzio.[22] It was surmounted by a clock and housed the "Portone di Bronzo," both of which came from the Palace of Innocent VIII (Fig. 7), which had been demolished to make way for Maderno's facade.[23] Along the path connecting the Borgo Nuovo and the tower there was a fountain, initially set up by Innocent VIII in 1490 but renovated by Maderno in 1613.[24]

FIRST SUBMISSION (AUGUST 19, 1656): THE TRAPEZOID

The design presented to the Congregazione on August 19, 1656, was Bernini's first submission. Bernini's plan does not survive. But it was evidently neither oval nor circular. We can infer from the committee's recommendation that the proposed plan was a trapezoidal piazza, rather squat in proportion and wider toward the Basilica. Other written sources allow us a reconstruction in further detail.[25]

At the meeting of August 19, Cardinal Pallotta, a member of the Congregazione, raised three objections. One was the risk of reviving the plague that had just been put under control; extensive demolition of the existing structures on the site was another; and the third was the stupendous cost for what he regarded an unnecessary display.

The second objection describes the area for clearance and reads as follows:

> A part of the Penitentiaria, the houses of the Cibi, and some other nearby structures will necessarily have to come down if the obelisk is centered on the piazza in relation to the porticoes, and any other site is probably too tight for the proposed buildings for housing the canons; but it must be borne in mind that in laying out a piazza the remaining site [on this block], the street [beyond it], and the Palazzo Cesi are not impaired.[26]

Pallotta assumes that no new proposal could ignore the obelisk and concludes that the project will take up the whole of the *isola grande* and may even extend farther south (Fig. 5).

The cardinal, of course, is not describing Bernini's submission. The content of the three objections, as well as the tone of this particular objection, clearly indicates that he was critical of the very idea of the project, the enterprise itself, rather than of the specific design proposed by Bernini. Moreover, the objections were read at the meeting by proxy.[27] This means that he wrote them without inspecting the proposed design, for there is no reason to assume that he had the privilege of a sneak preview from the architect. But, if the document is not a firsthand description of the lost design that we wish it were, it is still a valuable source of information; for Pallotta undoubtedly knew the program for the design, and a program of some kind was surely read and discussed at the previous meeting (July 30) in order to instruct the architect.[28] Pallotta's text, in other words, can be accepted as describing one aspect of the architectural program.

The clearance described by the Cardinal creates an area around the obelisk that roughly corresponds to the oval piazza as it was eventually built. We learn from this, then, that the general position and extent of the future Piazza Obliqua had already been established in the program. The architect did not decide on them; they were given to him. And the program was defined, in part, by the condition of the site. The obelisk marked the natural center for the new piazza, and the site farther west, immediately in front of the Basilica, was, as we have seen, too narrow for a piazza of the desired magnitude. The trapezoid of Bernini's first design was, therefore, certainly broader than that formed (as we may be tempted to think) by extending the lines of the present corridors; but it would have fallen well within the oval outline of the executed Piazza Obliqua (Fig. 9). Such a trapezoidal area was, in fact, already traced out schematically in the proposed plan of Ferabosco and Vasanzio (Fig. 10), of which, under Pope Paul V, only the northern wing and its tower, mentioned above, had actually been constructed. Bernini's sketch plan must have more or less coincided with their lower piazza in outline.

The *avviso* of August 19, 1656, describes Bernini's porticoes as "covered loggias with offices and dwellings for the Canons and penitentiaries"; [29] thus, they were presumably closed in the rear and two stories high. The fact that they were planned on "both sides of this piazza" suggests that the east side was open toward the Borgo. Since there is no evidence that demolition was contemplated at this time on the northern half of the site, the length of the porticoes was probably fixed by the distance between the Church of Santa Caterina and the buildings of the Swiss Guards.[30]

According to the same *avviso,* the whole stretch from the Priorato to the Campo Santo was marked for clearance. This included two smaller blocks west of the *isola grande.* In this part of the site, a tower and corridor matching those on the north side would have risen, to complete the symmetry stipulated by the obelisk and the new porticoes below. The over-all result was, then, a split-level design dictated in part by the condition of the site but also reminiscent, once again, of the plan of Ferabosco and Vasanzio. The idea of developing only the lower piazza as a new design and completing the existing upper piazza according to the inherited scheme already appears, on the other hand, in Carlo Rainaldi's project, as does the motif of a two-story structure with a loggia below (Fig. 11); this was proposed under Pope Innocent X, Alexander's immediate predecessor.[31]

Bernini was undoubtedly well acquainted with these earlier projects; the plan of Ferabosco and Vasanzio was prepared in 1620 as a part of a monograph on the architecture of Saint Peter's, while Rainaldi's plan was in the file of Pope Alexander VII together with various other papers and plans connected with the project.[32] But the resemblance between Bernini's solution and those of his predecessors signifies, more importantly, that the architectural program was already so closely defined by Bernini's time that it allowed very little leeway so far as the general layout, that is, distribution of architectural elements, was concerned. Still, the choice of a specific form, it must be emphasized, was open to the architect; neither the program nor the topography predetermined it. The trapezoid, therefore, calls for particularly close attention, even though in this regard Bernini was conservative, as we shall see, by any standard.

FLOW AND THRUST: PIAZZA AS PASSAGE

If our limited sources allow us no more than a sketchy plan in our effort at reconstructing Bernini's first submission, it is presumably no less schematic than the architect's own lost plan; and they still provide us with a set of points and lines of crucial boundaries which, even with a margin of error, reveal to us enough of the architect's process of thought.

Both in scale and character, Bernini's trapezoidal piazza was conspicuously modest (Fig. 9). It was nevertheless a very efficient solution. Basically, its form developed the oblique lines of the two main streets of the Borgo, the Borgo Vecchio and Borgo Nuovo, which reached the site of the piazza all the way from the Castel Sant'Angelo. In this way, the piazza gained itself a visible forward thrust, by continuing the very movement embodied in the thoroughfares. Beyond the new piazza, there opened the existing upper piazza, a platform with the portals to the Basilica in the rear, in relation to which the new development formed, in a sense, an oversized vestibule. From the new piazza through the platform to the narthex of the Basilica, there was created a sense of measured progression from a more public space to a more private one, emphasized by the rising grade and the telescoping effects of the three elements that progressively became narrower, shallower, more closed, and less utilitarian.

The tower of Paul V, housing the "Portone di Bronzo," was meant, moreover, to announce the formal entranceway to the palaces of the Vatican premises. The vestibule-piazza was consequently a link from the Borgo, not only to the Basilica, but also to the Vatican Palaces.

Bernini's trapezoidal piazza was, in short, more a parvis than an atrium; even though it was closed laterally, it was open toward the Basilica and, we might say, addressed it. In more general terms, the development is better characterized as an avenue than as an enclosure. The design was primarily directional in concept and expressive of a purposeful movement; it tried to shape "flow" rather than "collection." In this respect, and possibly also in the general form of the portico, Bernini's trapezoidal piazza must have resembled the Campidoglio, then the most formal and venerable of all the piazzas in Rome (Fig 12); and Michelangelo, not without faults otherwise, was to Bernini a divine architect.[33] What he had in mind was most likely a proposition that, as Michelangelo's piazza asserted the civic authority of the Senate over Rome, the new Vatican piazza, with its trails stretching to the Tiber, was to symbolize the papal authority over the Eternal City. The idea, as we shall see, stayed with him.

Obvious as it may be, formal analogy between the two designs is revealing. Bernini's lower piazza is also relatively small; but open toward the rear, it may appear more ample, and also more regular because, without a structure intercepting its lateral lines, the oblique sides cannot be easily estimated as such by sight. On the other hand, isolated totally from the facade of the Basilica, it reads as a self-contained unit and thus dominates the area. To this effect, the centerpiece no doubt contributes greatly, not only the obelisk but also Maderno's fountain; for this would have logically been relocated to a place in front of the obelisk as it later appears on the first foundation medal of August 1657 (Fig. 20). The facade of the Basilica is combined with the two towers and corridors that frame it in front, and these form a single integrated unit detached from the piazza. It is thus apparent that Bernini conceived the whole upper piazza as a framed picture box comparable to the relief plaque that the facade of the Senatorio is in the design of the Campidoglio. On account of the open perspective, however, the forward thrust of the lower piazza is fully released, whereas in Michelangelo's piazza a similar thrust is held back.

This emphasis on forward thrust, however, is not wholly explained by the architect's obeisance to Michelangelo. Bernini was also complying with the tradition defined by a long series of projects for the piazza that had existed before his own, of which he was no doubt well aware. Recurrently and prevailingly, these predecessors of Bernini produced designs that developed the piazza into a grand approach.

Pope Nicholas V (1447–55) planned a rectangular piazza that was narrow and long like the Piazza Navona—five times as long as it was wide; three broad streets with porticoes ran through the Borgo and reached the piazza.[34] Construction of new streets in the Borgo toward the end of the century, the Borgo Nuovo in particular, reflects Nicholas's plan.[35] Sixtus V (1585–90), who raised the obelisk where it now stands, had in mind, in so doing, the clearance of the *spina,* the blocks of buildings between the two streets of the Borgo; this would create a long avenue terminating at the piazza and assuring a vista of Michelangelo's dome from the bank of the Tiber.[36] Although erecting the obelisk was all that came true of Sixtus V's ambitious scheme, the obelisk itself, by its distance from the Basilica, implied a longitudinal concourse so that even Maderno's project for the forecourt became, in recognizing its position, a decidedly axial and directional design.[37] But the idea of opening up the *spina* was subsequently revived under Innocent X (1644–55), and significantly, the author of this new plan for the *spina* clearance was none other than Virgilio Spada, the papal almoner, who in this capacity was then active in the Congregazione and remained so until 1662.[38] These projects and the lesser ones between them emphasized penetration over enclosure and established a tradition that no architect directly concerned with the development of the piazza around 1656 could possibly disregard; Rainaldi's proposal (Fig. 11), insisting on enclosure, was the single notable exception.[39] Emphasizing flow and thrust, Bernini was serving this tradition, and he certainly knew he was. The recommendation of the Congregazione that called for lengthening the porticoes, too, rose surely from the general awareness of the same tradition.

TRAPEZOID RESHAPED: THE SQUARE PLAN

The official recommendation called for a rectangular plan, but this was good only on paper. The porticoes, in actuality, could not be very much longer; space was tight. Even if the buildings of the Swiss Guards had been cleared away, the retaining wall of Nicholas V skirting the Vatican premises blocked the way. The proposed revision, therefore, could only have resulted in a piazza of nearly square plan (Fig. 9). In fact, Bernini himself described it as a square in his *giustificazione;* this is the architect's formal statement in defense of the oval plan, and therefore, though it was written some years later (toward 1659), it deserves special attention.[40]

Bernini relates how one day, instructed by the Pope, he constructed on the site a rudimentary model of the proposed portico in full scale by framing simple beams. The Pope would thus see, judge, and decide for himself the suitable form and height for the new portico.

Immediately, he [the Pope] saw the drawbacks in giving the portico a square plan (*forma quadrata*) in that the height of the portico would block the view of the Palace from the people and from the Palace the prospect of the piazza, this inconvenience being all the greater inasmuch as the Pope, who customarily gives his blessing from the windows [of the Palace] to the pilgrims who arrive on the piazza to receive it in the Holy Year, could do so only from a great distance; and, moreover, in that the piazza would be divided up and thus reduced in size, leaving between the Palace and the portico a dead space where trash could collect and cause noxious vapors to rise to the Palace.

His Holiness saw therefore at once the drawbacks in giving the portico a square plan (*forma quadra*); and with a discernment that is more than human, he decided to give it an oval plan.

In the architect's own account, it is thus unequivocal that the trapezoid of the first submission was immediately revised into a square and subsequently transformed into an oval plan.[41]

The square plan, however, was never official; the oval plan that the Congregazione accepted on March 17, 1657, was Bernini's second submission. A critic (Critic II), who was present at this meeting, wrote afterward a memorandum to the Pope on the new proposal: he was not in favor of the extravagance—"spesa così grande" as he expressed it—but recognized the improvement. In part, it reads as follows: [42]

Having left behind the square, or rather, a part of the parallelogram (*parte rellogramma*), we have avoided a great many difficulties, in particular the problem that the windows of His Holiness [i.e., his apartment in the Palace of Sixtus V] would be lost from view for those [on the piazza] who gather close to the Palace, and we have gained a great many advantages, one of which is the increased spaciousness. . . .

Correcting the word *square,* the elliptical phrase is there undoubtedly to introduce precision; a part of a parallelogram must therefore mean a trapezoid.

For this critic, then, the oval succeeded the trapezoid. But why did he make the slip of mentioning the square at all? Why did he waver? To be sure, the trapezoid of the first submission was rather close to the square in configuration. There is, however, something else to his confusion.

The critic takes two points with regard to the improvement in the new design: visibility and spaciousness. These are, in fact, the very same points that the architect's own account also elaborates. But the *giustificazione* was not written until much later. Was Bernini possibly parroting his critic's words in his own defense? But this is unlikely. The two points are strictly professional in character and central in the new solution. There is, therefore, only one explanation to the correspondence. Bernini himself made these points when he presented his oval plan to the Congregazione.

The change in the form of the plan, we can be sure, was unexpected; it contradicted the recommendation of the committee. The Congregazione, moreover, prone to be on the conservative side, would have been hesitant to accept a change toward something more extravagant unless there was a persuasive argument for it. Yet, the oval plan was apparently received enthusiastically.[43] We can hardly deny that the alleged papal intervention described in the *giustificazione*—that the Pope himself had chosen the oval over the trapezoid—was diplomatically no mean advantage.[44] But, beyond this, the functionalist argument, coming from the architect himself, must have convinced the committee that the merit of the new plan was well worth the change. Understanding this situation, we can readily see that our critic was ambiguous in his description of the discarded plan, because he had heard the architect refer to it as the square plan while he himself knew that it was trapezoidal.

The revision proposed by the Congregazione was to make the trapezoid into a rectangle. But the plan that actually came out of it (assuming the revision was effected in the design process, however ephemerally) was almost square in form; and, moreover, it was unofficial and short-lived at that. It is therefore more accurate to say, contrary to the established view, that no rectangular project ever came into being.[45]

The rectangular project of unknown authorship, described in Carlo Fontana's book, may be regarded a derivative design related to the recommended revision (Fig. 13); its lower half, it is noteworthy, is a square piazza developed about the obelisk.[46] As for the better known version in the Vatican (Fig. 14), often associated with Bernini, we can best identify it with the false Bernini design of September 1656 that delayed the site clearance; it tries to create a unified and enclosed rectangular piazza.[47] Needless to say, both of these plans, failing to recognize the existence of the elevated Vatican premises, would endanger some of the buildings there.

SPLIT CIRCLE: THE FIRST OVAL PLAN

The square plan was a tentative design. To the architect, however, it was crucial since it led immediately to the first oval plan. The *giustificazione* describes how the Pope allegedly hit on the idea. But we also have a graphic demonstration of this development; it is a pen-and-ink drawing in Bernini's hand, heretofore unpublished, from a Chigi codex in the Vatican (Figs. 15 and 16).[48]

The drawing is a quick sketch, but it says a great deal. A straight portico, indicated by two parallel lines, represents the square plan. The new design consists of two circular porticoes and a short straight piece, the *terzo braccio,* closing the east side; these are all as wide as the straight portico and must, therefore, represent utilitarian structures like the earlier ones. The area toward the Basilica would, also as before, follow the plan of Ferabosco and Vasanzio; the sketch shows only the lower half, that is to say, up to the foot of Maderno's steps.

Gain in space and visibility characterizes the new design, exactly as described by the architect and his critic. It introduces, however, one additional feature of enduring significance. The *terzo braccio* betrays a new emphasis on enclosure and collection in contrast to the earlier concern with penetration and flow.

The same emphasis on enclosure characterizes the false Bernini design of September 1656 (Fig. 14). Here, too, a detached portico closes the Borgo side; and, proposing a unified space, the design corrected Bernini's two-part open scheme. That it was officially submitted suggests that it was put forward as a public criticism. So far as the *terzo braccio* was concerned, Bernini's sketch was therefore most likely a response to this pressure. On this basis, we can date the sketch plan early in the fall of 1656; accordingly, the Pope's *in situ* demonstration—be it a fact or fiction— must also be dated at this time.

The sketch prompts a few more observations. The written documents—both the *giustificazione* and the criticism we have cited—speak consistently of the portico rather than of the piazza. The portico was at first square; the portico was then changed to oval. Clearly, the portico, not the piazza, was the architect's overruling interest.[49] The sketch fully corroborates this bias. It shows that Bernini was no geometrician; he was not working with compasses. He was not even shaping space as such. Instead, he created the circular porticoes by reshaping straight ones as though they were malleable; or, more accurately, it was as though he would model his own hands, first holding them out straight and then cupping them. The porticoes, so remodeled, generated an oval piazza.

Significantly, too, the oval of the sketch differs from the executed version; it is a pseudo-oval, a figure consisting, not of a single continuous curvature, but of two full semicircles joined by straight lines.[50] Two semicircles accordingly stand out especially clearly. The rationale for the change of plan from the square to the oval was, as we have seen, spaciousness, visibility, and a sense of enclosure; but these features could be assured just as well by other geometrical forms, for example, by a polygonal plan like Rainaldi's (Fig. 11). We can therefore say that the choice of this particular form—a pair of semicircles—reveals the architect's ulterior, if perhaps still vaguely defined, aesthetic motivation.

In this connection, Bernini's own words describing the form of the "oval portico" gain a special importance for us. The concluding passage of his *giustificazione,* which immediately follows our earlier quotation, runs as follows:

Without knowing the inconveniences [of the square plan] described above, one would surely have thought that His Holiness had insisted on the oval form in consideration of beauty, but the remarkable thing is that he knew how to integrate with beauty both meaning (*il proprio*) and function (*il necessario*); beauty being the circular form, the form that is most pleasing to the eye, most perfect in itself, and most wonderful to make the best use of with straight entablature and single columns; meaning that since Saint Peter's is, so to speak, the mother church to all other churches, the portico accurately expresses her act of maternally receiving in her open arms Catholics to be confirmed in faith, heretics to be reunited with the Church, and unbelievers to be enlightened by the true faith; and, finally, function being overcoming the difficulties as described already.

The beauty of the oval portico, Bernini insists, is its "circular form"; and the phrases that follow—the traditional epithets for the circle—assure us that he was speaking, not merely of curvilinearity, but specifically of two circular arcs that defined the oval.[51]

The pen-and-ink sketch of Bernini's first oval plan records the genesis of the Piazza Obliqua; and it embodies a pair of semicircles. Notwithstanding the *terzo braccio,* the idea underlying the plan was almost certainly a split circle. The sketch plan proves conclusively that in Bernini's mind two circular porticoes preceded the oval piazza. Strange as it may seem, the design of the oval piazza did not start with an oval figure. There was no oval that served as a generative element of design. The circle, instead, was the primordial and archetypal image of the new oval piazza.

II Circle in the Oval: The Image

SECOND SUBMISSION (MARCH 17, 1657): THE ARCADES

THE PEN-AND-INK SKETCH showing the first oval plan was only the beginning, however; and it, too, was short-lived. In fact, it was never submitted. Almost immediately, the architect subjected it to reexamination. The design the *Congregazione* actually received on March 17, 1657, was a modified plan on a different oval and featuring porticoes, too, of a different kind.

According to our Critic II, the porticoes were now free-standing arcades, single-aisled, open on both sides, and articulated with simple pilasters; he finds them too exposed as a shelter, too meager in scale, and too circuitous in circulation.[52] Another witness of the design (Critic I) also submitted a criticism at this time; it proposes the Doric Order and gives an opinion that the arcade might be widened to 24 *palmi*.[53] To judge by a workshop drawing (Fig. 17), Bernini answered the critics with two different solutions, one, a Doric arcade with a single aisle 30 *palmi* wide and the other, like the first, but featuring two aisles 20 *palmi* each.[54] The second alternative, we might hypothesize, was arrived at by doubling the original arcade. Be that as it may, the arcade could not initially have been wider than 20 *palmi* within, or 32 *palmi* including pilasters outside the aisle, in contrast to the executed colonnade, which is 76 ½ *palmi* wide.[55]

It is also a documented fact that the oval of this plan extended well into the Palazzo Cesi to the south and covered the Priorato and Santa Caterina toward the Borgo; not just a little but "molte canne"—so emphasizes our first critic.[56] Even allowing for an understandable stretch, "many" could not have signified fewer than seven. One *canna* being ten *palmi, molte canne* should therefore be at least 60 to 70 *palmi*. There is no discussion anywhere of any change of plan for the upper piazza. We must assume, accordingly, that the clock tower with the "Portone di Bronzo" was to remain; therefore, the arcade should have kept clear of its axis.

Combining these data, we now have the key points for the layout of the arcades, from which we can reconstruct the oval plan of March 17 (Fig. 18). This attempt establishes one fact beyond any doubt; the oval of the arcades was internally larger than the oval of the executed colonnades on both the major and minor axes.

Beyond this single fact, reconstruction must proceed by inference. We may logically expect that the plan at this stage was in some respects related to the previous one, the pseudo-oval of the pen-and-ink sketch. But had the arcades, only 32 *palmi* wide, traced the semicircles of the pseudo-oval, the *terzo braccio* would have barely skimmed the Priorato (Fig. 16). The executed colonnades, on the other hand, almost cover the specified area externally; we are therefore tempted to speculate that the arcades followed the outer course of the future colonnades, including the *terzo braccio,* which then would have been curved. This could well have been the case; the assumption, then, is that, when the arcades were widened and made into colonnades in the next stage of development (to be discussed below), the increase in width was added on the inner arc of the arcade and the new arc had a slightly reduced radius that was exactly, and all too fortuitously we must say, one-third the distance between the newly developed colonnades such that the Serlian oval of this particular relationship, as was adopted in the definitive layout (Fig. 6), fitted in place perfectly (Fig. 5).

A more likely possibility is the one which appears in our reconstruction (Fig. 18). The arcades follow a curvature slightly larger (376 *palmi*) than the outer course of the executed colonnade (37 $\frac{1}{2}$ *palmi*), and the *terzo braccio* is straight rather than curved. The solution is a refinement over the previous one, for besides the area coverage it fulfills three other conditions suggested by additional pieces of evidence. First, the length of the arcade is precisely such that, when properly widened and then extended so as to cover the opening to the corridor like the subsequent colonnade, it would be, together with a matching extension at the other end of the arcade, 950 *palmi;* this dimension is documented on the workshop drawing of an arcade elevation (Fig. 19), which in certain details suggests a later stage of development but represents a revision of the arcade design. Secondly, the minor axis of the piazza is 752 *palmi,* twice the radius (i.e., the diameter) of the circular arcade. This dimension, appearing in the legend on G. B. Bonacina's large engraving (Fig. 24), does not agree with the executed plan, which the engraving illustrates (on which more below); very likely, then, this is residual information from an earlier phase of design. Finally, the form of the piazza is a pseudo-oval so that the *terzo braccio* is straight as it remains so in the initial stages of the colonnade design (Figs. 20-22) that succeeded the arcade design.[57]

FOUNDATION MEDAL (AUGUST 28, 1657): THE COLONNADES

Documents related to the arcade design are scanty, and our knowledge of it is, in consequence, limited. But it was destined to be ephemeral; sooner or later, it would have been dropped because of the problem inherent in the design, a certain incongruity within the system.

A loggia, laid out on a curve and open on both sides, makes two elevations that are unequal in length; the elevation on the outside curve is necessarily somewhat longer. If the two elevations were articulated with arches and these were uniform throughout, pilasters on the outer course would have to be slightly wider to compensate for the extra length of the course. But then, the arcades are rhythmically disparate and create an awkward effect, especially when one experiences them walking down the aisle; and naturally, the wider the aisle, the greater the discrepancy between the left and right, and the more unbalanced the general effect. If arches were eliminated, the differential could be distributed among both the pilasters and the spaces between pilasters; rhythmical discrepancy would then be visually subtler.[58]

The problem effectively explains why in the subsequent revision, as the porticoes were widened from one aisle to three, arcades also became colonnades. This new development took place during the five months following the submission of the arcade design as we learn from the foundation medal of August 28, 1657, of which two versions are known, the first with one fountain and the second with two (Figs. 20 and 21).[59] The porticoes are now wider, consisting apparently of three aisles, and are articulated with colonnades of paired columns; and they are joined to straight corridorlike extensions that reach the facade of the Basilica, replacing the constructions of Ferabosco and Vasanzio and giving rise to the Piazza Retta. On the basis of our reconstruction of the arcade design (Fig. 18), we can hypothesize that as the porticoes were lengthened they had to be curved more to fit the site on the northern side.

One of the critics of the arcade design, Critic II, already indicated, in fact, not only that single-aisled porticoes make a poor shelter but also that arcades would not stand up to the magnitude of the piazza unless pilasters were doubled; Bernini answered him on both counts in the revision but only by enlarging the construction against the intent of the criticism.[60]

The use of paired columns introduced, however, the same sort of incongruity as that in the arcade system since columns would be spaced farther apart from each other in the outer pair than in the inner pair. The design was therefore abandoned before it was fully developed, most likely for this reason, in favor of another featuring colonnades of single columns; this appears on the third foundation medal of unspecified date (Fig. 22).[61]

The designs recorded on these medals are essentially like the executed version in general character. But they are still tentative with regard to details and far from definitive in layout with regard to such specifics as the geometry of the oval, the terminal points of the colonnades, and the axis of the corridor; on all three medals, for example, the *terzo braccio* is still straight, and on Medal III so are the steps separating the two piazzas, thus creating a pseudo-oval reminiscent of the first oval plan.[62]

From this point on, however, planning enters a new phase of development. Earlier, the design developed in a series of experiments, new ideas and new forms coming and going in rapid succession; the new phase, on the other hand, is characterized by a series of elaborations of a single idea. The development led in time to the introduction of cross-passages that intercepted the aisles at key points, as we witness on still another medal (Fig. 23);[63] the *terzo braccio* is now curved, and the colonnades are properly articulated at the key points where cross-passages occur, namely, at the terminations of the colonnades and at three points on the cardinal axes of the piazza.

So far as the Piazza Obliqua and the two colonnades are concerned, we can regard this version the final design. It corresponds to that represented on the Vatican Plan (Fig. 6) as well as the version published in the engraving of G. B. Bonacina (Fig. 24). The latter was expressly commissioned to announce the new papal project far and wide and was presumably in preparation in the spring of 1659.[64] On July 30 of that year, on the other hand, there were already standing on the site forty-seven columns of the northern colonnade, including all the thirty-two of the innermost course;[65] and the layout of the executed colonnades corresponds completely with that represented on the Vatican Plan (Fig. 6). We can be certain, therefore, that the definitive layout of the Piazza Obliqua and the colonnades was established toward the end of 1658, or, at the latest, early in 1659.[66]

The colonnade design was subjected to scrutiny, then, largely through 1658, following the design represented on Medal III. A series of models are reported to have been produced before the end of 1657, but they do not survive.[67] On the other hand, architectural drawings for the Piazza Obliqua ascribed to Bernini and his assistants, of which a sizable number survives, concern for the most part details and refinement;[68] at least two-thirds are from this stage of design, while the remainder are largely later. The western termination joining the corridor was undoubtedly crucial; its solution, evidently neglected till then, received the architect's special attention (Fig. 25).[69] In the meantime, column diameters were worked out in the workshop (Fig. 26).[70] The twin pilaster was then invented for framing the cross-passages; and this was followed by the column-pilaster combination for terminating the middle courses (Fig. 24).[71] Only subsequent to this development could the Vatican Plan be laid out; and, as we already know, the underlying oval was then no longer a pseudo-oval but a Serlian oval based on two interlocked circles (Fig. 5).

It is naturally tempting to associate this particular oval with Bernini's obsession with the circle, especially the image of the split circle with which the oval plan came into being, insofar as it subsumes two circles; but what effect it had on the layout of the colonnades was, as we shall see, of a different order. Introduced only when the design was already well in its final form and ready to be laid out to scale, the Serlian construction, we must therefore suspect, was primarily a practical choice and was of secondary importance in the development of the image, or *concetto,* of the piazza.

OVAL PORTICO: IN FORMA DI TEATRO

The exact form of the arcade plan, submitted in March 1657, must remain largely a conjecture. But we are on much more secure ground with regard to its image; for we have ample evidence that the oval piazza was conceived from the start as an amphitheater.

In modern speech, possibly because of our modern emphasis on space as the primary element of architecture, we speak of Bernini's creation more often as the Square or Piazza of Saint Peter's than as the Colonnades of Saint Peter's; we tend to emphasize his piazza over his colonnades.[72] Piazza or square in current usage came to mean, rather awkwardly if one stops to reflect, a space shaped or defined by buildings into something eminently architectural rather than any open place; it is usually discussed in a class with such enclosed but hypaethral structures as the atrium, *cortile,* and amphitheater. In the seventeenth century, the word lacked this subtlety; in Baldinucci's dictionary (1681), piazza is simply a "luogo spazzioso."[73]

Bernini's own reference to his work as oval portico rather than oval piazza thus betrays, not so much a sculptor's bias, but the semantics of the time.[74] But another designation was current in certain contemporary sources. Bernini's portico was officially called a theater in the papal *avvisi,* the news dispatches that now and then reported the project's progress; typically, it was described as "quel gran teatro attorno la piazza." The phrasing is remarkably precise; for the piazza was already in existence before Bernini's time (Fig. 8), but the "theater" began to rise because of the architect's intervention. Furthermore, the word *teatro* concisely describes as a single creation both the portico *and* the space it encloses.[75]

The term *teatro* could, of course, be used simply as a figure of speech. From another source, however, we learn that the usage was actually far more precise. In Alveri's guidebook of 1664, written when the colonnades were under construction, we read that "[the site] is today surrounded by a splendid portico, which gives it a shape of the theater (*che lo rende in forma di Teatro*)"; and, according to Baldinucci, *teatro* normally indicated amphitheater.[76] Applied to Bernini's piazza, the term *teatro* undoubtedly alluded to a formal analogy; it had obviously to do with the oval form of the piazza.[77]

Once introduced in the *avviso,* the term *teatro* came to be adopted in various other writings as well. In the *avvisi,* it became the established designation; the piazza came to be quite consistently referred to by this term even after the arcades were superseded by colonnades.[78]

But the term was not in use at the very outset; in the *avviso* of September 8, 1656, we still read of the "disegno de' portici," but on December 23 of that year, it was reported that the Pope issued a chirograph for the purchase and clearance of the houses on the piazza "da fabricarvi attorno il disegnato teatro." This is the first appearance of the term; and it was about four months after Bernini's first submission. During these four months, the trapezoid plan, already rejected, was surely discarded and succeeded by the first oval plan (Fig. 15), which we have already dated precisely in this period but placed after the false Bernini design of September (Fig. 14). The possibility that the term *teatro* was initially applied to the trapezoid plan of the summer of 1656 is therefore very slim; and, too, this plan was only schematic and tentative. On the other hand, the first oval plan was also no more than a sketch; it is hardly a sort of thing that can be called "disegnato." Could the *avviso* of December 23 be saying, then, that the arcade design had already been completed?

This, however, puts us in a dilemma. We know that no oval plan was submitted until March 1657. The design with arcades had not yet passed the Congregazione in the December of the *avviso.* The clearance reported in this *avviso,* on the other hand, was surely for creating additional space on the site that the new oval plan required; this covered a larger area than the earlier trapezoid plan, and we have seen that the clearance of the *isola grande* had already been authorized in August and was actually begun in September.[79] The fact that this later clearance was sanctioned by a papal chirograph suggests that the new oval plan was by this time not a mere tentative scheme but already a more or less definitive conception and had taken a rather well-developed form.

The *teatro,* described specifically as already "designed" in the *avviso* of December 1656,[80] could then only be the arcade design, which by this time was fully developed —at least in its general layout and elevation. Another source, in fact, corroborates our conclusion. It is an expense account for the work in carpentry covering the period from November 8, 1656, to the end of 1657, and it lists a series of large wooden models for the new "theater"; the first in the list, and hence to be considered the earliest, is unmistakably for the arcade design since it cites the work "per i primi Archi del Teatro."[81]

The sequence of events, however, now appears impossibly lopsided. Are we to understand that the Pope and the architect perhaps agreed on the oval plan in advance and proceeded without waiting for the official approval of the Congregazione? We are evidently forced to accept this curious conclusion and still another that the informative *avviso* let out the secret, till then known only between the Pope and his architect, by describing the new completed oval design with the new designation, *teatro,* rather than *portico,* and yet with hardly anyone noticing the difference.

The oval plan with arcades was thus sketched out, developed, and completed with the Pope's sanction in the last four months of 1656, and it motivated the introduction of the term *teatro* in the *avvisi* in analogy with the amphitheater. That the oval piazza came to be associated with the amphitheater from the very formative stage of its design is, of course, no surprise. Once the oval plan was accepted as being functionally the most suitable form, the image of the amphitheater should have developed almost spontaneously. For one immediately thinks of the Colosseum, *the* amphitheater of all times and oval monument then without peer. Moreover, the obelisk that predetermined the center of the new piazza came from what was believed to be the site of the Circus of Nero, and the circus and amphitheater are near of kin; Alveri in fact writes in his guidebook we have cited above as though Bernini's "theater" was then rising just where the Circus of Nero had once stood.[82]

The analogy that Carlo Fontana draws between the Piazza Obliqua and the Colosseum in his book of 1694 is therefore hardly a mere literary conceit; he devotes, after all, one whole chapter to this very *paragone.*[83] He claims that the Flavian amphitheater prefigures the modern project of Pope Alexander VII; and he explains that the later work nevertheless surpasses the pagan prototoype not only in magnitude but also in idea and function because it is dedicated "alla Pietà, e Religione, & al Culto di Dio con il Publico bene." Naturally, the analogy rests on obvious similarities between the two monuments. Not only are they both oval in plan and colossal in scale, they are both open enclosures and encompass an "arena." As such neither is a shelter in the normal sense. Moreover, they were both built to accommodate a massive assembly for festive public events.

TWO THEATERS, OR AUDIENCE IN THE ARENA

The Colosseum was surely the most conspicuous building in seventeenth-century Rome; it was also one of the best known and most venerated monuments from Antiquity.[84] Moreover, while in Paris, Bernini actually proposed an amphitheater like the Colosseum for the space between the Louvre and the Tuileries.[85] A natural analogy, therefore, like that which Carlo Fontana subsequently developed, could hardly have escaped Bernini's mind. Yet it must be acknowledged that we know of no reference to an amphitheater of any sort in Bernini's own account of his portico. But we have reason to believe that an image of the amphitheater did, in fact, exist in the architect's consciousness at this time.

In the well-known production of the *Due Teatri,* first given in 1637, Bernini developed a simulated amphitheater of a very elaborate kind.[86] This is, of course, the best known of Bernini's theatrical works, but a recapitulation is in order.

According to Massimiliano Montecuculi, who witnessed the performance, the stage was prepared with "a flock of people partly real and partly only feigned" so arranged that, when the curtain had fallen for the opening of the play, the audience saw on the stage another large audience who had come to see the comedy. Two braggarts, played by Bernini himself and his brother Luigi, then appeared on the stage, one facing the real audience and the other the fictitious; and recognizing each other in no time, they went on to claim, each in turn, that what the other saw as real was actually illusory, each firmly convinced that there was no more than one theater with its audience in that half he was facing. The confusion of realities in mirror image thus heightened, the two finally decided "that they would pull a curtain across the scene and arrange a performance each for his own audience alone." Then the play was performed to the real audience, that is, the main act to which what preceded was only a pleasant prelude. But through the play another performance was supposed to be taking place simultaneously on the second stage introduced by Luigi; the play was, in fact, "interrupted at times by the laughter of those on the other side, as if something very pleasant had been seen and heard."

At the end of the play, the two braggarts reappeared on the stage together to reaffirm the "reality" of the illusion. Having asked each other how they fared, the impresario of the fictitious performance answered nonchalantly that he had not really shown anything but the audience getting up to leave "with their carriages and horses and accompanied by a great number of lights and torches." Then, drawing the curtain, he displayed the scene he had just said he had shown to *his* audience, thus rendering complete the incredible reversal of reality and illusion to the confused amazement of the real spectators, who were now finding themselves ready to leave and caught in the enchanting act of feigning the feigned spectators.

According to Bernini's own account of the play, which Chantelou got from him in 1665, this final scene with a crowd of people and their horses and carriages was actually a moonlit view of "la place de devant Saint-Pierre." The production of 1637 may or may not have featured the piazza; Montecuculi does not specify. If the piazza had been shown, it was naturally without any portico. In his reminiscences, on the other hand, Bernini could have hardly avoided a montage of the old scene and the new *teatro,* then nearing completion. Conversely, the *Due Teatri* might well have existed in his mind as he evolved the oval plan for the piazza several years before.[87]

The *Due Teatri* involves two kinds of illusionism. On the one hand, there is a sense of reversal between the stage and the auditorium, with which the play begins and ends; the spectators, seeing another audience on the stage, begin to suspect that they occupy the stage. There is, on the other hand, an effect, different from the first, that there are two theaters, placed face to face and forming, thus joined together, an amphitheater;[88] the stage then becomes the arena in the midst of the encircling audience.

That the program for the piazza implied certain analogous effects should have been immediately evident to Bernini. Of the ritual requirements, two were of paramount importance: the papal benediction of Easter Sunday (Fig. 27) and that of the Holy Year. Bernini, who was deeply religious, could not have failed to appreciate the drama of these solemn yet festive occasions, on which he, too, might have stood among the exultant crowd to receive the grace of God.[89] And, certainly, he was vividly aware that the Pope, who administers the ceremony as the Vicar of Christ, actually is only a catalyst in this sacred drama. The protagonists in these spectacles are indeed the recipients of the blessing; and they occupy the arena of the holy amphitheater. The piazza is the stage upon which the ritual is consummated.

The Easter blessing is bestowed from the Benediction Loggia above the central portal of the Basilica; in the Holy Year, the Pope gives his blessing from a window of his private apartment in the Palace of Sixtus V. We have already seen that the reciprocal visibility between the Pope and the populace was the central architectural problem in the development of the plan; it may have suggested the oval plan and did certainly justify its adoption. The problem is also one that is familiar to every scenographer and would have been solved by drawing lines of vision on the plan between the respective position of the Pope and the limits of the piazza; we know Bernini did use such lines later on in determining the position of his propylaeum (Fig. 72).[90] But even if he did not actually draw such lines, the mere thought of this inevitable analogy would only have revealed the very inversion that the Pope at the focus of attention is really more like an honored guest in the royal box overlooking the stage (Fig. 27).

The oval piazza could thus be readily envisioned as the amphitheater of the Church Militant, the faithful in action; then it would immediately call to mind the arena of Christian martyrs like the Circus of Nero and, more importantly, the Colosseum. The choice of the arcade for the elevation of the new portico, instead of the colonnade as in the form in which it was eventually executed, can hardly be separated from this association; the arcade was a natural choice for the new Colosseum. It is true, on the other hand, that the arcade is a very common architectural form; the trapezoid plan, had any elevation been worked out, might have featured it, and the old Benediction Loggia outside the atrium, built in the Quattrocento and demolished to make way for Maderno's nave and façade, may well have sanctioned its use. But the crucial point to keep in mind is the conjunction of the three elements: the oval plan, arcade elevation, and analogy with the Colosseum.

The arcade, not the colonnade, was the architectural form to have been initially, and therefore specifically, associated with the oval of the new plan, whereas the colonnade was a motif that was introduced subsequently and therefore newly superimposed on the oval plan. It must be emphasized that the arcade, not the colonnade, must thus hold the primary clue to the meaning of the Piazza Obliqua.[91]

In this connection, the combination of Doric columns with Ionic entablature, adopted in the executed colonnade (Fig. 28), deserves our special attention. The lowest Order of the Colosseum actually features the same combination, although this is not widely known (Fig. 29). With regard to the Order used in Bernini's arcade design, we know only that it was not Doric. In any case, the eventual adoption of the combined Order certainly found precedence and full justification in the Colosseum.[92] It must be added, too, that this combination, which Wittkower called "unorthodox," was more common by Bernini's time than is generally thought; examples abound in Rome (Fig. 30).[93]

THE AMPHITHEATER OF THE CHRISTIAN UNIVERSE

If the *Due Teatri* prompted the image of the amphitheater, this in turn held in store another level of meaning. As Bernheimer has shown, the idea of "inserting the amphitheater on the stage at the beginning or at the end of the play" goes back in tradition to the Florentine wedding festivities of the sixteenth century.[94] Attempts were first made in the *intermezzi* of these occasions to reverse the auditorium and the stage and eventually to merge them scenographically into one complete amphitheater. Circular in form, the amphitheater would effectively draw the attention of the audience from the stage to the courtly spectacle in its midst; surrounded by the ladies of the court "shining like a series of scintillating stars," the princely pair to be wed would receive their diadems, while mythological personalities come out of the play and, singing eulogies, descend upon them—so a witness describes a scene at the wedding of Ferdinand de' Medici and Christine de Lorraine in 1589.[95] The scene evokes a heavenly coronation like that of the Virgin in the theater of the Blessed above. In this way the circular form of the classical amphitheater also realizes the Christian idea of the celestial world. The imagery was by no means new; it was well established in the Renaissance pictorial convention (Fig. 31). But it was never so complete nor so real.[96]

From the turn of the century, the image like this was no longer a rarity in the theater of *intermezzi* (Fig. 32).[97] Undoubtedly, Bernini was thoroughly familiar with the tradition of this courtly theater. The *Due Teatri* was, in a sense, a parody of its conventions; the finale, showing the "audience" on the way home, concluded with a properly inverted climax—the appearance of Death, who rides in with his footmen and "finishes all." [98] So, too, he was surely aware of various artistic potentialities such a theatrical experience suggested. He must have recognized that the extravagance of the festive theater was not amiss for expressing the glory and splendor of the religious spectacles that the piazza was to accommodate (Fig. 27). It is hardly surprising, therefore, that his colonnade, adorned with a balustrade and row of statues, came to resemble the architecture of the Teatro Olimpico in Vicenza (or its derivative in Sabbioneta), which was undoubtedly based on Palladio's own reconstruction of the ancient theaters like that at Pola (Fig. 33);[99] nor is it fortuitous that the piazza, however slightly, dips toward the center (Fig. 3), echoing the trough shape that characterizes the amphitheater.

But, more important, Bernini must have readily seen that the amphitheater promised a powerful metaphor. In the Holy Year, pilgrims gather on the Piazza Obliqua from the four corners of Christendom; the Easter blessing, administered *urbi et orbi,* is extended to Rome itself, the *Caput Mundi,* and symbolically to the whole world. The oval piazza is not only the globe; it is also the whole universe revolving around the sun, symbolized by the obelisk.[100] But that is not all. Overhead, there reigns, invisibly but magnificently the heavenly theater of the Church Triumphant, or so it was felt and understood, as echoed materially in the circle of saintly statues above the balustrade. The Piazza Obliqua is thus most completely the Theater: the amphitheater of the Christian universe.[101]

This was Bernini's first and, I believe, primary *concetto* for the Piazza Obliqua. Some years later, Bernini expressed a different idea; in his *giustificazione,* as we have seen, he explained the colonnades as the maternal arms of the Church, the matrix of Christianity, held out to receive believers and unbelievers alike. The imagery, appropriate to the executed design with colonnades, applies less aptly to the arcades; for these were architecturally detached from the Basilica and, in consequence, the oval piazza was a relatively self-contained space. Between the Piazza Obliqua and the Basilica, there still intervened the upper piazza of Ferabosco and Vasanzio. The image of maternal arms evidently could come up only later; and, in writing his *giustificazione,* Bernini presumably suppressed a reference to the amphitheater only because this was obviously no longer as vivid an image as the other, once the arcades became colonnades that joined straight corridors extending from the Basilica. But the generative image was not readily obliterated.

PIAZZA AS ENCLOSURE: A DEPRESSED CIRCLE

The document of particular interest to us at this point is the chalk drawing by Bernini showing a tetrastyle gateway (Fig. 34). In the sequence of events between 1657 and 1659 that we have outlined earlier, the drawing is best understood as the point of departure for the elaboration phase of design and should immediately follow the development of the colonnade of simple columns (Fig. 22).

The tetrastyle of the drawing is surmounted by the clock of Innocent VIII from the tower of Paul V, which means that the tower is now destined for demolition. The new gateway, in other words, is clearly meant to supersede the tower as a landmark for indicating the entrance to the Vatican Palaces, and the old tower is already missing from the view on Medal I; for this reason, Wittkower erroneously thought that the drawing represented a stage of design preceding the colonnade of paired columns. A close analysis proves, however, that this is not the case.

The plan to the right of the tetrastyle, to judge by its tight spacing, was evidently drawn only after the elevation was complete. Although it is a quick sketch, reconstruction of the process of completing the drawing (Fig. 35) shows that it contains three stages of thought. The earliest portion is a simple diagram stating that the tetrastyle (four short and emphatic strokes) will be a direct link between the Vatican (two lines at right angles) and the piazza (simple oval); by implication, it says that the tetrastyle will appear at the terminal segment of the colonnade and serve as a frame for the "Portone di Bronzo" at the end of the corridor. The second installment starts with the indication of the three colonnades, which is incomplete for lack of space; it summarizes the idea that the tetrastyle should appear at the end of the extended axis of the Borgo Nuovo (two lightly drawn vertical lines) and be preceded by one of the fountains (a little circle). In sketching out this idea, it was found that the first four strokes were out of position, and a correction (dark and emphatic) was introduced to their right by repeating, however, only the right half.[102]

Finally, a diagonal line was drawn in to study the effect of the tetrastyle together with its duplicate on the opposite side as viewed from the terminus of the Borgo Nuovo. A passing thought probably came to Bernini's mind at this moment to appropriate the gateway with the clock for the *terzo braccio,* that is, providing only one tetrastyle at the center instead of two placed apart; at this position its double meaning is most explicit—the tetrastyle signifying the Basilica (which façade it echoes) and the clock the Vatican.[103] This idea was not recorded on the sketch because the main colonnades were the issue at hand; but, as we shall see, it was revived later on in the revision of 1667. In the meantime, the clock disappeared from the design, and the cross-passage to the corridor was given a simpler opening with two projecting columns (Fig. 24: bottom left). The sketch at the same time led to the idea of creating cross-passages on the cardinal axes of the piazza (Fig. 25). That these two representations closely followed each other is supported by the decoration that crowns the cross-passages; it adopted the tetrastyle of the chalk drawing with no change except for the stemma of the Chigi Pope that replaced the clock.[104]

The sketch plan under discussion is of special importance, however, in relation to the pen-and-ink drawing of the incipient oval plan (Fig. 15). For the piazza is now described unequivocally as a single oval figure, not as two semicircles. The oval, moreover, is delineated with long sweeping strokes that emphasize the continuity of its circumference; it is, in this respect, well in conformity with the design on Medal III (Fig. 22), in which columns, now isolated and therefore rhythmically more compressed, seem to continue interminably and, moreover, still conceal the opening to the corridor rather than isolate it. The new oval, in other words, suggests a fluid form.

The new sense of form is nevertheless already manifest in the first colonnade design (Fig. 20). In spite of the newly created Piazza Retta, the oval piazza is a relatively self-contained area comparable to the closed figure of the sketch plan; for ground levels change along the oval outline at the three openings between the colonnades. Because of this and the continuous entablature, we are compelled to read the whole group more as a loop of colonnade interrupted at three places than as an ensemble of two concave units and a connecting piece. G. B. Falda's print accurately captured this effect (Fig. 36).[105] But here is a remarkable fact. On the earlier of the two versions of the medal, the piazza features one fountain, rather than two, placed in front of the obelisk; the closed oval was introduced in the design without bifocalism.[106] The fountain was subsequently duplicated and arranged laterally, but the result was still basically monofocal; for the obelisk in the center soared high and dominated the scene.

It is therefore evident that the changed perception did not arise from an interest in the oval as an elongated and fluid or "dynamic" form; nor did it develop from the image of the oval inherent in the Serlian construction of two interlocked circles. Rather, it suggests insistence on a centralized form with the obelisk as its single focus. In the initial stage of the colonnade design, then, the oval, now complete in outline, is conceived as another variant of the circle. In place of the split circle, we now have a circle that has been flattened out or depressed to fit the limited site. As such, the piazza asserted once again that image of the circle which the earlier two detached semicircles expressed in another way.

In short, the circle remained the underlying formal image; it was made explicit in two different manifestations. In one respect, what is new in the new form, then, is a sense of enclosure as opposed to penetration. In this respect, the depressed circle, as opposed to the earlier split circle, reverses the emphasis that had prevailed in the earliest stage of planning (Fig. 37, a-b) and reinforces the image of the amphitheater (c-f), which came into being with the arcade design.

The amphitheater, in Renaissance thought, was understood to be circular, notwithstanding surviving examples, especially the most spectacular of all, the Colosseum; the theory found support, above all, in Vitruvius and was fully elaborated by his commentators Cesariano and Barbaro.[107] Andrea Pozzo's "Colosseum," which he published in his perspective treatise, is actually still circular (Fig. 38), as were the examples given by Francesco di Giorgio.[108] Ideally, Bernini's new piazza therefore had to be a perfect circle. Seeing that the existing topography prevented it, he sought a solution in a nearest approximation—a split circle at first, then a depressed circle.

It must be stressed at this point that Bernini's concern with the circle did not issue from the image of the circle as a geometrical abstraction, but rather from that of the concrete architectural form of the amphitheater. This is in striking contrast to the position taken by the Renaissance theorists from Alberti to Palladio, for whom the ideal church plan would be, or approximate, a circle because the circle as a form is readily associated with such abstract ideas as unity, uniformity, and perfection, and can therefore be regarded a visual symbol of the deity.[109] It is true that Bernini's own understanding of the amphitheater was rooted, as we have seen, in this tradition of thought so that we might validly argue that it was the architects' innate classicist bias, to begin with, that gave rise to his interest in the amphitheater. The important distinction, however, is that in Bernini's case the viewer is first led to a concrete image rather than abstract form in order to reach an idea. Bernini's *concetto,* in other words, was eminently perceptual.

It is also in this regard that Bernini differs from the author of the set of drawings from the Brandegee Collection, which Wittkower convincingly and definitively characterized as the Counterproject of 1659.[110] The critic, too, advocated a circular plan (Fig. 39), but his concern was the circle per se, which was to symbolize such ideas as the eternity and universality of the Church;[111] in consequence, he was critical of Bernini's deformed circle and insisted that the piazza be perfectly circular regardless of the given topography (Fig. 40), for it was essential for his more emblematic symbolism that the circle be a physical existence and not merely a visual phenomenon. Needless to say, the critic failed to see for this reason, and in spite of the *giustificazione,* which he apparently knew, that the oval, in Bernini's *concetto,* was indeed a circle.[112]

It is therefore misleading to say, as Wittkower proposed, that Bernini's *concetto* is no more than a metaphor; it is, rather, more than a metaphor because it assumes in the first place, and in effect reinforces, an architectural bond that is more than a similarity of isolated abstract qualities. The bond is indeed a real one.

We might say that Bernini's "oval portico" is not merely *like* an amphitheater in this or that respect, but *is* itself one despite obvious differences; and this fact, moreover, is visually verifiable, or at least it was expected to be. It is this concreteness and directness, rather than the attributes of the "ellipse" as a form, that perhaps more precisely qualify Bernini's design of the Piazza Obliqua to be called Baroque.[114]

III Circle and the Oval: The Geometry

OVATO TONDO: THE STANDARD OVAL

FOLLOWING THE DRAWING with a tetrastyle, Bernini sketched out a study for the western end of the colonnade (Fig. 25); the point of the drawing was to coordinate the cross-passage at this location with the opening to the corridor.[115] The corridor, in consequence, was now rigidly joined to the colonnade, as we see on Medal IV (Fig. 23), so that the two elements became a single extended arm;[116] Bernini's drawing accurately records this perception and suggests that his second *concetto*—the colonnades as the arms of the Church—dates only from this time. Surely by the time the Vatican Plan came into being in the winter of 1658–59, Bernini was ready to give a verbal summary, his *giustificazione;* and it was here that this new imagery was first articulated. Yet this did not mark the end of the first *concetto.* It remained in the design, and this is confirmed by a closer examination of the Vatican Plan and the Bonacina Engraving that followed, especially the subtle geometry that underlies the layout of these plans.

We have already said that the compass marks and construction lines, still discernible on the Vatican Plan, verify our observation that this layout is based on an oval constructed from two circles (Fig. 41).[117] First published by Serlio in the First Book of his influential manual,[118] the oval of this particular construction was designated *ovato tondo* in some seventeenth-century treatises.[119]

The ovals in Serlio's First Book constitute the first published demonstration of oval geometry in the Renaissance.[120] Serlio illustrates here four different ovals and asserts that he is demonstrating four different methods of constructing ovals (Fig. 42). Oval construction rests, however, on one principle. Therefore, there is basically only one method. Serlio illustrates the general principle in his first oval. The remaining three represent three special cases.

The principle of oval construction is a diamond defining the four centers for the four arcs of the oval. Serlio employs a pair of V's (or isosceles triangles), one of which is inverted and superimposed on the other (Fig. 42, I). The apexes of the V's and their intersection points furnish the four centers required. It is readily seen that two factors can be varied at will: the angle of the V, which controls the apportionment of four circular segments, and the length of its arms, which regulates the radii of the arcs. These two factors, in short, determine the precise configuration of the oval. Serlio simplifies the matter by eliminating the first of them, however. He specifies V's of the equilateral triangle ("triangoli perfetti di lati uguali"), and that is what he illustrates; although he does not explain, this assures a generally balanced distribution of segments. The radii of the arcs may still be shortened or lengthened at will in order to obtain, respectively, a longer or stouter (and rounder) oval.

In each of Serlio's three remaining illustrations, however, the oval is fixed in configuration. Since the V's are inscribed in a specified geometrical frame of squares or circles, the two variable factors are both eliminated, and the configuration is predetermined. The ratio of the axes, x/y, is consequently a constant for each example.

Two of the three fixed ovals (Fig. 42, II and III) are based on the diamond of right angles; this accounts for the characteristic long sweep of the larger arcs. They differ markedly from each other in internal geometry (three circles versus two squares), but one is basically like the other except for the change in the radii of the arcs. The first of these, to Serlio, is especially egglike ("somiglia molto al uovo naturale").

The last of Serlio's fixed ovals (IV), the *ovato tondo,* represents one specific instance of his very first illustration. In comparison with the other two fixed ovals, this one is noteworthy for the order of its internal geometry. Circles and equilateral triangles are perfectly interlocked in it and yield simple ratios (1:1, 1:2, and 1:3) in the relationship of its parts. The four arcs are equal in length because the larger arc is twice the smaller in radius but half in angle (60° versus 120°); and the major axis of the oval is triple the small radius. The lucid geometry of this oval undoubtedly impressed Serlio; he made a special comment regarding its versatility, simple construction, and inherent beauty. It is, he wrote, "assai grata all'occhio, et da servirsene à più cose per la facilità di farla, et per la dolcezza sua."

By the unique *dolcezza* of this oval, Serlio must have had in mind proportion on the one hand, and a sense of perfection suggested by its regular geometry on the other. But in conjunction with the "appeal to the eye," we can best understand the term as fullness; for, certainly, he could not have meant grace. In distinction from the other two, the *ovato tondo* possesses visibly bulging "haunches" (Fig. 43). It is not significantly shorter or stouter than the others in proportion (expressed in x/y),[121] but the haunches create an impression of roundness. This fact also explains the later nomenclature, *ovato tondo;* by contrast, Serlio's first two fixed ovals were called, respectively, *ovato longo* and simply *ovato.*[122]

The *ovato tondo* is characteristically "round" and "regular." But as Serlio himself observed, it is remarkably easy to construct. In this respect, it is indeed unsurpassed. The initial circle automatically yields the center of the second; and one can do away with the V's altogether since the interlocked circles generate the four points required. The whole procedure can be completed, indeed, with a pair of compasses alone and in four quick swings at that. Significantly, this technical abbreviation was already suggested in Peruzzi's sketch, which was Serlio's source (Fig. 44): two quick circles and two finishing arcs.[123] No such abbreviation is possible with the two other fixed ovals. The principle, moreover, works equally well with two circles overlapped at various distances as with a string (Figs. 45 and 46). Having mastered it, one could in fact dispense with the general method of the first illustration altogether; but Serlio apparently ignored this remarkable fact.[124]

The three fixed ovals certainly vary in character and feeling; the fullness of one, for example, is in contrast to the slimness of another. But the difference is immaterial at the scale of most architectural projects; as a shape one is as good as any other. All three, moreover, are equally conducive to triangulation. An architect would therefore choose among them on the basis of some other factors. To some the lucid geometry of the *ovato tondo* may be an indispensable intellectual prop. Serlio himself recommended this particular oval for its beauty and utility, and this might influence a choice. But no draftsman would ever overlook its superb technical simplicity, which no other oval possesses. It is virtually ready-made; it comes, so to speak, with compasses. Except in those cases where an oval of unusual configuration is either desired (e.g., for proportion, internal articulation, and other special effects) or necessitated (generally because of limited space, as in the design of chapels, vestibules, staircases, and similar internal halls), the *ovato tondo* is the only natural and logical choice.

Since its first publication, Serlio's First Book remained in wide circulation well into the seventeenth century. It was republished in Venice about 1551 and in 1568, and subsequently, as a part of *Tutte l'opere d'architettura et prospettiva*, in 1566, 1568–69, 1584, 1600, 1618, 1619, and 1663.[125] All of Serlio's ovals were therefore equally well known to architects of the sixteenth and seventeenth centuries. Yet, in practice, the *ovato tondo* was the overwhelming choice, and the only conceivable reason is its technical advantage.

Surveying major oval buildings and projects from the sixteenth and seventeen centuries, we discover that Serlio's two other fixed ovals were hardly ever in use, while the *ovato tondo* appears in most of them (Figs. 47-50);[126] a few exceptions, however, include Sant'Andrea al Quirinale.[127] It should also be mentioned in this connection that Vignola alone can be credited for inventing a new oval, which characteristically surpasses the *ovato tondo* in rational structure (Fig. 51); its core is composed of Pythagorean triangles (3:4:5) so that the radii of the arcs as well as the axes of the oval are expressible in whole numbers.[128]

The *ovato tondo* was, in short, the standard oval in architectural practice—at least in Bernini's Italy. The true ellipse was not unknown (Fig. 52); but awkward to plot, it was impractical for use in workshops.[129] While several forms of oval were known in treatises, there was in practice only one standard form. Given this condition, it is more likely that an *ovato tondo* was adopted in the definitive plan of the Piazza Obliqua as a matter of course rather than toward a specific artistic purpose; the choice, therefore, may well have been an assistant's rather than Bernini's own. The Vatican Plan itself, so far as its actual draftsmanship is concerned, was largely a mechanical chore, after all.

It is, in fact, noteworthy that the *ovato tondo* almost forces a system of triangulation, and yet the layout of the Vatican Plan (Fig. 6) shows no trace of such an attempt. The construction lines of the oval have no bearing on the layout of the colonnades. The innermost columns follow the circumference of the oval; but rather than centered on it, they are laid out immediately outside the line and tangent to it. The *ovato tondo,* in other words, was of interest, not for its geometry, but for its outline. This is in striking contrast to the case of most oval projects (Figs. 47-50); layout by triangulation was actually a rule. All this suggests that the choice of this particular oval was no more than a practical one.

On the other hand, we cannot exclude for this reason alone the possibility that Bernini based his design on some aspects of the *ovato tondo;* after all, if he did not himself execute the plan, he certainly supervised it. There is, to be sure, a certain bond between the oval and the plan that is almost self-evident. The image of the split circle, each half with its own center and its own radial alignment, is entirely consistent with the bifocalism of the interlocked circles that underlies the *ovato tondo;* one may be seen as a corollary to the other. A causal relationship between them may indeed seem difficult to deny. But we have reason to question the matter.

LONGITUDINAL VERSUS TRANSVERSE OVAL

There is, however, another factor that has to be taken into consideration. Bifocalism, in the first place, is not peculiar to the *ovato tondo,* nor for that matter the presence of circular arcs. In fact, all elliptical figures, true or approximate, are bifocal; [130] and all ovals, however constructed, consist of circular arcs. [131] But, in the context of architectural design, these two properties—bifocalism and circularity—have more to do with orientation rather than with configuration.

Bifocal structure emerges clear and concrete only in the transverse oval—*in any* oval, that is to say, regardless of its configuration insofar as one approaches or enters it along its short axis (Fig. 53, top). In such a plan, moreover, the axis of approach not only counteracts the major axis of the oval and thus mitigates its elongated character; it also sets apart the two smaller concavities, which normally encompass an obtuse angle and are therefore conspicuously rounder, too. [132] In short, transverse use brings out in the oval, not only its two centers, but also its more visibly circular arcs. In the longitudinal oval, by contrast, the two centers inevitably merge in the axis of approach, and this, so reinforced, splits the figure lengthwise, penetrates its rounder ends, and accentuates its elongation (Fig. 53, bottom). [133] Orientation, insofar as it modifies proportion, is thus an element of form.

Not the *ovato tondo* as such but, rather, the specific fact that it was used in transverse disposition therefore accounts for some of the more salient features of Bernini's oval piazza. Conversely, had Bernini's concern been the circular arcs in the oval rather than the oval itself, this would have been the only way. This fact, moreover, is particularly noteworthy, and we are therefore forced to put a great deal of weight on it, because while the choice of an *ovato tondo* followed one convention, the transverse use violated another.

In Bernini's Italy, oval churches were almost invariably longitudinal in plan; and it was in church design that architects of his time found major examples of oval building. There were not many oval churches within their knowledge, to be sure; but they were new as a type and therefore more noteworthy, and they were undoubtedly more carefully noted. The Piazza Obliqua (though not a church) and the nearly contemporaneous Sant'Andrea al Quirinale were exceptions to the rule.[134]

The preference for the longitudinal oval in church design is not unrelated to the fact that the oval is an oblong figure. We must recognize, however, that the axial and elongated property of the oval may suggest but does not in itself stipulate the longitudinal use in architecture. For the oval is by definition ambivalent in character. It is at once round and oblong, as we read in Baldinucci's definition, *tondo bislungo*.[135] Either of the two properties may be capitalized in the plan by circulation, articulation, or both. Entrance may be provided at any one or more points on the circumference, on either of the cardinal axes or at any point between them. The path of circulation may follow round the circumference or through the center. It may be blocked, dissolved, or diverted and redirected; if continued through, the axis of approach may still completely penetrate the form or it may be thwarted by a counteraxis. Peruzzi emphasized the circularity of the oval in some of his projects; in one of them, for example, the colonnade goes all around uninterrupted (Fig. 47). Serlio, on the other hand, emphasized the cross-axis by giving the two lateral chapels dominance and clustering secondary chapels in triplets on the narrower ends of the oval (Fig. 48). But in later oval churches the long axis is almost invariably given prominence (Figs. 49 and 50).[136]

It was undoubtedly the enduring liturgical tradition that sanctioned the longitudinal oval in church architecture. For the inevitable focus at the altar and the sense of directed movement it generates naturally suggested a scheme in which the two nodal points—the main portal and the high altar—are located as far apart from each other as possible and yet absorbed in one single axis.

The Counter-Reformatory Church, it has long been held, fostered this tradition as a program.[137] But in a series of oval projects Vignola confirmed it in practice. He developed his idea of axially and directionally defined space more as a formal problem; it was an architectural principle all his own.[138] In his solutions he nevertheless demonstrated convincingly the aptness, if not the "rightness," of the longitudinal oval for church building in the Counter-Reformation. His Sant'Anna de' Palafrenieri was by no means a type solution; a counteraxis tempered the longitudinal expression because two main altars had to be provided by the special requirement.[139] But it was primarily a longitudinal church, with the facade completed on its narrow end, and as such set a pattern for the succeeding generations.

Yet if, subsequently, oval churches tended to be repetitive in basic scheme, it was not to Vignola's credit alone. As an architectural problem, the oval *church* design was self-limiting; it gave little scope for substantial variations. It is true that the longitudinal axis of an oval church could be checked or exploited by the articulation of the dome and walls.[140] The oval space may be "centralized" by emphasizing the circumference (e.g., identical and repetitive motifs and continuous entablature), the lateral axis (e.g., larger chapels on the minor axis), or even both; or by deemphasizing these elements, its longitudinal axis may be stressed and make the space look like an inflated nave. In all instances, however, the basic *plan* on which the space is modeled is an inflated nave;[141] it is characterized by a pair of gently concave walls containing chapels. However modified, the longitudinal oval church is, to paraphrase Lotz, a laterally expanded but basically axial and directional space.[142] The design of San Giacomo degli Incurabili (Fig. 49), for example, is primarily uniaxial in plan (as Lotz has it),[143] although it is modified spatially, like Vignola's prototype, by a "centralizing" counteraxis (as Wittkower has it).[144]

Restricted as a problem and with examples few and far between, the oval church design developed, so to speak, by inbreeding. The tradition it created was therefore well defined; oval churches tended to look alike. It was also firmly established and resistant to innovation. Oval churches almost *had* to be longitudinal; they could hardly be otherwise. By the middle of the seventeenth century, the tradition was already so firmly set that the oval nearly came to be understood as inherently elongated *and* longitudinal; except to Bernini, no other way of using an oval was conceivable.[145] Carlo Fontana, in fact, criticizing Bernini's piazza precisely with regard to orientation, remarked in 1694 that its transverse oval is improper "secondo le buone regole" and called the longitudinal oval of his own proposal—actually another *ovato tondo* (Fig. 54)—"la vera figura Elipse."[146]

It is true, on the other hand, that Bernini had no choice in this regard as Fontana himself, too, knew perfectly well. The elevated terrain of the Vatican premises, as we have seen, wedged into the site from the northwest, limiting usable space in this direction (Fig. 8); and the obelisk, erected on the piazza in 1586, preestablished the center of a future project. In consequence, a new piazza of such magnitude as was required could be developed only in the lateral direction around the obelisk (Fig. 5).[147] Thus the transverse form of the Piazza Obliqua, too, emerged out of another imposed condition; it was no more the architect's choice than the specific configuration of its oval. But, of course, it is a functionalist fallacy to conclude that the transverse *oval* was stipulated by the topographic condition; for choice was open between an oval and any non-oval—a polygon, for example (Fig. 11).[148] Obviously, then, the topography dictated the way the oval was oriented but not the preference for the curvilinear form of the oval.

In view of the solid tradition of the longitudinal oval, the transverse oval of the

Piazza Obliqua may then seem to represent a compromise arrived at—as in Fontana's line of thought—by rotating an oval on its axis to fit the given site. The alleged first choice of a longitudinal oval is justified by still another imposed condition, the liturgy; the papal benediction given from the balcony above the central portal of the Basilica and from one of the windows of the Palace of Sixtus to the northwest demanded a maximum visibility of the piazza from these vantage points.[149] But this condition of visibility, too, might have been served equally well by a polygon. A transverse oval, moreover, makes a poor substitute for the longitudinal oval; for the accentuated longitudinal axis of the latter is not only its primary attribute but also the single feature that distinguishes it from its substitute and the change takes away this very factor. The alleged compromise seems to give up too much.

If we return for a moment to our earlier observation that the transverse oval accounts for bifocalism and circular arcs, those salient characteristics of the Piazza Obliqua, we can readily see that the form that was initially developed to fit the site was perhaps a pair of semicircles, and this, in turn, yielded a transverse oval, rather than vice versa. That this was actually the case in the development of Bernini's design has already been shown; in the architect's first oval plan (Fig. 21), the piazza is a pseudo-oval defined by two fully semicircular porticoes.[150]

If the topography of the site was at all a restrictive factor as it presumably was (although it does not necessarily have to be so), the form that was compromised in arriving at the transverse oval was obviously the circle, not a longitudinal oval. This is not to say that Bernini planned a circular piazza; it was in all likelihood no more than a mental image, which evolved two semicircular porticoes—a split circle—to fit the given site, and this was subsequently developed into an oval on which, when the plan was laid out to scale, an *ovato tondo* was superimposed (Fig. 5). We are therefore confirmed in our conclusion that the circle was the archetypal form of the Piazza Obliqua, and, as such, the form of the architect's first preference.[151]

THE VATICAN PLAN: LAYOUT FOR THE EXECUTION

Granted that the *ovato tondo* was a practical choice and its adoption was preceded by a plan that conceived the porticoes as two semicircles, we might still argue that its interlocked circles provided a perfect structure for the radial layout of the quadruple columns. Analysis demonstrates, however, that the *ovato tondo* was not entirely a right choice for this purpose.

The circular segment on the narrower side of the *ovato tondo* is 120 degrees (Fig. 41, t-t), and this is a fixed value. The colonnade, on the other hand, extends beyond this limit in both directions (T-T); its outline, in short, is a composite curve. The terminal segments are, to be sure, very short so that at the scale of the piazza the shift in curvature is imperceptibly small. For achieving a perfect radial unity of columns, however, the curve with three centers is decidedly awkward. It may still be objected that the deviation, if real, is trifling and negligible; it involves, after all, no more than a few marginal bays. The conflict nevertheless deserves a close analysis because of the curious consequences it entailed.

The draftsman might have resolved the conflict in several ways. Three immediately come to mind:

First (Fig. 55, A), in keeping with the geometry of the *ovato tondo,* the quadruple columns and pilasters in the problematic terminal segment (t - T) are lined up to converge at their proper center (p or p'), the radial unity is only partially fulfilled but its effect is tolerably accurate.

Second (Fig. 55, B), without altering the composite curve determined by the *ovato tondo,* the columns and pilasters in question are nevertheless lined up with the primary center of the oval (o or o'); the compromise produces some rhombic distortion in the pilasters and column bases, which may be awkward, but the radial unity is complete.

Third (Fig. 55, C), the colonnade is outlined all the way on one of the initial circles underlying the *ovato tondo* so that all supports, free of distortion, converge at one center (o or o'); the radial unity is perfect and consistent, but the oval, completed with a shorter and more depressed arc on the broader sides, is no longer an *ovato tondo.*

In view of the image of the circle, so prominently displayed in the actual piazza, we may well expect the last of the three possible solutions to have been Bernini's choice. To our bafflement, however, the large Vatican Plan (Fig. 6) shows instead a highly intricate compromise between the first two solutions (Fig. 56). It is as follows:

As we have seen, the *ovato tondo* is intact on the Vatican Plan. But the columns and pilasters in the terminal segments (t - T) are adjusted variously. The problem involves two sets of supports at the western end of the colonnade near the Piazza Retta—one of the pilasters (c) and the other of columns (16); these converge together with all the other columns toward the primary center of the oval (o) as in the second solution. At the eastern end, three sets are involved—one of columns, the second of pilasters, and the third consisting of both (16, c and f, respectively).[152] The last of the three sets (f), finishing the colonnade, lines up with the secondary center (p) as in the first solution. But the other two (c and 16) bring us to the most peculiar detail of the layout; they line up with neither of the two centers (o and p) but are interpolated, instead, to fall between them. The detail flouts geometry and defies logic.

Lines indicating this strange adjustment are still clearly visible on the Vatican Plan (Fig. 57).

The net result of this subtle and complicated maneuver is then threefold. First, the *ovato tondo* remains intact. Second, the rhombic distortion that the second solution entails is mitigated at the eastern termination (16 and c). Finally, the radial unity, though geometrically untidy, is sufficiently consistent in its visual effect. The solution, in short, is characteristically empirical; and it is a masterly compromise.

What comes as a further surprise is that the colonnades were actually executed according to this involved layout with all its idiosyncrasies. Inspection on the site proves the correspondence conclusively. Seen from the center of the radial system (o), the pilasters at the western end next to the last set of columns line up like the rest (Fig. 58). But their counterparts at the other end do not line up; however slightly, they show their sides (Fig. 59).[153]

Bernini's part in the layout of the Vatican Plan was probably no more than supervisory, but this is not to deny his decision; he may not have worked it out himself, but he certainly authorized it.

THE BONACINA ENGRAVING: CORRECTION FOR PUBLICITY

Bernini does not stop confounding us, however. He sanctioned yet another layout unlike any we have considered so far. It appears on the large plan of the colonnade published in engraving by G. B. Bonacina (Fig. 24). The colonnade traces here a simple circular segment from end to end, not the characteristic composite curve we have noted on the Vatican Plan. In this respect, the layout is like our third solution (Fig. 55, C); the *ovato tondo,* that is to say, is relinquished. On the other hand, if we trace the lines of the quadruple pilasters and columns, we discover that they do not all converge at one single point; instead, those at the eastern end show the familiar deviation. In other words, with regard to the radial system the engraving closely follows the Vatican Plan. Although one may at first think of attributing some of these peculiarities to the shrinkage of the paper, they also appear on the drawing made in preparation for the engraving (Fig. 60).[154]

The Bonacina Engraving was in circulation in September 1659; it was presumably in preparation in the spring, but not before April.[155] The forty-seven columns standing on the site on July 30 of that year included, as we have seen, all the thirty-two of the innermost course and the eight framing the three cross-passages; therefore, the definitive layout—the executed version—was by then surely in existence.[156] It must have come into being when the northern colonnade began to rise, say, several months earlier.[157] We can therefore assume that the lower half of the Vatican Plan showing the colonnades (but not the upper part with the corridors, which shows a later stage of design) was available for consultation by the end of 1658. In fact, on both the engraving and the drawing for it, we can see that the small supplementary plan of the oval piazza is unmistakably on an *ovato tondo* (Fig. 61).[158] The large engraved plan, in short, contradicts the official layout.

But the Bonacina Engraving, too, was official in purpose; it was to herald formally the new papal project far and wide.[159] Accordingly, it is also imposing in its dimensions; the plan is about twice the Vatican Plan in scale since it represents only one colonnade. Information assembled for it must surely have been as complete and definitive as it could then be; much care was undoubtedly given to its preparation. Inasmuch as the small supplementary plan shows an *ovato tondo* accurately, it is obviously hard to believe that the large and principal layout was misrepresented through error or negligence; an argument, for example, that the draftsman resorted to a single swing of compasses merely to simplify his work is unconvincing. We are therefore compelled to postulate that the large plan of the Bonacina Engraving was deliberately distorted. Had the distortion been due to the draftsman's incompetence or negligence, we must still agree that Bernini, on approving the plan, was indifferent to the change; to him, composite or simple, the arc of the colonnade was circular. But the likelihood that Bernini endorsed the peculiar distortion is strengthened by the nature of the function the engraving was to serve.

The engraving was designed for those in distant places who would not be able to visit the monument in person. To those who come and see the piazza, the radial unity is concrete and indubitable; not only that, with the quadruple columns lined up radially all around, they can hardly escape experiencing the colonnade as perfectly circular even though it is composite in curvature. But the situation is different for those who scan the engraving; here, the arc is far more visible than the radii. In order to communicate to them clearly and correctly the very phenomenon that the colonnade is experienced as perfectly circular, the plan of the colonnade must stand a simple proof—a verification with compasses. The curvature thus called for a "correction" in the printed version; the rest could remain the same. In execution, the colonnade needed only to *appear* circular; here, it had to *be* so.

Paradoxically, the inaccuracy was necessary for accuracy. The plan was distorted in order that what it represents is correctly understood by the beholder of the engraving. This was almost certainly Bernini's idea. For it is analogous to what he said, speaking of a marble portrait: "The sculptor sometimes best imitates the model by introducing something that is not in the model." [160]

The warp in the engraved plan was once again empirically motivated; the concern, here, was publicity. The Bonacina Engraving differed from the Vatican Plan somewhat as the presentation drawing in our days differs from the working drawing. We read on it the idea underlying the plan; it should and does represent the monument in terms of the architect's intentions embodied in the design. The "correction" required for achieving this end was certainly subtle; and the inconsistency it developed was seemingly trivial. But the artifice, to say the least, was an immense success.

The Bonacina Engraving, in effect, authorized once and for all that the colonnades *are* perfectly circular; since then—and well into our century—plans of the piazza continued to record them as such. The composite curves of the Vatican Plan virtually vanished, except right on the site.

Carlo Fontana was fully convinced that the colonnades were completely and perfectly circular. When he spoke of *bracci circolari,* he meant precisely what he said. For that is exactly how he represented them on his plans of the Piazza Obliqua for his authoritative book (Figs. 54 and 62), and he was consistent.[161] The Bonacina Engraving was evidently his source; apparently, he had no access to the Vatican Plan.[162] Reading the engraved version, Fontana undoubtedly saw a contradiction between the arc of the colonnade and the lines of the columns and pilasters at the eastern end; accordingly, he attempted to resolve it in his own way. He turned the very last set, which consists of columns and pilasters, slightly inward; but its line runs still outside the center of the arc (o, o'). In consequence, the cross-passage at the eastern end is conspicuously tapered toward the piazza (Fig. 54), whereas on the Vatican Plan and in execution this is almost uniform in width (Figs. 57 and 56, B).[163]

Letarouilly apparently thought that Fontana's plans were untidy. He therefore eliminated all the warps and contradictions and produced a plan in which the colonnade is entirely on a circular segment and the pilasters and columns all converge consistently toward a single point (Fig. 63). Completely systematized, his layout brings us back to our third solution (Fig. 55, C).[164] Simple and logical, Letarouilly's plan is far from the fact if true in spirit. Yet, it was anticipated in some earlier plans of the piazza and many of the maps of Rome from the eighteenth and nineteenth centuries; in fact, almost every map of Rome after 1659, including G. B. Nolli's plan of 1748 (Fig. 64), shows perfectly circular colonnades.[165]

So far as graphic records are concerned, Bernini's colonnades were thus perfectly circular, whatever the variation in the alignment of columns and pilasters. Thus it remained unknown to modern critics how intricate and irregular the executed plan actually was. Bernini's gimmick, we might say, worked almost too well.

OVAL OF A CONTINUOUS CIRCUMFERENCE

In the history of the Piazza Obliqua, the Vatican Plan and the Bonacina Engraving constitute the two largest and most complete surviving graphic documents from the time of construction. One was the official record of the design as executed; the other, the principal public statement. Neither could conceivably have escaped Bernini's own personal supervision. The two plans, on the other hand, contradict each other. Yet, divergent in layout, they communicate one single idea that the colonnades are perfectly circular in curvature. The idea was undoubtedly paramount in Bernini's conception of the piazza.

As we have seen, the *ovato tondo* with interlocked circles interfered with a full realization of this idea; this was a restrictive, rather than generative, form. On the other hand, once realized, the two circular porticoes in the form of parentheses (Fig. 15) could readily generate a transverse oval which would accommodate bifocalism and lateral protraction, the two most prominent features of the executed plan. As revealed in the definitive layout, then, the archetypal image of the plan was neither an oval nor two circles but two semicircles; it was unequivocally a circle split in two.

The conclusion is thus inevitable that two circular colonnades preceded the oval space not only in Bernini's process of design but also in his formal conception of the piazza. The split circle was not only a formative idea; it was also the most essential idea in his design. But why, then, the oval at all, and the *ovato tondo* at that?

For Bernini the *ovato tondo* was only one more restrictive condition to cope with. It was, after all, close enough to what he needed. But would it not have been far simpler to adapt the oval to his idea rather than vice versa? Would it not have been simpler to reshape the oval toward the more orderly solution in the form of Letarouilly's plan? This would have eliminated awkward kinks and warps, simplified drafting and masonry work, and expressed the idea of two semicircles just as vividly, and as for the reshaped oval, no visitor on the piazza would ever see the difference. But Bernini did not relinquish the *ovato tondo.* Needless to say, this fact calls for an explanation.

The *terzo braccio,* the strip of colonnade closing the piazza to the east, gives us a clue. On the Vatican Plan it is laid out along a large arc of the *ovato tondo* (Fig 6). It serves as a linkage between the two detached colonnades, and the *ovato tondo* assures a sense of continuity across them because their terminal segments share the same arc as the *terzo braccio*. The Vatican Plan shows a concern with this problem in three ways:

First, the very last set of supports (f) in each colonnade is lined up with the center (p) of the arc of the *terzo braccio* (Fig. 56, A).

Second, the axis of the cross-passage falls outside this center and serves as a transition between the two radial systems.

Third, some of the terminal pilasters and columns (16 and c), as we have noted, line up off the center of the radial unity they were meant to serve (o); this compromise is peculiar to the eastern end, so that we can assume it was for creating a smoother transition between the colonnade and the *terzo braccio* than is otherwise possible.

This concern with a sense of continuity around the oval circumference is perplexing. It is in apparent contradiction to the image of a split circle; for it suggests a fluid form, protracted, bifocal, and transitional—perhaps more properly elliptical. Yet these two divergent ideas do not merely coexist but are resolved in the executed plan by what is otherwise a most subtle and even superfluous detail. Are we to believe that the oval has become in the course of the development of the design as essential as the split circle?

The answer to this question is provided by the chalk drawing with a tetrastyle gateway, which is already familiar to us (Fig. 34); long sweeping strokes emphasize the continuity of its circumference and describe the piazza unequivocally as a single oval figure.[166] In this connection, we have already said that Bernini introduced here, in substitution for the split circle, a circle flattened out or depressed to fit the limited site. The architect's interest in the circumference, too, must be viewed as an outcome of his concern with the perfect circle.

But there is more to be deduced from this sketch plan. If the colonnade terminations, obviously crucial for the final layout of the plan, were already graphically indicated on this drawing, the precise curve of the colonnades was not established until later. It was, in fact, still provisional in the workshop plan on which the graded column diameters were worked out (Fig. 26). Here, the arc is not yet what we find on the Vatican Plan; the radius is longer.[167] Evidently, the *ovato tondo* came in the design, as we have been assuming, with the layout of the Vatican Plan. The architect's concern with a continuous circumference developed, in other words, independently *before* he adopted the *ovato tondo*.

It may be objected that to call one oval a split circle and another a depressed circle is tautology; after all, subtle changes notwithstanding, the Piazza Obliqua remained oval starting with the first oval plan (Fig. 15). But even if it is the case that the circle, in its two different manifestations, could be identified only in the architect's ideation, our observation carries a momentous implication. To Bernini ovals were phenomena of the circle, and as such they were, so to speak, as good as the circle. It is evident that he did not consider them deformed circles as they appeared to Galileo some decades earlier.[168] Nor did he see them as elongated forms opposed to the circle in the tradition of the longitudinal-central contrast, as Fontana and other architects in Bernini's time apparently thought; rather, to Bernini ovals *were* circles.[169] And, needless to say, this perception is in perfect accord with his primary iconography of the piazza, the amphitheater of Christendom.[170]

If the architect's two sketch plans record vividly the two different manifestations of the circle, the Vatican Plan, which was the executed version, embodied them both, however subtly. In the delicate maneuver of those terminal columns and pilasters that resulted in their irregular alignment, we read Bernini's attempt to bring the two images of the circle together.

The two images, of course, might be more simply explained by the *ovato tondo,* in which two circles are perfectly interlocked to form an oval of continuous circumference. But we must keep in mind that the oval geometry entered the design only long after the two images of the circle had separately been established in the earlier stages of design. It is true that Bernini cannot be said to have been indifferent to the *ovato tondo.* He did not relinquish it, even though that would have been simpler for realizing a simpler layout; and this was only because he knew he could make it into an asset. He saw that he could develop the "loose" ends it created in the colonnades into smooth links with the *terzo braccio.*

On this historical basis, then, we must reject the attribution to Bernini of that *concetto,* recently suggested by Fagiolo dell'Arco, that the Piazza Obliqua, combining the circle and ellipse in its plan, iconographically reconciles in compromise the two divergent cosmological views, the old (Ptolemaic) and the new (Keplerian).[171]

IV Oval into Circle: The Revision

PENETRATION AND ENCLOSURE: TOWARD REINTEGRATION

IN THE LONG VICISSITUDES of Bernini's oval plan for the Piazza Obliqua, two formal images, split circle and depressed circle, developed one after the other and eventually merged together in the Vatican Plan. Parallel with this development, we also observe a progressive accumulation and merger of two spatial expressions: penetration and enclosure.

The synthesis of these antithetical expressions was demanded by the two-faced architectural program. On the one hand, the piazza was to serve as a place of assembly; it must accommodate "collection," a sense of localized activity. The piazza, on the other hand, was also to be a grand approach to the Basilica and the Vatican; it must capture "flow," a sense of purposeful movement. A self-contained, enclosed space would best express collection; a directional, penetrated space would best express flow. A full expression of one therefore tends to diminish the effect of the other; a compromise might well serve as synthesis.

But a synthesis of enclosure and penetration was, in fact, achieved in the first oval plan (Fig. 15). The semicircular porticoes enclose, but the space opens forward; and they are transformations from the straight porticoes of the trapezoid plan, in which penetration was given a full expression. The *terzo braccio* that closes the piazza on the east side is straight and thus tends to isolate the curved colonnades and emphasize the split in the split circle (Fig. 37, b-c).

In the arcade design, however, enclosure became the dominating theme; in con-

46

formity with the image of the amphitheater, the piazza was a "circular" enclosure—as circular as it could be made—featuring one concentrated focus (Fig. 18). The first foundation medal (Fig. 20) inherited this emphasis on enclosure; to repeat what we have said before, the whole reads here as a loop of colonnades interrupted at three places, and it is a centralized plan, with one fountain, rather than two, in front of the central obelisk (Fig. 37, d-e).

It is true, on the other hand, that the design on the medal was quickly revised; the fountain was duplicated and dispersed bifocally (Fig. 21). Given the development we are outlining, there is only one explanation to this revision. It was an attempt to reconcile, not the circle and ellipse,[172] but two divergent expressions of the circle, and, in effect, their two spatial implications. Two fountains, one for each half of the piazza, retrieved the image of the split circle, now superimposed on that of the depressed circle whose center is marked by the obelisk; they were also so spaced out as to define two passages within the piazza that extended the axes of the Borgo streets and thus reinforced penetration to counterbalance the emphatic enclosure of the colonnades. The triad of the obelisk and fountains was not in itself new; Rainaldi had already organized his design with such a triad (Fig. 11).[173] But Bernini's solution was, in its particular context, a superb synthesis, and his triad was moreover the first definitive formal element in the design of his piazza.[174]

The loop was subsequently strengthened further. On Medal III, columns were isolated; rhythmical units were consequently multiplied and seem interminable (Fig. 22). The sketch plan in chalk (Fig. 34), which we have dated to immediately follow this medal, captures this effect vividly. In the elaboration phase that ensued, as we witness on Medal IV (Fig. 23), the *terzo braccio* is curved, thus reinforcing the continuous circumference of the loop. But several details, introduced in this development, gave a new emphasis, in turn, on penetration (Fig. 6).

First of all, the cross-passages articulated the loop into segments and mitigated the effect of the enclosing circumference. Then, the colonnade and the corridor were joined in a new relationship, which is best understood as the indication of the new *concetto,* the maternal arms of the Church. The western cross-passage, axially coordinated with the corridor (Fig. 25) [175] and embellished with a columnar frame and papal stemma, makes the corridor look as though it pierces through the end of the colonnade and reach the piazza; the gap in the split circle is thus once again stressed. Analogously, the steps that completed the oval of the piazza toward the Piazza Retta were pushed out, and those between the colonnades and the *terzo braccio* were altogether eliminated. The Piazza Obliqua now lost its self-contained character, and the Piazza Retta, though still a picture box as before in relation to the oval space, became more an extension than an appendage (Fig. 37, f-g).[176] Parallel with this forward orientation, the oval *teatro* was also frontalized more decisively; but this needs explanation.

On the Bonacina Engraving (Fig. 24), double columns embellish the middle cross-passage of each colonnade both in the inner facade (facing the piazza) and on the outer facade. Bernini apparently planned initially to frame the passage this way only on the inner facade but decided to add projecting double columns also on the outer facade shortly before the completion of the engraving; for they are missing from the plans on the preparatory drawing for the engraving (Fig. 27).[177] Since the Vatican Plan, as we have already demonstrated, preceded this drawing, the ornamental columns outside the middle cross-passages on this plan must be understood as a postscript.[178]

Preceding this amendment, then, only the three cross-passages on the side of the Borgo were framed with projecting columns both inside and outside the piazza, as we see on the small plan on the preparatory drawing for the engraving (Fig. 60). Except for these three, the cross-passages looked inward; [179] these three, facing the Borgo, therefore defined a facade by which the *teatro,* otherwise recognizably central in plan, became more characteristically frontal, in the manner the Pantheon is frontal by virtue of its portico.[180] An axis was now created that sweeps through the *terzo braccio* and across the piazza up to the facade of the Basilica (Fig. 23). Too, frontalized and more directly linked to the Basilica than before, the Piazza Obliqua reads now more convincingly than before as the vestibule to the Basilica, reminiscent of the demolished atrium to the Old Saint Peter's.[181] In his effort of reintegrating enclosure and penetration, the architect was evidently trying to give form to the *concetto* of the maternal arms of the Church, superimposed on that of the amphitheater of Christendom; and, needless to say, he achieved a good measure of success on the original Vatican Plan before the addition of the postscript.[182]

The ornamental columns, introduced as an afterthought, necessarily altered the balance of enclosure and penetration. It is known that this addition was made in connection with the new pilgrim's road, which was to extend northward on the axis of the middle cross-passage; the project proved economically infeasible, and the protruding columns were never executed.[183] The project, which was certainly Bernini's own original idea as is attested by an autograph sketch,[184] implies, then, that the columnar frame was meant to close a long vista. The piazza would then have gained a strong cross-axis, which called for another reinforcement of the main axis; and this was accomplished with four more columns.

The four columns, added as the second postscript on the Vatican Plan, were placed on the facade of the Basilica, and they represent a tetrastyle portico (Fig. 6). The portico (Fig. 65) is similar to that of Michelangelo's design, which notably axialized and frontalized, too, the otherwise central church plan.[185] More importantly, however, it is an amplification of the columnar frame of the *terzo braccio,* and thus would have reasserted the axis, not only from the Basilica to the *terzo braccio,* but beyond; for the free-standing columns would have accentuated the facade by giving it more plasticity and thus made it more visible from a long distance. But with the abandonment of the pilgrim's road project, this design obviously became superfluous and was, too, discarded.

Except for these postscripts, the plan of the Piazza Obliqua was undoubtedly already settled early in 1659 in the form of the Vatican Plan; construction of the northern colonnade was well under way in July, and its layout, as we have seen, followed this plan to the letter.[186] With the publication of the Bonacina Engraving that spring, Bernini's design of the piazza could be considered virtually completed; other engravings, based on this one, soon followed, notably those of Falda (Fig. 36).[187]

From 1659 on, the construction proceeded steadily at a good pace.[188] The completion of the northern colonnade was commemorated in 1661; the medal still shows, in all likelihood incorrectly, the postscript columnar embellishment (Fig. 66).[189] Work on the south side then followed immediately.[190] In the meantime, the northern corridor was in progress, and this was completed in November 1662.[191] It was reported in April 1666 that the *teatro* was now completely finished; but the *terzo braccio* was apparently still missing.[192]

THE LAST REVISION (FEBRUARY 19, 1667): THE PROPYLAEUM

Construction of the *terzo braccio* was obviously now in order. But the block of buildings with the Palazzo del Priorato di Malta, which filled the opening between the two colonnades toward the Borgo, was still standing at the time (Fig. 5); the clearance of this block came up for discussion only on February 19, 1667.[193] On the very same day, however, Bernini submitted to the Congregazione a revised design for the *terzo braccio,* according to which this structure would be surmounted by a clock tower and thus made into a formal propylaeum; but the cardinals of the Congregazione deferred decision on it in favor of the more pressing pavement study.[194] But the proposal was never picked up again; the death of the Pope on May 22 of that year brought the whole enterprise to a close, and the propylaeum was never built.

What we know of the revised design, however, radically transformed the character of the general plan.

The *terzo braccio* made its first appearance, as we have seen, on the pen-and-ink sketch of the first oval plan (Fig. 15). It was there a straight closing unit. In the subsequent development of the design, it was initially a straight piece, as we still see on the first foundation medals (Figs. 20-22), but was later made into a curved colonnade completing the oval form of the piazza on the side toward the Borgo (Fig. 23); it was also at this time given a cross-passage to match those in the main colonnades. This brought about a significant change in the general area.

Three cross-passages link the oval piazza with the Borgo (Fig. 6). The passage through the *terzo braccio* is central and so dominates the other two; not only is it more emphasized than the other two, embellished as it is with double rather than single projecting columns, but it also asserts itself because the structure it penetrates is isolated and thus reads as a special frame for it. Accordingly, the two cross-passages that terminate the colonnades, too, read compositionally as lateral frames for the central passage. The *terzo braccio* became, in effect, a propylaeum already at this stage of design; no longer a simple colonnade, it would be the formal entrance-way to the Piazza Obliqua.[195]

Upon the completion of the two colonnades, however, Bernini evidently decided to reexamine the propylaeum design. The architect's first thought, recorded on a chalk drawing (Fig. 67),[196] was to surmount the *terzo braccio* with a clock supported on a tetrastyle frame, repeating for the superstructure the design he had earlier developed for the western cross-passage; the germinal idea of the revised design was thus his own early chalk drawing (Fig. 34). We have already indicated before that it was most likely while studying the effect of the matching tetrastyle gateways as seen from the Borgo Nuovo that the architect had a passing thought of appropriating the motif for the *terzo braccio*.

The clock on the new sketch, then, is the clock of Pope Innocent VIII, which traditionally marked the entrance to the Vatican. The clock tower thus features a belfry, too, as did its predecessor, the tower of Paul V (Fig. 7). At its new position, elevated above the propylaeum, the clock announces that the propylaeum is not only the first gateway to the sacred precinct but also the formal entranceway to the Vatican. This, then, explains the two-story structure. If the propylaeum were to be understood as the formal gateway, it would have to be visible from afar; it would have to be an urban landmark.[197]

The first design, however, was immediately modified (Fig. 68); the new propylaeum is no longer curved but straight in plan. This is a sure indication that the architect had already decided that the propylaeum would be located in a newly created ante-piazza rather than on the oval outline of the Piazza Obliqua.[198]

The development of an antepiazza for accommodating the new propylaeum is re-corded in Bernini's two sketch plans drawn side by side on a single sheet (Fig. 69); they are both schematic and clearly primordial in character.[199] On a smaller plan, the oval piazza is closed toward the Borgo by a rectangle, which may be read as the *terzo braccio* in its original position but is more plausibly the Palazzo del Priorato, destined for demolition but still standing at the time. The other plan, larger and ap-parently later than the first, shows a new trapezoidal piazza created by clearing the whole Priorato block; an antepiazza, the future Piazza Rusticucci, thus came into being. The obvious result of this development is that the oval piazza, essentially a closed figure till then, was opened up decisively, now penetrated by the axis joining the matched trapezoidal units, the antepiazza and the Piazza Retta. The new complex would have been a roughly cruciform plan more or less like the present situation (Fig. 70).

The architect then studied in another drawing (Fig. 71) the view of the left part of the Piazza Obliqua that would have revealed itself to the viewer as he came up the Borgo Nuovo and reached the opening to the newly created antepiazza; the study thus pursues again the problem that was left off in the chalk drawing with a tetra-style (Fig. 34). The drawing now shows the Piazza Obliqua in bird's-eye view to-gether with a large section of the Borgo, and the two sets of visual lines indicate changing views from two different points along the street. The argument of the sketch is, then, that the antepiazza should be only so deep that from the opening of the street the visitor should be able to see a good part of the colonnade to the left; and the area to be cleared (now in plan) was indicated by hatching.[200]

From this exploration Bernini was immediately led to the decision on the precise position of the new propylaeum (Fig. 72). The sketch plan shows schematically the Piazza Retta, the Piazza Obliqua, and the existing Priorato block (indicated in some detail), and superimposed on the plan, two lines of sight that establish the view-point from which the oval piazza would appear in its full breadth; the new pro-pylaeum was laid out in such a way that the visitor will have this view as he steps out of it.[201] The sketch plan was then redrawn to scale in the workshop and used for a pavement study (Fig. 73).[202] From it we learn that the relocated propylaeum, though straightened and elaborated, was neither lengthened nor widened from the *terzo braccio* of the Bonacina Engraving; it retained the same nine-bay construction on the same dimensions, 75 by 220 *palmi*.[203]

In the process of developing the new propylaeum, Bernini was principally concerned with two problems. One was the role of the structure as an independent, formal gateway; the other was the proper depth of the antepiazza. Together, the two problems suggest that the architect had already decided at the very outset to bring the propylaeum all the way to the back of the new antepiazza. We must therefore reject the possibility, suggested by the engraving for the Conclave of June 1667 (Fig. 74), that Bernini initially considered moving the *terzo braccio* of the Bonacina Engraving without changing its form and tentatively only a little into the Piazza Rusticucci; rather than the revival of an early phase of the revision of February 1667, this representation is more likely a new, reduced scheme proposed after the Pope's death as a more practicable alternative to the full-fledged revision.[204]

THE OPTIMUM VIEWPOINT: PANORAMA AND PERSPECTIVE

Bernini's use of *visuali* in positioning the new propylaeum suggests that the architect's overriding concern in the revision of 1667 was the total view of the Basilica, piazza, and colonnades as a single pictorial composition. His own testimony, in fact, clarifies his concern. Eight years earlier, he had already written his *giustificazione* that the low-lying colonnades should serve well as an optical corrective to the squat facade of the Basilica since, in juxtaposition, the latter "would be set off and, in a sense, raised above its own height."[205]

This idea remained paramount in Bernini's mind for some years; while in Paris in 1665, he repeated the explanation in some detail at least three times.[206] The alleged optical illusion, moreover, gave rise to an elaborate Gestalt theory of dubious accuracy in modern times; it was argued, typically, that the oval of the Piazza Obliqua, together with the divergent walls and the rising grade of the Piazza Retta, distorts the sense of distance between the viewer and the facade, and this makes the facade appear taller than it is.[207]

Bernini's optical device was, however, a very simple matter. It was no more than a principle of contrast by juxtaposition—*i contrapposti,* as he called it; exemplified in the relation of arms to the head in the bust, it was a principle based on the phenomenon that form changes according to its context, or "things are seen not only as they are but also in relation to what exists around them that modifies their appearance."[208] For a full effect, then, Bernini's corrective requires two conditions. First, the colonnades must be seen in full horizontal extension in order to set Maderno's facade in maximum contrast; second, the facade and the colonnades must be viewed simultaneously as a single pictorial composition.

This explains Bernini's concern, already manifest in the earlier sketch (Fig. 71), with the view of the piazza that combined the Basilica and the colonnades. But in the sketch plan that determined the position of the propylaeum (Fig. 72), the viewpoint fulfilled the two requirements perfectly. For from any point closer to the piazza, the colonnades would extend too far out of the field of vision, while from a point farther away, they would be clipped off from view by the terminal temple fronts that swing out into the foreground (Frontispiece).[209]

The prescribed viewpoint, however, delivered more. It substantially improved the visibility of Michelangelo's dome, a major issue of the day, without in the least diminishing the full spatial impact of the immense piazza.[210] The effect of the expansive space, which may be had, too, from the propylaeum in its original location on the oval outline, was expanded to the full. From the designated viewpoint, the composition encompasses an angle of vision that is just a little excessive for comfort but only so much that the strain properly enhances the breathtaking magnitude of the piazza as though in cinemascope; and the temple fronts of the colonnades, framing the ensemble like a picture, hold the panorama together (Fig. 1).[211]

The new propylaeum thus marked the optimum viewpoint; and it was characteristically a fixed viewpoint. The ideal view it promised was accordingly also a fixed view—frontal, closed, and static; and this is scenography on an urban scale.[212] By relocating the propylaeum, Bernini produced a panoramic scene; and the two temple fronts that terminated the colonnades conveniently served as built-in *periaktoi,* between which it could be unfolded. Even at this immense scale, Bernini fulfilled his "ideal of a three-dimensional picture," which he had earlier realized in his design of niche statues, chapels, and churches.[213]

The revision of 1667 was moreover a scenography, not only in result, but in method as well. On the sketch plan in question (Fig. 72), the *visuali* are not drawn for verifying the view from a predetermined position; they are controls, instead, for locating the point from which a desired prospect can be had.[214] The procedure is exactly like the method of correlating the perspective scene with its point of sight located in the royal box, from which the effect of illusion was calculated to be perfect; and the sighting may be done with a string or, vicariously, with a drawn line (Fig. 75).[215]

Of Bernini's own scenography, however, we know very little.[216] We are nevertheless certain of one point; he was keenly aware of the limitations of one-point perspective, which was the standard practice in stage design during his time.[217] After discussing the production of his *Due Teatri* while in Paris, he commented that "scenes that demand a single viewpoint should be avoided"; but he did not have in mind a system with more than one vanishing point, for he cited, in support of his argument, the ceiling of the Farnese Gallery with its "compartments, herms, and other ornaments that permit several viewpoints." Needless to say, the Farnese Ceiling is basically a *quadratura;* what, then, does Bernini mean by several viewpoints?[218]

He knew the simple truth that in one-point perspective orthogonal lines are the crux of the system. Orthogonal lines that recede in depth account for the dramatic illusion of space in *quadratura,* but they also cause disturbing distortions unless the scene is viewed from the designated point of sight. The Farnese Ceiling is a design in one-point perspective, but orthogonals are virtually eliminated because receding pictorial elements are herms and atlantes rather than rectilinear architectural members; the design thus allows for a broad range of satisfactory viewpoints even though, theoretically, there is only one perfect viewpoint. By several viewpoints, then, Bernini simply meant a range of viewpoints free of glaring distortions.

We can safely assume on this basis that Bernini should have rejected in his scenography those street vistas in the tradition of Serlio; he should have favored, instead, scenes composed of frontal, oblique, and curved elements, which would be less prone to distortion and would permit more than one viewpoint.[219] This is, in fact, precisely the case in his urban panorama of the Piazza Obliqua; it consists of the frontal church facade, oblique corridors, and circular colonnades. Like his sculptural compositions, it affords the viewer "one and many views"; within the range of viewpoints provided by the antepiazza the propylaeum, like the royal box, assures one optimum viewpoint.[220]

As in his sculpture, too, Bernini provided for a range of viewpoints in front of the scene. In this connection, the antepiazza has been likened to the vestibule of Bernini's centralized churches in its relation to the Piazza Obliqua; he explained to Chantelou that people, on entering a room, habitually take a few steps forward so that only by providing a vestibule he can be sure that they experience the form of the church in its entirety (Fig. 76). But the analogy is invalid, because it ignores the fundamental difference in scale; a few steps out of the propylaeum, the visitor still finds himself in the depth of the antepiazza, and the comprehensive view of the oval piazza, in fact, dissolves as he approaches it.[221]

Ideally, then, and also primarily, the Piazza Obliqua was designed to be viewed from a stationary point rather in motion; it was meant to be experienced as a fixed scene rather than in sequence of shifting perspectives as the "ellipse" in its geometrical sense may lead us to suppose; but, above all, it had to be *seen from without* rather than comprehended from within. On this ground we can claim that Bernini's design presupposes a scenographic vision, no less scenographic than, say, that which underlies Palladio's design of his classical villas (Fig. 77).[222] And this leads us to two conclusions.

The first concerns the form of the piazza. Viewed from the propylaeum as stipulated by the architect, the Piazza Obliqua could appear either oval or circular. But because it is immense in scale and lacks orthogonal lines in this view, we cannot accurately estimate its depth; and, consequently, we are more likely, if not forced indeed, to assume that the piazza is as deep as it is broad and logically deduce from this that it is circular on the knowledge that circle is elliptical in perspective (Fig. 52, left). In other words, the piazza does not necessarily *appear* circular, but the beholder tends to *think* it is very likely circular.[223] To Bernini's contemporaries, to whom the iconography of the amphitheater was more immediate than to us, the piazza could only be circular.[224]

An oval is a circle seen askance; or stated differently, it is an oblique cross-section of the visual cone. In the view from the propylaeum, the piazza is oval as a visual phenomenon; but it is also oval already in the actual plan though this may not be immediately apparent in the ideal view. Such an observation must have given rise to the name Piazza Obliqua, the designation we inherited from Carlo Fontana;[225] it says that Bernini's piazza is a design in anamorphosis. Objectively oval, it may be said to represent a circular piazza set oblique in advance, or we might say "pre-foreshortened," not unlike the converging walls of the contemporary Scala Regia, which similarly created an effect of amplification. In both cases, the effect assumes a stipulated viewpoint outside the setting.[226]

Providing the view of the piazza in its entirety, the relocated propylaeum moreover displayed its "circular" form as a closed entity. The executed pavement design (Fig. 78) confirms this observation; its outline is emphatically continuous, and radial spokes issue from the focal obelisk, certainly not accidentally, like the sun's rays.[227] But at the same time, the propylaeum was removed out of the oval outline; the oval was thereby opened up as the two semicircles were ever more decisively isolated. The circle, asserted in the comprehensive view, was thus at the same time split apart, the two halves now held in place only by the concentric force of the obelisk, which acts as an anchor. The second conclusion concerns this penetration through the piazza.

The relocated propylaeum defined a new antepiazza, which not only opened up the oval piazza but also transformed the general plan of the whole complex. Together with its counterpart, the Piazza Retta, the Piazza Rusticucci created a trapezoidal concourse that recalls to our mind, in its position and dimensions, the trapezoid plan, the architect's first submission. The "avenue," so created, developed in its form the lines of the Borgo streets that opened into it, and in this way it correlated the two gateways, the propylaeum to the piazza on the one hand, and on the other, the portals to the Basilica beyond it. Axial and directional, the "avenue" was set in contrast with the enclosing and centralizing form of the Piazza Obliqua proper. A workshop drawing representing another pavement study (Fig. 79), though eventually discarded, most accurately summarized in linear design the combination of these two formal elements.[228] The two elements, the trapezoid and the transverse oval, needless to say, represented two major stages of Bernini's design, and were expressive, respectively, of penetration and enclosure that had been alternately and consistently strengthened in the whole process of design up to this point.

Superimposed on each other as though in summation, then, the two elements now produced a form which can only be described as a cruciform plan (Fig. 37, h). The cross, it is true, is lopsided in plan; but like the oblique circle of the Piazza Obliqua, it too corrects itself anamorphically in the stipulated frontal view (Fig. 2).[229] In the revision of 1667, the oval thus remains central and dominating, and yet the cross embraces all in the total scheme and subsumes the globe. The new composite plan therefore clarified not only the design but also its iconography. It developed into a palpable and concrete image the very idea of the Christian universe, which was symbolized simultaneously high above the lantern of Michelangelo's dome in the form of the cross and the orb. The emblem, which Bernini finally succeeded in embodying in the plan,[230] is no less evident to the visitor than that which crowns the supreme temple of Christianity, for the ideal view from the propylaeum encompasses not only the oval piazza but the entire cruciform plan. The Square of Saint Peter's in its entirety is now more than ever the Amphitheater of the Christian Universe.

THE AVENUE FOR VISTA AND SUSPENSE: THE GRAND DESIGN

We have so far concentrated on the internal aspect of the revised design. But what did Bernini plan outside the propylaeum? The question has never been posed; but it is a valid and intriguing one.

The Piazza Obliqua was undoubtedly more an enclosed space than an "avenue" in 1659 (Fig. 24), notwithstanding the Piazza Retta; but the revision of 1667 split it open into two relatively independent hemicycles embracing a longitudinal concourse.

The composite plan that resulted from the revision was cruciform; and it is markedly axialized within. Still, as a whole, the plan is a self-contained entity. It is, as a space, clearly differentiated from the dense urban texture of the surrounding area (Fig. 64); the open space is blocked out all around, except for the outlets to the Borgo that provided two spatial leaks. The enclosing colonnades are penetrable, visually as well as physically, as is frequently observed, yet they turn inward and show that their allegiance is more the space it encloses than the settlement that huddles up on the outside. What we see here, in short, is an urban inset, not unlike, say, the Square of Saint Mark's in Venice or the Piazza Farnese in Rome.[231] But what of Bernini's concern with penetration, then?

We must, first of all, recognize that the propylaeum is by definition an element of penetration. It is for entry and exit—in short, for passing through; it does not make sense, in fact, without a street that runs directly into it, or else an open area in front of it. The *terzo braccio* of the Bonacina Engraving therefore already implies an axis that penetrates it insofar as it is already a propylaeum in character; but neither this representation nor the Vatican Plan gives us a clear indication in this regard.[232]

The postscript columns on the Vatican Plan are, however, noteworthy. As we have indicated earlier, the middle cross-passage of the northern colonnade, now double-faced, was meant to close the long vista on the newly projected pilgrim's road; and, even more significantly, the Michelangelesque tetrastyle portico, accentuating Maderno's facade plastically and thus making it more legible from a distance, also implied a long vista. However unlikely it may seem, it is as though Bernini was imagining an avenue right through the Borgo.

When the propylaeum was relocated in 1667 to assure the optimum view of the reshaped space, the architect revealed more of his conception regarding the development outside the propylaeum. For he must direct visitors toward the passage through the propylaeum to make the ideal viewpoint work for them; and to achieve this end the area outside must be so organized that the circulation toward this crucial point is defined unequivocally. Bernini could not have conceived this area undeveloped.

Information in this regard is nevertheless very scanty. The sketch plan (Fig. 72) indicates that the Piazza Rusticucci, made by clearing the Priorato block, was deep enough to allow a small piazza in front of the propylaeum. But the piazza, in this form, was not only asymmetrical but too narrow in width for the proposed propylaeum at the designated position (Figs. 5 and 78); it required a systematization of some sort.

The two workshop drawings for pavement design demonstrate only that no definite solution was on hand. The first study (Fig. 73) shows the enlarged Piazza Rusticucci; a part of the block across the Borgo Vecchio from the Priorato block was sliced off somewhat imprudently, and the propylaeum, placed in the middle, provides for a small piazza outside it. The second study (Fig. 79) proposes a symmetrical antepiazza; the plan is incomplete, but, completed, it would have looked like the later plan by an unknown French architect (Fig. 80), who repeated the same pavement design.[233]

In examining these two possible solutions, it becomes soon apparent that the circulation from either of the Borgo streets to the propylaeum lacks the required control. No sooner than the visitor emerges out of the street, the facade of the Basilica will come in view, and before he recognizes the main entrance to the propylaeum he will find himself at its side entrance; but by then the Piazza Obliqua is already largely in view, and the incentive to enter the propylaeum is slim. The view of the piazza thus unfolds gradually, and the crucial viewpoint is bypassed. As a convergence point, if not in other respects, the propylaeum would have worked better in its original location on the oval outline. With regard to the antepiazza, then, the pavement drawings hardly represent solutions; they record only tentative ideas that apparently contradict the thesis of the revised design.[234]

The thesis of the design forces us to envision, in fact, a piazza that is considerably deeper than that suggested by the pavement plans, if not indeed a fully developed avenue. As a passageway, and a formal gateway at that, the propylaeum demands an axial and directional space that flows toward it. But embodying the ideal viewpoint, the propylaeum must also be effective as the convergence point; and for this, it must read as the single focus, visible well in advance, toward which visitors will be drawn naturally. The new propylaeum, moreover, became a structure that rises higher than the colonnades (Fig. 68); as a prominent landmark, it calls for a long vista, which it would close scenographically rather like Michelangelo's Porta Pia.[235] The vista, finally, would introduce a new element of penetration and thus answer his own persistent concern and that of his traditionalist critics.[236] It is hardly surprising, therefore, if Bernini himself envisioned a broad avenue through the Borgo leading up to the relocated propylaeum.

Bernini's proposal of 1667 is known as his last revision; more accurately, it is his last known revision. We have indeed no reason to believe that it represented his final design; rather, it seems to represent no more than the first thought of a new, developing concept. The architect evidently had not yet fully worked out the situation outside the propylaeum when he submitted the proposal. The project was called off altogether a few months later by the death of the Pope, and the design remained unresolved—terminated but unfinished.

The propylaeum was never built, and the *spina* was preserved intact, except for the Priorato block, well into this century. Bernini's development, the cruciform composite, therefore retained that insular character which it would have had if the propylaeum had been built to close it off (Fig. 78). This situation makes it difficult to accept our proposition and also explains in part the almost universal condemnation of the clearance of the *spina,* effected in 1937.[237]

The argument goes that the clearance of the *spina* destroyed irretrievably the effect of dramatic surprise intended by Bernini. Formerly, the panorama of the piazza would have overtaken the visitor like a sudden revelation as he reached the end of either of the narrow Borgo streets. Today, he ascends a broad avenue—Via della Conciliazione —all the way from the bank of the Tiber to the piazza, drawn by the long continuous vista up to the facade of the Basilica (Fig. 81); the contrast between the piazza and the approach to it has been therefore drastically diminished. Instead of a surprise, the argument claims, he experiences nothing more than a prolonged introduction.

Bernini certainly would not have wanted a dissipation of suspense. But nor would he have been happy with the previous condition which lacked the propylaeum, the device for halting the visitor. The propylaeum was, after all, the crux of the 1667 revision; it alone would have justified an avenue leading to it. An avenue without it makes no sense. But had the propylaeum been built, and only then, Bernini would have favored the open *spina;* indeed, he would have proposed it himself. For, with the propylaeum, the Via della Conciliazione would be vastly different from what it is today (Fig. 82).

The venerated dome of Michelangelo would be in view from the start at the river bank and draw the visitor up the avenue; but the propylaeum, superimposed on Maderno's façade would shield the Piazza Obliqua from view. He may for a while have a glimpse of it through the propylaeum but never quite enough to detract him from the propylaeum itself; and as he moves on the slits would eventually close while the propylaeum would loom larger and larger over the Basilica thus keeping the piazza out of his sight until that crucial moment when he steps out of the passage through the propylaeum. There, the vast panorama would suddenly engulf him.

With the propylaeum at the end of the avenue, the sequence of concealment and revelation is not unlike that in the situation before 1937 (Fig. 78). The sudden exposure is no less dramatic; in fact, it is more so. The propylaeum marks the fulcrum of two radically different urban spaces. The avenue is linear and directed; it plots and guides our movement. The piazza is a concentric and contained space, if also expansive; it leaves us to spread out and wander around until we come together again at the Basilica beyond. The contrast dramatizes the feeling of release and elation. The forward thrust of the avenue, however, penetrates the propylaeum and extends to the Basilica because the piazza, cruciform in plan, is internally axial. The avenue and the piazza thus dovetail into each other perfectly, and at their juncture the propylaeum is at once a barrier and a link.[238]

It is clear that only by opening the *spina* Bernini would have resolved the dilemma of the dual program in his characteristic way. Earlier, in the plan of 1659, he tried to make one and the same place expressive of both enclosure and penetration. In the revision of 1667, he would define the two expressions separately in two spatial components. The executed pavement design is completely centralized because the oval piazza is now freed of the burden of expressing penetration; the rejected versions were still dealing with the duality (Figs. 73 and 79). The piazza and the avenue, as two components of an integrated whole, are thus inseparably joined and yet clearly differentiated from each other. They are, in short, set in *contrapposti,* not unlike the church façade and the colonnades in the view from the propylaeum, or for that matter, as we witness in the architect's façade design in general.[239]

Contrasted with each other for mutual reinforcement, the two components nevertheless form a unit; they must be experienced as one continuous sequence.[240] In this sequence, the ideal panorama significantly comes in the middle rather than at the outset. It is the crowning climax, carefully timed and prepared for, and, surprisingly, we are not really taken by surprise; we find ourselves prepared for it, instead, because the avenue provides us with the anticipation that something momentous is coming while what it is that is coming is scarcely revealed. This effect of anticipated climax, it must be emphasized, is fundamentally different from that of unexpected surprise that the situation before 1935 presented; the latter is reminiscent, in fact, of the drama in the medieval townscape, of which the Campo in Siena is one familiar example. It also corresponds to the condition of the piazza as Bernini found it when he was commissioned the planning (Fig. 83).[241]

The idea of preparing for the climax with a proper context is one of the most central principles in Bernini's art in general; but, in particular, it characterizes that dramatic effect which Bernini so consummately perfected in his theater. A conflagration on the stage, for example, did not happen without a warning in his production; it would be preceded by a scene in which an actor comes on stage with a torch in his hand swinging it around mindlessly as though he might in any minute accidentally set the scene on fire, and so eventually he does.[242] Such a psychological manipulation of the audience, rather than a sheer spectacle, was apparently what gave Bernini's theater the reputation it deserved.[243] So, too, in his urban design he would not have dispensed with the long avenue he needed for preparing the visitor for the climax at the propylaeum. The basis of Bernini's urban drama—to paraphrase Alfred Hitchcock's words on his own art—was not a mere surprise but a true suspense;[244] and the result was a theatrical effect of the highest order. This was Bernini's Grand Design in full Baroque splendor.[245]

TOWARD THE OPEN *SPINA:* FONTANA AND THE AFTERMATH

In Bernini's first submission, the trapezoid plan, Michelangelo's Campidoglio served him as a point of departure. The revised design of 1667, if fully completed, would also have resembled in some respects the Campidoglio and its Cordonata. The piazza, though frontal, can be seen as a relatively self-contained space, and this is contrasted with the ramp that penetrates it with its forward thrust. As we walk up, the ramp (since it slopes upward) keeps the piazza partially out of our sight, obscuring its actual shape and dimensions, until we reach the summit (Fig. 84); here, the enclosed space, together with the oval pavement, suddenly unfolds before us.[246]

Michelangelo's piazza, however, is completely open on one side; and, spatially, the ramp continues into it without a barrier. The two component parts, therefore, accommodate each other rather like the nave and crossing of a Latin-cross basilica; neither is really complete in itself. The piazza, however, is not only frontal but strongly axialized within, and urges us to move on. It thus reiterates the tapered form as well as the dynamism of the ramp, of which it thus becomes a telescopelike extension; and, together, they read as an integral part of the city's "flow" system (Fig. 85). In a sense, then, the Campidoglio frustrates the expectation of those who approach it. Reaching the top of the ramp, where we expect a restful pause, we are only urged onward all over again. We are drawn in suspense, but the climax, by Bernini's standard, is over too quickly; and, of course, we must recognize the fact that the Campidoglio is more a vestibule than a place of assembly that the amphitheater of the Piazza Obliqua was conceived to be.

Carlo Fontana, however, denied this distinction; in proposing the completion of Bernini's project in 1694, he insisted on the expression of flow at the expense of suspense and drama. His three designs in the *Templum Vaticanum,* which are generally considered as three separate proposals, represent nevertheless three stages of his conception that trace the development from a critique of Bernini's premise to the solution that fully realizes the author's own ideal.[247]

In his first design (Figs. 86 and 87),[248] Fontana elaborated on Bernini's propylaeum, enlarging it as well in width and height, and placed it farther out from the Piazza Obliqua than Bernini had planned; he then enclosed the antepiazza with corridors like those of the Piazza Retta. Fontana positioned the propylaeum at the exact distance from the obelisk as the facade of the Basilica is from it in order to achieve, as he explains, a symmetrical design; but, undoubtedly, he also wanted to mark out his own ideal viewpoint, from which Michelangelo's dome and drum was thought to be better in view than in Bernini's solution.[249] In this view, on the other hand, the corridors in the foreground crop out a large portion of the colonnades that frame the Basilica since the antepiazza is now twice as deep. The view truncates the oval space and emphasizes the two trapezoidal compartments; the piazza, in its initial impression, is therefore a longitudinal space. Needless to say, Fontana transformed the given situation to bring it as close as possible to the design based on his "true ellipse" that he expounded earlier in the same book (Fig. 54);[250] it should be noted that his comparison is, in fact, Bernini's 1659 design with the *terzo braccio* on the oval outline, as indicated in dotted lines.

At this stage of thought, Fontana still considered preserving whatever remained of the *spina;* he created a small hemicycle outside the propylaeum and provided two streets flanking it (Fig. 88).[251] But the conception is obviously incomplete; the streets would channel the visitor directly into the antepiazza, bypassing the crucial propylaeum, and it is not clear, either, how they were linked to the existing Borgo streets, which were not arranged in symmetry.

In the second design, therefore, Fontana amended this difficulty. He would now clear the whole *spina* and also a part of the blocks south of the Borgo Vecchio in order to create a broad avenue leading to the propylaeum (Fig. 89).[252] Lined with shops, the avenue—called Piazza di Mercato—is secular in contrast to the sacred precinct beyond the propylaeum, which is now designated Arco Trionfale.[253] The two areas are thus clearly distinguished from each other, spatially separated and contrasted functionally. Yet, similar in form, one repeats the other thematically; the deep, receding vista Fontana offers us at the propylaeum instead of Bernini's expansive panorama is, we might say, a scenographic elaboration of the first vista we are given to experience as we go up the introductory avenue. As the Campidoglio elaborates on the theme of its Cordonata, Fontana's piazza amplifies the vista of the avenue, like a choral reprise, with pomp and fanfare; and, significantly, the propylaeum, also described as the "nobile interrompimento," comes exactly halfway in the long stretch from the bank of the Tiber to the Basilica as the obelisk marks the midpoint of the second sequence. The pause at the propylaeum is nevertheless only a pretext for another drive forward; despite the interruption, the whole progression is almost one continuous grand avenue.

The third design thus follows from the second; having eliminated the propylaeum altogether, Fontana now ran the avenue—no longer a piazza but *stradone* as he calls it—all the way up to Bernini's circular colonnades (Fig. 90) and then proposed new porticoes on both sides of it.[254] Uninterrupted, the avenue has become the whole design. In consequence, the Piazza Obliqua, too, reads now more as a space for flow than for collection; like a traffic circle, it is now completely subordinated to the avenue and barely interferes with the path of progression on which one is expected to keep moving single-mindedly. Nothing, of course, is so remote as this from Bernini's conception of the open *spina*.

Guided by a unity of purpose, Fontana's last design is nevertheless simple and consistent; and, if simplistic and overscaled, it is surely grandiose and brings with it a sense of momentum like that of Haussmann's later cannon-shot boulevard. The appeal of Fontana's proposal for the planners in the next two centuries may be partly accounted for by this simple monumentality. Cosimo Morelli's project of 1776 (Figs. 91 and 92) is essentially a more economical version of Fontana's; the avenue traces the lines of the existing Borgo streets and is therefore asymmetrical.[255] The project of Camille de Tournon, Prefect of Rome under Napoleon, in which Valadier participated in full measure, revived Morelli's design;[256] and from there it entered Alessandro Viviani's Piano Regolatore of 1873,[257] and came to be perpetuated first in the Plan of 1881 and then in the revised and amplified version of 1887, which readopted the symmetrical avenue.[258]

By the middle of the nineteenth century, however, there were naturally other reasons for the special interest in Fontana's "thruway" scheme. It served well in the planning scheme of the time, which emphasized a network of thoroughfares—a flow system. Moreover, it was historically tenable. Recorded in what came to be accepted as an authoritative volume on Saint Peter's (by no less an authority than Letarouilly), Fontana's designs—all three of them—commanded respect; but the last of the three, in particular, which was the most consistent, must have appeared the most definitive proposal ever inasmuch as it was supported by the tradition extending from Nicholas V. By contrast, Bernini's vision existed only in sketches and was quickly forgotten.

But art historians came to know better. From the end of the century, in fact, no project proposing an open avenue passed without a critical attack based on the knowledge of Bernini's design, and there were already a few before 1920.[259] But the argument, repeated time and again, claimed on the basis of the design of 1659 that Bernini conceived the piazza as an unpenetrated enclosure and therefore any open avenue did injustice to his intention;[260] and, before long, on the strength of its persuasiveness, the proposition became a whole historical truth. That the architect's intention in 1667, if not already in 1659, was to enclose *and* penetrate eluded even Wittkower, who was himself responsible in 1931 for the discovery and publication of the ill-fated last revision; demonstrating the relocation of the *terzo braccio,* he neverthelesss assumed that Bernini would have left the Borgo intact.

Piacentini and Spaccarelli: Via della Conciliazione

There already existed, then, two distinct factions when the open *spina* became a pressing issue in Mussolini's Rome; there were, cn the one hand, those practicing architects, who, acquainted with the projects of the preceding two centuries, hardly thought of questioning the aesthetic validity of the open avenue, and there were, on the other, defenders of the closed piazza, represented by art historians. The projects of Marcello Piacentini and Attilio Spaccarelli, which resulted in the widely censured Via della Conciliazione, can be accurately assessed only against this background.[261]

Appointed in 1935, the two architects produced in the course of the next year and a few months a series of plans that dealt with two general questions. One was whether the avenue should be open all the way or closed off the Piazza Rusticucci by means of a portico, and the other was whether it should taper out toward the piazza or maintain a uniform width.[262] As a result of the study, the architects concluded that an open avenue would require parallel sides for a proper optical effect if the grandeur of the Basilica were to be maximized as desired and that only a closed avenue would create the necessary separation of the sacred precinct from the civic zone that belongs to the city of Rome; and a portico, they also observed, could provide a viewpoint for the Basilica across the piazza and isolate Michelangelo's dome in the view from the bank of the Tiber (or Ponte Sant' Angelo) by screening off the facade of Maderno.[263] Their own choice, accordingly, was the solution that most closely resembled Fontana's second design—an avenue that tapered out and terminated with a single-story portico more or less where Fontana planned his "nobile interrompimento" (Fig. 93); and this was submitted in June 1936, first to Mussolini and then to Pope Pius XI, both of whom gave their immediate approval. It is important to realize that Piacentini and Spaccarelli were fully aware of Bernini's heritage in adopting the basic idea of Fontana's second design.[264] They might have calculated, too, that the project, a compromise solution, could appease the two factions.

Instead, controversy raged over it; besides the old issue, to keep or clear the *spina,* there was now a new one, to close or open the avenue.[265] In the meantime, the demolition of the buildings of the *spina* was begun, and in 1937 a wood-and-plaster mockup of the proposed portico was built on the site to test its form, position, and effect. By then, the architects reversed their earlier decision on the form of the avenue, mainly for economy and preservation, and received approval on the avenue of uniform width.[266] Finally, in another *volte-face,* they discarded the "interrompimento" and the result was the definitive project, submitted and approved in May 1938 (Fig. 94).[267] But this was not an open-avenue scheme that the projects of Fontana and his successors were; for, while the portico was eliminated, there was introduced in the same location at the head of the avenue what was called Propylaea, formed by the porticoes of the new matching palaces framing the Piazza Rusticucci.

The execution of the definitive project proceeded slowly; interrupted by the war, it was brought to completion only in 1950. In view of Piacentini's leadership in Fascist Italy, the widespread condemnation that the Piacentini-Spaccarelli project suffered in the decades after the war is understandable; but it is hardly justifiable.[268] For, the style of the buildings aside, theirs is a thoughtful solution.

The singular ingenuity of the definitive plan is, indeed, the bottleneck constriction produced by the last-minute invention—the Propylaea. First of all, it defined the separation of the piazza from the avenue without isolating one from the other, exactly as desired by the architects from the start. The opening, which is 30 meters or about 135 *palmi,* is sufficiently small in proportion to the dimensions of the enclosed area to insure its integrity, if one recognizes as he should that the enclosure is not the oval but the cruciform composite; had Bernini's *terzo braccio* been built as specified by the Bonacina Engraving, the gaps on either side of it would have been almost as wide.[269]

The constriction, moreover, not only successfully conceals Bernini's colonnades from the visitor all the way up the avenue (Fig. 81); it also masks, as intended, the outer bays of Maderno's facade in such a way that the Basilica regains in the vista up the avenue the more vertical proportion associated with Michelangelo's design.[270] It is well to recall that, rightly or wrongly, Bernini himself was obsessed by the problem of correcting Maderno's "squat facade." [271]

To build a propylaeum in the Piazza Rusticucci after Bernini's design would be an archeological restoration, and that is not difficult; a substitute, whatever the style, would necessarily risk being either a pastiche or an obtrusion. Having decided against an "interrompimento," Piacentini and Spaccarelli created a void where a propylaeum might have been built; thus, without a propylaeum, they achieved the most essential of the effects that Bernini had planned to achieve with his propylaeum. The entrance to the piazza, it is true, lacks formality; the pause in the sequence is dramatically weak; the ideal viewpoint is no longer indicated. Still, the avenue, uniform rather than tapered, is a spatial corridor, set in *contrapposti* with the expansive piazza beyond the bottleneck; and there is a suspense and drama that Fontana's second design lacks.[272] A solution that comes closer to Bernini's ideal than this has never been proposed.

The suspense in Bernini's Grand Design, needless to say, was not an end in itself. It was a means of magnifying the splendor of the piazza that was to glorify the Christian world. Only by clearing the *spina* he could truly fulfill the twofold program of the project: to create a majestic approach to the Basilica and the Vatican and an enclosed place for assembly. Only with a formal avenue could he fully express the idea that the Basilica reaches out across the piazza to the city of Rome in compliance with the office of the Pope as her Bishop and in conformity with the nature of his Easter blessing given *urbi et orbi* (Fig. 95). Yet the propylaeum would have warranted that the cruciform place excluded the Borgo, and the Piazza Obliqua within it would have remained an amphitheater, a world in itself.

We must recognize, then, that the Square of Saint Peter's as we know it today, is still most of these things that Bernini expected it to be; it is sequentially a prelude to the sanctuary, functionally its extension, and spatially a buffer to set it off from the secular world, the Borgo and what lies beyond it. If for a wrong reason, Piacentini and Spaccarelli masterfully solved this problem of linkage and separation, penetration and enclosure. The *spina* clearance under Mussolini which involved their effort, indeed, not fortuitously commemorated the Lateran Concordat of 1929 between the Holy State and the Italian government, again, if for a wrong reason; and this was recorded for the posterity in the name of the new avenue—Via della Conciliazione.

Postscript: Bernini as Scenographic Architect

ERNINI'S DESIGN of the Piazza Obliqua was conceived, developed, and executed between 1656 and 1667. During the same decade, the architect also produced three churches, which, together with the piazza, constitute the core of his architectural output: [273] San Tommaso da Villanova at Castelgandolfo (1658–61),[274] Sant' Andrea al Quirinale in Rome (1658–70), and Santa Maria dell' Assunzione at Ariccia (1662–64).[275]

The three churches are all central-type designs insofar as their plans are based on simple geometrical forms; they are also characteristically simple and lucid in both massing and spatial definition. Thus they corroborate the architect's avowed predilection for regular geometrical forms as well as his unqualified reverence for the Pantheon.[276] For Bernini, indeed, the Pantheon was not merely a point of departure but a paradigm; he unabashedly imitated it in the church at Ariccia, but even in Sant' Andrea he made it the underlying theme.[277] It is not surprising, therefore, that Bernini's architecture is traditionally discussed in terms of classicism. After all, even Milizia, the undaunted censor of everything Baroque, found virtues in his architecture.[278]

The Piazza Obliqua is also centralized in plan; the oval area has a single focus at the obelisk, and this is stressed by the radial pavement design. The cruciform composite, created in the 1667 revision, is even more explicitly a biaxially balanced form. The architecture of the colonnades is also simple, lucid, and severe. In the architect's conception of the design, moreover, the oval piazza was the circular amphitheater; in both form and iconography, Bernini pursued a classical paradigm.

But classicism is only one dimension of Bernini's art of design. If his church plans exhibit simple geometrical forms, they are, as architectural expressions, frontalized both externally and internally (Fig. 76). The exterior shows a clear distinction between the front and the rear; it is designed to be seen and approached from the front, and the facade, with its *piazzetta,* is the most vital feature of these churches. The interior is no less frontal. The internal space, not withstanding its general shape, is hardly the kind that is evolved centrally about an abstract nodal point. The center of the space, recognizable on the plan, is obscured in the actual experience of the space by an axis, a line of progression, that connects the entrance to the high altar. By emphasizing the high altar facing the entrance, Bernini disrupts the continuity of the form implied in the repetition of identical aspects around the space and, moreover, forces the visitor to confront the altar and establish this axis immediately on entering the church. But the space is not axially organized, as the case may be in a longitudinal space, because the elevation in which the high altar is set extends laterally. The frontal elevation, which corresponds to the rear half of the plan, thus defines the space that unfolds in front of the visitor, as the facade shapes the *piazzetta* outside; physically closed, the interior is nevertheless as frontal in experience as the chapel, or even the proscenium stage. In short, the space is developed frontally from the specific viewpoint of the visitor; the elevation and the space in front of it, experienced as a whole in perspective, or *scaenographia* in Vitruvius's term,[279] thus constitute the spatial reality of Bernini's churches. Bernini's space emerges more as an optical experience than as a conceptually defined geometrical entity.

In imposing axiality and frontality on the plan, even when it is central, Bernini goes counter to his Renaissance predecessors and finds affinity with the architects of Imperial Rome. The Pantheon was, indeed, his paradigm. But his experience with the Piazza Obliqua undoubtedly had a special impact on the conception of his churches. The project, after all, was one of creating a space in front of a preexisting facade; frontality was an aspect of the program. By 1657, moreover, he had already come up with the split circle, a central form penetrated by an axis; and the next two years corresponded with the most intense phase in the design of his two churches, San Tommaso and Sant' Andrea.[280] The comprehension of the oval space defined by the colonnades and Maderno's facade inset between them that one would have had from the *terzo braccio* of the 1659 design is exactly like that of the interior of Sant' Andrea from a point a few steps inside the portal.[281]

The scenographic potentiality of the Piazza Obliqua, on the other hand, was fully explored only in the revision of 1667; it was then that the front side of the oval was actually opened up and the viewpoint stipulated *outside* it. The experience gained in the design of churches was now brought to bear on an urban situation where, unhampered by the necessity to shelter, the principle of scenography could be carried a step further. And Bernini's unique strength as an urban planner is closely linked to his scenographic approach to architecture. He was quick to see that no urban design can be a closed, self-contained entity that a building might be because no segment of an urban environment can be really isolated from the contiguous segments that constitute its context; he knew how to open a form to its environment. Moreover, it came natural to him to shape a space as a view that unfolds before the viewer; he could readily think a design out as a sequence of vistas and panoramas, in which the viewer is the point of control.

If classicism is an aspect of Bernini's architecture (as it undoubtedly is), its underlying principle is nevertheless illusionism—illusionism in its very broad sense of a preoccupation with the reality of visual perception. To borrow from Panofsky's illustration of Galileo's *paragone* on sculpture and painting, a circular disk, painted in chiaroscuro to simulate a sphere, is no less real as a visual phenomenon than the sphere it simulates.[282] To Galileo, a scientific and analytical mind, the distinction between tactile relief and visible relief was as clear as it was essential; to Bernini, it was secondary to the common factor, the visual reality. Thus he would have seen the difference between painting and sculpture more as a difference of degree than of kind; and architecture, conceived as scenography,[283] would have been a part of this scheme. Only on this premise, would the "mixed" creation like the Cornaro Chapel have been conceivable and justifiable.

If Bernini saw no contradiction between classical architecture and Baroque sculpture that he combined in his churches,[284] that was because he conceived his architecture no less (and no more) scenographically than his sculpture. As his statues engulf the space in front of them and participate in the real world and, in so doing, make the fictional space coextensive with the real space,[285] so his architecture also merges art and life in its own way. In classical architecture, the space that the architect has shaped is ideally complete in itself; the viewer, physically occupying it, is nevertheless expected to suppress his own presence in reading it as though he were somewhere outside, above, or beyond it. The fluid space the viewer conquers by moving through is considered to be apart from the objective architectural space which is fixed to endure, though they may be physically inseparable. In Bernini's architecture, by contrast, the space the viewer commands by possession is the very space the architect shaped into a permanent setting. Life and theater thus merge into one experience; for the architectural elevation, or *scaenographia,* imposes itself on the viewer and makes him the protagonist of the architectural space it defines, and he is compelled to participate in the world of the artist's creation.

In Bernini's architecture the classical ideal is subsumed in his Baroque vision as the circle is subsumed in the oval in his design of the Square of Saint Peter's.

Appendix

1. THE ELLIPSE IN THE SIXTEENTH AND SEVENTEENTH CENTURIES

THE ELLIPSE is a conic section; the oval, composed of circular segments, is an approximation. (The terms *ellipse* and *oval* are interchangeable in common usage, but the distinction drawn here is useful for our purpose.) The true ellipse is awkward to plot and build. The oval suffices in architectural design unless a property peculiar to the ellipse is specifically sought (e.g., its shifting curvature). An architect, therefore, does not normally choose between the ellipse and the oval but among different forms of the oval. This was true also in the seventeenth century.

It has been noted that for architects of sixteenth-century Italy the ellipse was virtually nonexistent (Lotz, "Die ovalen Kirchenräume," 11–17). The situation remained basically unchanged through the seventeenth century notwithstanding Kepler. The oval stood for the ellipse and served in all architectural needs; and treatises repeated Serlio's ovals. But to say that the true ellipse was nonexistent in practice does not mean that it was unknown. The true ellipse did appear sporadically in treatises, Serlio's among them.

A few pages before his oval geometry, Serlio treats the arch "of less height than the semicircle" (*Il primo libro,* 11). He first describes the method with a string: "Vorrà l'Architetto fare vn ponte, o vn' arco, o veramente vna volta di minore altezza che il mezo cerchio, auenga che molti muratori hanno vna certa sua prattica, che col filo fanno simili volte, lequali veramente corrispondeno all' occhio, & si accorda anchora con alcune forme ouali fatte col compasso." This is an application of his oval construction (Fig. 46). Then, he goes on: "Nondimeno se l'architetto vorrà procedere teoricamente, portato dalla ragione, potrà tener questa via." The method Serlio then demonstrates is the coordinate method. Two concentric circles are first drawn whose diameters correspond to the major and minor diameters of the required ellipse; the curve is plotted between the two circles by combining for each common radius the horizontal coordinate of one with the vertical coordinate of the other (Fig. 52, right). Naturally, Serlio illustrates only a half-ellipse. The method is nevertheless a standard demonstation in analytic geometry; and furthermore, he specifies that the curve "non si può fare col cõpasso, ma con la discreta et prattica mano sarà tirata."

Without naming it, Serlio evidently distinguished the "theoretical" ellipse from the practical approximations "drawn with compasses."

There is no evidence, on the other hand, that Serlio knew the string method familiar to gardeners (Fig. 52, center). This method is based on the property of the ellipse that the sum of the distances of a point on the curve from its two foci is a constant. It received the first theoretical treatment after Antiquity in Guido Ubaldo, marchese del Monte, *Planisphaeriorum universalium theorica,* Pesaro, 1579 (Lotz, "Die ovalen Kirchenräume," 12, n. 9). But not until past the turn of the century does it begin to appear in architectural treatises as an alternative to the oval. Pietro Accolti introduces it with a comment that "puossi ancora più manualmente tirar in disegno qualsiuoglia ouato in questo modo" and thus identifies this ellipse with the oval of circular arcs he illustrates in the same chapter (*Lo inganno degl' occhi,* Florence, 1625, ch. 30). After reproducing Serlio's four ovals, Troili recommends the method "per varie misure d'ovati" (*Paradossi,* 10–11). Guarini demonstrates it under the caption, "Del modo di formare una Elisse, od ovato con due centri" (*Architettura Civile,* Turin, 1737, 59).

The ellipse occurs most frequently in perspective treatises in the form of a foreshortened circle (Fig. 52, left). As a rule, however, perspective was treated apart from the construction of geometrical figures because it is a phenomenon observed on a foreshortened plane. Two convergent lines were customarily described as parallel; and a square in perspective was a square, not a trapezoid. A foreshortened circle was therefore a circle—neither an ellipse (which it was) nor an oval, its approximation.

Vignola's widely circulated treatise, *Le due regole della prospettiva pratica,* Rome, 1583, is typical (v. T. K. Kitao, "Prejudice in Perspective: A Study of Vignola's Perspective Treatise," *Art Bulletin,* XLIV, 1962, 173–94). Egnatio Danti, who edited the treatise with extensive commentaries, was a mathematician. He remarks authoritatively, in the chapter on "il cerchio in Prospettiva," that Vignola does not discuss "la figura curvilinea, che eschi dalla sezione parabolica, ò da quella dell'anello, ò da qualsivoglia altra sezione del cilindro, ò del conio" (*Le due regole,* 113) and suggests that any conic section can be plotted in perspective like the circle. Yet he illustrates the comment with an *ovato tondo* which includes all internal lines, and he is totally indifferent to the fact that the foreshortened circle accompanying Vignola's main text in the very same chapter is, after all, an oblique section of the visual cone.

The relationship was, however, pointed out by Lorenzo Sirigatti, known only by his *Pratica di Prospettiva* (Venice, 1596 and 1625). He reminds the reader (Bk. I, ch. 9) that "non essendo altro il cerchio degradata, che vna figura Ouata, chiamata da Greci Elipsi," it can be constructed by using two axes (by which he must mean coordinates) as "Signor Guidobaldo de' Marchese del Monte insegna nel fine del secondo libro del suo Planisferio."

Ellipsography interested both Dürer and Leonardo, but Barozzi's ellipsograph was published only much later in Francesco Barozzi, *Admirandum illud geometricum problema* (Venice, 1586; v. Otto Kurz, "Dürer, Leonardo and the Invention of the Ellipsograph," *Raccolta Vinciana,* XVIII, Milan, 1960, 15–25). The subject remained a mathematical problem, however. Various graphic methods and mechanical devices for constructing ellipses are found in Franciscus van Schooten, *Eerste Bouck der Mathematische Oeffeningen,* Amsterdam, 1659.

Dürer, who discussed the ellipse as a conic section in his *Underweysung der Messung,* Nuremberg, 1525, represented it in the shape of an egg and equated the German *Eierlinie* with *Eklipsis* (E. Panofsky, *Albrecht Dürer,* Princeton, N.J., 1945, 247f.). Equivalent terms *ellipse* and *ovale* or *ovato* applied equally in the seventeenth century to both the exact form and the approximation; and this included Kepler (E. Panofsky, *Galileo as a Critic of the Arts,* The Hague, 1954, 22, also 29, n. 2, and 31, n. 1. The erudite term was nevertheless rare in architectural writing, and it is still missing from Baldinucci's dictionary of 1681. *Vocabolario toscano,* in which the oval is entered: "Ovale, ouato, & Aouato: add. Tōdo bisūgo."

Carlo Fontana's use of the term *ellipse* in describing Bernini's oval piazza (see below) was certainly pedantic in 1694; it may be the earliest application of the term to an actual work of architecture. In the following century, Milizia already eschewed the more familiar term; he wrote that Bernini chose for his piazza "la figura ellittica" (*Memorie degli architetti antichi e moderni,* Bassano, 1785, II, 176–77).

2. CARLO FONTANA'S "TRUE ELLIPSE"

Carlo Fontana's criticism of Bernini's Piazza Obliqua in his *Templum Vaticanum*, Rome, 1694 (Bk. IV, ch. 3), is one of special interest for what the text reveals about the oval in architectural practice of the Seicento. The relevant passage (p. 183) runs as follows (italics are mine):

> Sono questi *due Bracci circolari* de' Portici non prossimi al Tempio, distanta vno dall'altro ne' principij de' *loro quasi semicircoli* palmi 427 nel quale spazio risiede la Piazza. Lo circoferenza di questi sì interne, come esterne compone *vna figura quasi di elipse.* La linea del diametro maggiore essendo parallela alla Facciata del Tempio, è impropria, secondo le buone regole, questa disposizione; mentre douerebbe la predetta linea essere corrispondente à quella del mezzo del Tempio, cioè essere situati i Portici per il longo, e formare *la vera figura Elipse,* colla quale douerebbero quasi essere congionti al Tempio, come è stato pratticato degli antichi Romani ne' loro Teatri . . . Ma da' principij di questi Portici che s'attaciano a' Corridori, mediante la loro situazione trasuersale, resta nascosta buona parte di *quei Semicircoli,* doue viene impedito il vedere al Popolo la Loggia della quale il Sommo Pontefice dà la benedizione. Quell' impedimento non si sarebbe causato, se *l'ouato* di questi Portici fosse stato disposto per il longo, non per il trauerso, come è stato pratticato.
>   Nulladimeno non deuesi censuare il Bernini . . . per non auerli così bene disposti, mentre il Palazzo, fu necessitato nel distribuirli à dare nel denotato difetto.

Fontana describes the form of Bernini's piazza twice in the passage, first as *figura quasi di elipse,* and later as *ovato.* This may suggest that his own *vera figura elipse* is a precise conic section. But we know this is not the case. Fontana illustrates it as an *ovato tondo* (Fig. 54); joints of circular arcs are, in fact, clearly discernible. We also find elsewhere that *ovale* and *elipse* are interchangeable; "piazza ouale" of the Italian text is rendered "platea fig. elypsis" in Latin (p. 184). It is therefore evident that by *figura quasi di elipse* he does not mean an approximate form.

The colonnades Fontana describes are *circolari;* he also refers to them as *semicircoli.* He is obviously more specific when he speaks of *loro quasi semicircoli.* We may be tempted to interpret *quasi* in this phrase as referring to the fact that the colonnades are nearly but not perfectly circular in curvature; each colonnade extends beyond the 120-degree segment of the *ovato tondo* and is therefore a composite curve (Fig. 41). But Fontana was actually unaware of this subtlety; throughout the book he illustrated perfectly circular colonnades. By quasi *semicircoli,* Fontana must then mean that the colonnades form nearly but not quite complete semicircles. The *figura quasi di elipse* is consequently an open curve; it is not complete all around. The phrase is accurately applied to the outline formed by the colonnades.

Obviously, Fontana's alternative proposal would feature porticoes, too, so that his *vera figura elipse* could not be complete either. The *vera* in the phrase concerns neither precision nor completeness, then; it is not placed opposite *quasi*. It signifies, instead, truthfulness to the tradition ("secondo le buone regole"); specifically, it has to do with the proposition that the oval is "disposto per il longo, non per il trauerso."

Fontana refers to the Roman theater, not for the oval plan, but for the relationship between the enclosure and the temple. He is specific that it is Bernini's placement of the oval that is improper. His *buone regole* therefore do not pertain to the authority of the ancients. There is no doubt that they represent the tradition of the oval plan in the more immediate past, which we discussed in this study. Fontana's "true ellipse" was the longitudinal oval, firmly established in church architecture since Vignola's contributions. Similarly, in another passage describing Bernini's oval piazza (p. 208), Fontana speaks of "questa non perfetta Elipse."

We can discard the possibility that Fontana is speaking loosely. For, pedantic in his diction, he is rigorously precise. His fastidiousness is manifest in this passage as well as elsewhere in his book; to him Bernini's creation is not simply a piazza but, accurately, a "Teatro con suoi Portici che recingono la Piazza Vaticana, auanti il Tempio" (p. 179). When he writes "true ellipse," he must therefore imply authenticity. He must mean that his oval not only follows the tradition but is for that reason authentic.

Furthermore, Fontana's proposal is unrealistic; it is not feasible. But since he is fully aware of this fact, he is presenting his own oval as an ideal, unattainable but worthy of consideration; it is *the* true ellipse. The ellipse, in Fontana's mind, is true only if it is disposed lengthwise. Longitudinal placement is virtually an inherent property of the oval or ellipse.

This peculiar reasoning undoubtedly reflects Fontana's personal preference. Geometrically, it may be regarded an aberration. But from the point of view of design, it is a remarkably sharp and accurate observation. For, while the oval is by definition oblong (Baldinucci's *tondo bislungo*), the elongated character is fully realized only in the longitudinal use; only then the axis of approach, superimposed on the long axis of the figure, fully develops the "ovalness" of the oval. The transverse oval is in this sense unreasonable, because it contradicts the nature of the oval.

G. B. Passeri explained this phenomenon lucidly and thoroughly nearly a century later: "La figura ovale ha tutto il comodo della rotonda poichè in questro pur anche l'occhio concepisce tutto l'edifizio ed inoltre è più capace del doppio di quello. E però contro ragione di formare d'ovato in traverso, cosicchè l'ingresso sia nel fianco maggiore e per conseguenza per lo minor diametro della figura; poichè l'occhio nel primo ingresso misura l'edificio nella parte dove è più stretto e convien poi che cerchi più ampio ne' due lati, mirandoli in due vedute, e per conseguenza deve formare due distinte figure, per comprenderne il tutto." (The passage was cited by V. Fasolo, "Sistemi ellittici nell'Architettura," *Architettura e arti decorative,* X, 1931, 311; source unidentified.)

What Carlo Fontana did not fully comprehend was that Bernini was least concerned with the ovalness of the oval; and as for the unity of the two parts, the central obelisk was a sure anchor and focus.

Notes

1. The fundamental work on the subject is Wittkower's contribution, "Petersplatz," in H. Brauer and R. Wittkower, *Die Zeichnungen des Gianlorenzo Bernini,* Berlin, 1931 (hereafter, Brauer-Wittkower), 64–102. This is supplemented by two articles by Wittkower: "A Counter-project to Bernini's 'Piazza di San Pietro,'" *Journal of the Warburg and Courtauld Institutes,* III, 1939–40, 88–106, and "Il terzo braccio del Bernini in Piazza S. Pietro," *Bolletino d'arte,* XXXIV, 1949, 129–34. In addition, Chantelou's account of Bernini's sojourn in Paris is essential: *Journal du voyage du Cavalier Bernin en France,* ed. L. Lalanne, Paris, 1885. Basic documents were published by S. Fraschetti (*Il Bernini: la sua vita, le sue opere, il suo tempo,* Milan, 1900, 307–16), Brauer-Wittkower, F. Ehrle ("Dalle carte e dai disegni di Virgilio Spada," *Atti della Pontificia Accademia Romana di Archeologia,* serie III, Memorie II, 1928, 1–98), and L. von Pastor, *The History of the Popes,* XXXI, London, 1940, 291–99; these and other unpublished documents are found for the most part in the Vatican library (Chigi codices), the Archivio Segreto Vaticano (*Avvisi*), and the Archivio della Reverenda Fabbrica di San Pietro (Minutes of the Congregazione della Fabbrica, estimates, contracts, accounts, records of work, etc.). For the early history of the site and its bearing on Bernini's design, see C. Thoenes, "Studien zur Geschichte des Petersplatzes," *Zeitschrift für Kunstgeschichte,* XXVI, 1963, 97–145. The earliest monograph on the piazza is Carlo Fontana, *Templum Vaticanum/Il Tempio Vaticano,* Rome, 1694, of which the Fourth Book is devoted to the Square of Saint Peter's. Many penetrating ideas are also found in V. Mariani, *Significato del Portico berniniano di San Pietro,* Rome, 1935. In the latest monograph on Bernini, Maurizio and Marcello Fagiolo dell'Arco make a number of observations that coincide with my conclusions: *Bernini, una introduzione al gran teatro del barocco,* Rome, 1967, 151–54, 278–79, Cat. No. 166 *et passim.* For brief accounts, see the following: G. Giovannoni, "Roma dal Rinascimento al 1870," *Topografia e urbanistica di Roma,* in *Storia di Roma,* XII, Bologna, 1958, 442–50 and 524–32; R. Wittkower, *Art and Architecture in Italy, 1600–1750,* Harmondsworth and Baltimore, 1958, 125–29; and H.-W. Kruft,

"Symbolik in der Architektur Berninis," *Neue Zürcher Zeitung,* No. 267, June 11, 1972, 51–52 (an excellent summary, to which Ernest Nash kindly called my attention).

2. *Templum Vaticanum,* 181, where both "Piazza Retta" and "Piazza Obliqua" are indicated; this is, to my knowledge, the earliest appearance of these names. *Retta* obviously signified in this context, not straight, but rectilinear as opposed to curvilinear; otherwise, it would be contradictory to apply it to a piazza whose sides are rectilinear but divergent or oblique. *Obliqua* therefore could not have meant oblique. In the seventeenth century, in fact, the primary meaning of the word *obliqua* was *non retto* or *torto* rather than *inclinato;* the latter, which was a secondary sense, gained priority only in the nineteenth century. For this, see F. Baldinucci, *Vocabolario toscano dell'arte del disegno,* Florence, 1681; *Vocabolario degli accademici della Crusca,* Verona, 1806; and *Vocabolario universale della lingua italiana,* Naples, 1834. The implication of the designation Piazza Obliqua is discussed below (Ch. IV). Fontana also christened the platform immediately in front of the portals of the Basilica "Piazza Pensile."

3. Each colonnade is a three-aisled structure. Piers and columns of travertine are laid out in four courses of concentric arcs. The central aisle, designed for carriages, is barrel-vaulted and is about twice as wide as the side aisles, which are for pedestrians (Fig. 24). No more than about two column-diameters in width, the side aisles are trabeated and coffered. A cross-passage intercepts the aisles at three points: on the axis through the fountains, at the juncture with the corridor, and at the eastern termination. It is framed by twin pilasters. Columns are closely set; the clear bay varies from two column-diameters in the innermost course to two and one quarter column-diameter in the outmost course (cf. Note 70, below). They are also relatively slender; though crowned with Doric capitals and mounted on Tuscan bases, their shafts are Ionic in proportion (Fontana, *Templum Vaticanum,* 187). Cf. Note 92, below. The plain Ionic entablature is continuous except above the cross-passage, where it projects forward. A balustrade adorned with statues surmounts the whole structure.

4. K. Lynch, *The Image of the City,* Cambridge, Mass., 1960, 9f., where the term was introduced and defined.

5. Thoenes, "Geschichte des Petersplatzes," 120. The geometry of this oval and its significance in Bernini's plan for the piazza will be treated in Ch. III, below; see also Notes 117–19, below. That the colonnades describe circular arcs was already observed by M. Reymond, *Le Bernin,* n.d. [ca. 1911], 114, and Max von Boehn, *Lorenzo Bernini,* Leipzig, 1912, 86; but earlier still, Gasparo Alveri wrote in his guidebook of 1664 that the piazza, then under construction, is oval in plan but most perfect in form because it is composed of two circles (v. Note 82, below).

6. Bibl. Vat., Chig. P VII 9, fols. 17ᵛ/18; the drawing measures 774 x 548 mm., approximately 30 x 21 inches. The radius of the two interlocking circles is 296 *palmi;* the major axis of the oval is accordingly three times this, or 888 *palmi* (198.2 meters or 650.1 feet). The minor axis is 671.3 *palmi* (149.8 meters or 491.46 feet); see Note 121, below. The conversion rate is 1 Roman *palmo* = 0.2232 meters or 0.7321 foot; it can be verified by the life-size scale of one *palmo* on the Bonacina Engraving (Fig. 24; v. Note 154, below);

I have counterchecked it using the pilaster in the interior of Sant' Andrea al Quirinale, which is four *palmi* wide on the plans of the time. It is noteworthy that the columns of the innermost course are laid out immediately outside the circumference of the oval—tangent to it rather than centered on it; and the layout shows no trace whatsoever of triangulation (on which more in Ch. III, below).

7. See Note 3, above.

8. The typical statement of this view is the following from D. M. Robb and J. J. Garrison, *Art in the Western World,* New York, 1953, 226–27: "This choice of elements in plan that are complex rather than simple geometrical forms—the ellipse instead of the circle and the trapezoid instead of the rectangle—is characteristically baroque and again is motivated by a wish for vital and dynamic space effects." This view, not uncommon in textbook writing (e.g., Helen Gardner, *Art Through the Ages,* 4th ed., New York, 1959, 399) and older literature (e.g., A. E. Brinckmann, *Platz und Monument,* Berlin, 1908, 49–57; and T. H. Fokker, *Roman Baroque Art,* London, 1938, 205–12), still survives in more recent works; it is explicit in E. A. Gutkind, *Urban Development in Southern Europe: Italy and Greece,* New York, 1969, 176 (". . . Bernini and his patrons would not have been men of the Baroque had they not finally fallen for an oval form. . . .") and implicit in the discussion of the piazza by Wittkower (*Art and Architecture,* esp. 128–29: "Bernini's dynamic conception of architecture"), G. C. Argan (*L'architettura barocca in Italia,* Milan, 1957, 15–18), and Fagiolo dell'Arco (*Bernini;* v. Note 171, below). Reymond observed, conversely, that the colonnades are circular, in order to reinforce his point that Bernini was a classicist (*Le Bernin,* 114). The source of this idea is, of course, Woelfflin's formal generalization about the oval as an alternative, if not antithesis, to "the absolutely static and unchangeable form" of the circle (*Renaissance und Barock,* Basel and Stuttgart, 1961, 49; first published in 1888). The notion also underlies W. Lotz, "Die ovalen Kirchenräume des Cinquecento," *Römisches Jahrbuch für Kunstgeschichte,* VII, 1955, 5–99; E. Panofsky, *Galileo as a Critic of the Arts,* The Hague, 1954; and R. Wittkower, "Carlo Rainaldi and the Roman Architecture of the Full Baroque," *Art Bulletin,* XIX, 1937, 242–313. Bernini's case was, however, distorted by this generalization. But more recently we read of the "segments of a circle, pulled apart to to enclose an oval space" in H. Hibbard, *Bernini,* Harmondsworth and Baltimore, 1965, 156.

9. The oft-cited passage from Chantelou, *Journal,* 167 (September 19), is that "les formes les plus parfaites sont les ronds, les carrées, hexagones, octagones, etc." The context of this statement was the *paragone* on Saint Peter's and the Pantheon; Bernini's verdict was that "la coupole de Saint-Pierre, à la vérité, est belle, qu'on n'en voit aucune dans les ouvrages antiques, mais qu'il y a cent fautes dans Saint-Pierre et qu'il n'y en a point dans la Rotonde." It was precisely during these years of planning and developing the Piazza Obliqua, prior to his sojourn in Paris (1665), that the architect demonstrated in practice what was eventually formulated into a theory; he built the centralized churches that realized his Albertian predilection for simple geometry (Wittkower, *Art and Architecture,* 116–21), and involved himself in the project of clearing the Pantheon of urban

"barnacles"—houses and sheds—that had accumulated around it. On the Pantheon project, see Brauer-Wittkower, 120–22, and S. Bordini, "Bernini e il Pantheon: note sul classicismo berniniano," *Quaderni dell' Istituto di storia dell' architettura,* XIV, 1967, 53–84.

10. Archivio della Fabbrica di San Pietro, I Piano, ser. 3, vol. 163, fol. 86, dated July 31, 1656 (Ehrle, "Virgilio Spada," 34); the text reads in part: "Relatum fuit per Rev. P. D. Virgilium Spadam, Sanctissimum inclinare, quod circumcirca plateam Sancti Petri fiant porticus; et ideo ordinatum fuit equiti Bernino ut faciat delineamentum eidem Sanctissimo et Sac(rae) Cong(regatio)ni ostenden(dum), ut melius deliberari possit." The minutes of the meetings of the Congregazione della Fabbrica are bound into several volumes of which this is one, and they carry the title: *Decreta et Resolutiones Sac. Cong.nis R. F. S. Petri ab Anno 1653 ad Annum 1660.* Material relevant to the Square of Saint Peter's is contained in Volumes 163 and 164 of this important source; Ehrle published most of it and also wrote an account of the Congregazione—its organization and function ("Virgilio Spada," 18–21). See also Niccoló del Re, "La Sacra Congregazione della Reverenda Fabrica di S. Pietro," *Studi romani,* XVII, 1969. According to the minutes of the Congregazione of August 19, 1656, the Pope conceived the project as a means of relieving unemployment (v. following Note; v. also Bibl. Vat., Chig. HII 22, fols. 102–3^v.

11. Arch.Fabb. S.P., I Piano, ser. 3, vol. 163, fol. 89 (Ehrle, "Virgilio Spada," 34); "Die Sabathi, 19 Augusti 1656. Habita fuit de mandato S(anctissimi) D(omini) N(ostri) Papae congreg(ati)o Particularis Rev. Fabricae S. Petri cum em.^{mis} D(ominis) Cardinalibus in Cancell(eri)a Apostolica et in mansionibus emin.^{mi} et rev.^{mi} d(omini) cardinalis Barberini, in qua intervener(un)t emin.^{mi} et rev.^{mi} DD. cardinales Barberinus, Franciottus, Astallius, Caffarellus, Borromeus, Aldobrandinus, et Vidman, r.^{mus} D(ominus) Franzonus thesaurarius et R. P(ater) D(ominus) Virgilius Spada. Et in eadem proposito intentionem Sanct(issi)mi esse, quod pro subventione Pauperum aliarumque indigentium familiarum Urbs a R(everenda) Fabrica construatur aliquod novum opus, et quate(nu)s videatur, fiant porticus circumcirca Plateam Basilicae Vaticanae.

"Audito Equite Bernino visoque, et lecto bene considerato delineamento per eum allato eorumdem porticorum, fuit commendata pietas Sanct(itat)is suae et inclinatum pro dicti operis constructione. Et quia Eminentissimus D(ominus) card(ina)lis Pallotus nõ bene valens, nonnulla proposuit advertenda quae per me oeconomum de m(anda)to S(uae) Em(inenti)ae fuer(un)t in eadem cong(regatio)ne relata, iidem Emin(entissi)mi dixerunt, eadem esse et(ia)m referenda Sanctitati Suae. Et iniunxerunt Equiti Bernino, quod platea potius protrahatur in longius quam abbrevietur et si potest non sit latior a parte Ecclesiae quam in eius principio, sed recto tramite, seu filo producatur a principio usque in eius finem." A transcription of this record, with minor orthographic variations, exists in Bibl. Vat., Chig. H II 22, fol. 96; this is the version Fraschetti knew (*Il Bernini,* 315).

12. Archivio Segreto Vaticano, Avvisi, 103, fol. 212 (printed version on fol. 461), dated Rome, August 19, 1656 (Pastor, *Popes,* XXXI, 291): Si è resoluto mettersi di breve mano al gettito delle Case contigue alla Penitentiaria nella Piazza della Basilica Vaticana cominciando dal Palazzo del Priorato fino à Campo Santo per poi ambedoi le parti di essa

Piazza edificare con loggie coperte Appartamenti, et altre commodità perli Canonici, Penitentieri e tutto il Corpo del Capitolo di S. Pietro con ogni magnificenza." Some of these news dispatches are manuscript; others are printed. A group of manuscript *avvisi* are apparently drafts for printed *avvisi;* others are not. Some in the latter are often cursorily written and look like rough drafts for those in the first group, but they differ in content even when the dates match; others in the second group, written in letter form, are by one Alessandro Costantini, whose signature appears on some of them as does the addressee, "Monsignor Massimo, Patriarca di Gerusalem" (fols. 301 and 311). See also Note 59, below, for examples. On the nature of the *avvisi* in general, see C. d'Onofrio, "Gli 'Avvisi' di Roma dal 1554 al 1605 conservati in biblioteche ed archivi romani," *Studi romani,* X, 1962, 529–48.

13. Arch. Segr. Vat., Avvisi, 103, fol. 338, dated Rome, September 8, 1656 (Pastor, *Popes,* XXXI, 292): "Il disegno de' portici da far à San Pietro si è intorbidato, perchè il disegno non era del Bernini, al quale si crede habbi fatto far de' mali offitij." *Ibid.,* fol. 336, dated Rome, September 29, 1656 (Pastor, *Popes,* XXXI, 292): "Si è cominciato a cauar su la piazza di San Pietro uicino alli tedeschi [Campo Santo] per ueder si terrà il fondamento." These are both Costantini's *avvisi* (v. preceding Note).

14. Arch. Segr. Vat., Avvisi, 103, fol. 272, dated Rome, December 23, 1656 (printed version, dated December 29, on fol. 489; Pastor, *Popes,* XXXI, 292): "La Stà di Nro. Sig.re ha spedito chirografo per la Compra e demolitione di molte Case s.a la Piazza di s. Pietro da fabricar i attorno il disegnato teatro, come fù scritto."

15. Arch. Fabb. S.P., I Piano, ser. 3, vol. 163, fol. 103v (Ehrle, "Virgilio Spada," 35), which reads in part: "Fuerunt etiam per Eq(uitem) Berninum ostensa Sac(rae) Congr(egationi) quaedam delineamenta Porticuum in Platea Sancti Petri de mandato eiusdem S(anctissi)mi construen(doru)m et in ouata forma excitan(doru)m, et Em(inentissi)mi de ea se remiserunt voluntati Sanct(itat)is Suae, mandantes illam exequi et de reliquis provid(end)o." The word *reliquis,* missing from the text of the minutes (and so in Ehrle's transcription), appears in the draft copy of the minutes, Arch. Fabb. S.P., I Piano, ser. 2, vol. 74, fol. 749. Fraschetti knew the draft version rather than the clean copy and referred to it by the old identification, Arm. II, vol. 4 (*Il Bernini,* 315, n. 5); he also accepted the date in the heading, 1659, which was a clerical error. The correct year, 1657, actually appears on the back cover; and this is the date given on the clean copy. Fraschetti's information misled Wittkower (Brauer-Wittkower, 81). Ehrle suspected an error but assumed that the version cited by Fraschetti was a transcription. But this version is hastily written and full of corrections and additions of words; and it is in the handwriting of Andrea de Ghetti, who signed the final copy of these and most other minutes of the Congregazione. The clerk who executed the clean copy apparently found the word *reliquis* illegible and left the space open. I owe Don Cipriano, the archivist of the Reverenda Fabbrica, for his kind assistance in locating and deciphering this material. There also exists another record of the meeting, written in Italian and with more detail, in Bibl. Vat., Chig. H II 22, fol. 136, where we read that the design "ricivette applauso considerabile."

16. This general shape was given around 1400 under Boniface IX, when he cleared the

buildings on the Ruga Francigena (or Francisca), which terminated the ancient Via Triumphalis, the northern access to this area (Thoenes, "Geschichte des Petersplatzes," 98–100), and built a wall there (below the later wall of Nicholas V). The site plan, used in this construction and elsewhere in this study, was prepared by combining several graphic sources. The background on the Vatican Plan (v. Note 6, above) was reproduced for the left half (south). The lower right is from Bibl. Vat., Chig. P VII 9, fols. 32ᵛ/33 (Fig. 14). This source was preferred to Maderna's plan, Uffizi, dis. arch. 263, for several reasons: (1) this particular area is not central in Maderno's project; (2) it appears on the second sheet, which is not accurately joined to the first; (3) the disposition of the Leonine Wall is closer to that on Nolli's Plan of Rome (1748) which is generally reliable; and (4) the left half of our source matches the background on the Vatican Plan. For the upper right, the same source was used with additional data from (a) Maderno's plan, (b) Nolli's map, and (c) a large plan of the northern corridor from Bernini's workshop (Bibl. Vat., Chig. P VII 9, fols. 25ᵛ/26; Brauer-Wittkower, Pl. 164c).

17. On the wall of Nicholas V, see Magnuson, *Studies in Quattrocento Architecture,* Stockholm, 1958, 116–17; for the topography of the area west of this wall, see esp. H. Egger, *Carlo Madernas Projekt für den Vorplatz von San Pietro in Vaticano,* Leipzig, 1928, esp. 11–22, and "Das päpstliche Kanzleigebäude im 15. Jahrhundert," *Festschrift zur Feier des Zweihundertjahrigen Bestandes des Haus- Hof- und Staatsarchivs,* II, Vienna, 1951, 487–500.

18. Revision is not consistent, however. The construction of Saint Peter's is updated with Maderno's nave and facade; the obelisk stands at the relocated position (v. Note 21, below); and the tower of Paul V is properly incorporated (v. Note 22, below). But the Palace of Sixtus V is missing. The bell towers of Saint Peter's, shown here as though completed, are of Ferabosco's design, to judge by the pedimented first story and the shape of the crown; Bernini's towers were actually in construction at this time, but the work was interrupted in 1641 after the first two stories of the south tower "owing to technical difficulties and personal intrigues" (Wittkower, *Art and Architecture,* 126), and in 1646 the whole thing was dismantled. On the towers, see esp. D. Frey, "Berninis Entwürfe für die Glockentürme von St. Peter in Rom," *Jahrbuch der kunsthistorischen Sammlungen in Wien,* XII, 1938, 203–26, and H. A. Millon, "Notes on Old and Modern Drawings: An Early Seventeenth Century Drawing of the Piazza San Pietro," *Art Quarterly,* XXV, 1962, 229–41. Note, too, that the Borgo Nuovo is labeled anachronistically on this map by its original name, Via Alexandrina, and the inscription "Borgo Nuouo" appears erroneously on the street north of it, the Borgo Sant' Angelo (which was initially known as Via Sistina); cf. following Note. See also our Fig. 83, below.

19. The other is the Borgo Nuovo. The Borgo Vecchio (the ancient Via Cornelia, which became the Via Santa in the Middle Ages), and the Via de' Cavalli to the south of it, roughly corresponding to the later Borgo Santo Spirito, were the two oldest streets in the area. Late in the fifteenth century, they were found to be inadequate for holding the increasing number of pilgrims and visitors to Rome. Sixtus IV (1471–84) therefore added a wider street named after him—the Via Sistina—from the moat of the Castel Sant'An-

gelo to the gate of the Papal Palace; this was later renamed the Borgo Sant'Angelo. Then the fourth street, the Via Alessandrina, was opened under Alexander VI (1492–1503) for the Jubilee of 1500 to receive ever increasing numbers of pilgrims from outside the city. The largest street in the area then, it started at the eastern terminus of the Borgo Vecchio near the Tiber bank and reached the piazza farther north of the counterpart; and, in time, it came to be known as the Borgo Nuovo. It was also the first street in the area that opened directly to the piazza and thus established a sense of axis in the piazza, which till then was relatively insular in character; this is because the Borgo Vecchio by-passed it as at the time there still existed a strip of buildings to the north of the *isola grande* all along its length, which still appeared on Bufalini's plan of Rome of 1551 but was cleared in November 1564. See Pastor, *Popes,* IV, 455f.; VI, 166f.; and XII, 222f.; and Thoenes, "Geschichte des Petersplatzes," 98–100 and 107, who also notes that the Borgo Vecchio was lined with covered porticoes in the Middle Ages as early as the fifth or sixth century. The two streets, the Borgo Vecchio and Nuovo, disappeared under Mussolini in 1937, when the houses between them, known as the *spina* (Fig. 2), were pulled down for the present Via della Conciliazione, on which see below.

20. Because of this change of grade, there were always steps in front of the atrium (Thoenes, "Geschichte des Petersplatzes," 100). When Pius II (1458–64) started the Benediction Loggia next to the atrium, he also reconstructed the steps and adorned them with colossal statues of Peter and Paul (Pastor, *Popes,* III, 302; and R. O. Rubinstein, "Pius II's Piazza S. Pietro and St. Andrew's Head," *Essays in the History of Architecture Presented to Rudolph Wittkower,* London, 1967, 22–33). These steps were off-centered to the north from the axis of the Basilica in order to serve, evidently, not only the atrium but also the entrance to the Vatican complex on this side. In the sixteenth century, the entrance to the Vatican was an archway incorporated in the palace built by Innocent VIII (1484–92) next to the Benediction Loggia, the work on which he continued toward completion (H. Egger and F. Ehrle, *Piante e vedute di Roma e del Vaticano* dal 1300–1676, Vatican, 1956, 15 and Pls. XIII & XXVII); the Loggia and the palace, as well as the older structures farther south, were demolished in 1610 to make way for the new facade of the Basilica with the exception of a part of Innocent's palace which preserved the old entrance to the Vatican (Pastor, *Popes,* XXVI, 391). Maderno's steps, built subsequently (1616) to replace the old ones, constituted a part of his project for the piazza and were essentially symmetrical with the new facade; see Thoenes, "Geschichte des Petersplatzes," 116 and Fig. 11. See also Note 37, below.

21. The transportation and reerection of the obelisk was planned by Paul II (1464–71), who almost brought the plan to the point of execution when he died. The task was contemplated in the following century by Paul III (1534–49) and again by Gregory XIII (1572–85); see Pastor, *Popes,* XXII, 248–63, where the undertaking of 1586 is also described in detail. Domenico Fontana, who supervised the project, left a vivid account in his *Della trasportatione dell'obelisco vaticano,* Rome, 1590; on Maderno's rôle in this enterprise, see Hibbard, *Maderno* (v. Note 37, below), 14–15, and 235. On the history of this obelisk, see C. d'Onofrio, *Gli obelischi di Roma,* Rome, 1967; and now

E. Iverson, *Obelisks in Exile,* I, Copenhagen, 1968. On the doubt cast on the Renaissance belief that the southern wall of the Constantinian basilica rested on the northern wall of the Circus of Nero, see J. Toynbee and J. Ward-Perkins, *The Shrine of St. Peter and the Vatican Excavations,* London, 1956, 9f.; see also d'Onofrio, *op. cit.,* for the theory that the circus was laid out perpendicular to the axis of the later basilica. The obelisk does not stand exactly on the axis of Maderno's nave; if one stands at the opening to the piazza and sights Michelangelo's lantern through the obelisk, the central portal of the Basilica is offset to the left, and conversely, if one sights the portal, the lantern appears to the right of the obelisk (Fig. 1). The problem was familiar to some of those concerned with the development of the piazza (Fig. 14); Bernini positioned the center of the piazza between the axis of the nave and the center of the obelisk (Fig. 5) in order to minimize the discrepancy (Brauer-Wittkower, 76, n. 1). Accordingly, G. P. Bellori later observed that "si trova la Guglia non essere perfettamente piantata nel mezzo della piazza . . . ne meno corrisponder al mezzo della facciata di Paolo V.," although he admitted that the discrepancy "non è sensibile alla vista" (*Vite de' pittori, scultori et architetti moderni,* Rome, 1728 (first published in 1672), 81–98. Then, an explanation was attempted by Carlo Fontana (*Templum Vaticanum,* 283); he argued that Maderno's nave, which came later, was incorrectly laid out with a deflection toward the south and made the obelisk offset to the north though it was accurately centered on the axis of Michelangelo's crossing. Wittkower, on the other hand, hypothesized that (1) the obelisk, when erected on the piazza, was centered on the axis of the old Basilica while the new Saint Peter's had its center slightly south of it, and (2) Maderno actually added his nave with a slightly northward deflection to reduce the anticipated discrepancy between the facade and the obelisk (Brauer-Wittkower, 76, n. 1). But Thoenes convincingly indicated more recently ("Geschichte des Petersplatzes," 107–11 and 128–34) that (1) Sixtus V, in transferring the obelisk to the piazza, harbored an idea of clearing the *spina* (v. Note 36, below) and consequently had it located on the axis connecting the center of the crossing and the meeting point of the two main streets of the Borgo, and this axis deviated slightly to the north of that of the Basilica; (2) the exact position of the obelisk was marked out in advance by erecting a wooden model, for which Giacomo della Porta and Ammanati, rather than Domenico Fontana, were responsible, and the latter is therefore reticent on this matter in his own chronicle; (3) Maderno's nave deflects neither to the south nor to the north, but is precisely on the axis of the crossing, and the discrepancy between the left and right corner of the facade concerns a change in the design of the tower, on which also see Hibbard, *Maderno* (v. Note 37, below), 161.

22. See Thoenes, "Geschichte des Petersplatzes," 112–19, for the discussion of this project, Maderno's design on which it was based (on which more in Note 37, below), and Vasanzio's rôle in the project, which was heretofore neglected. See also H. Egger, *Madernas Projekt* and "Der Uhrturm Paul V," *Meededeelingen van het Nederlandsch historisch Instituut te Rome,* IX, 1929, 71f. Ferabosco published the project in his collection of engravings, G. B. Costaguti, *Architettura della Basilica di S. Pietro . . . fatta esprimere, e intagliare in più tauole da Martino Ferrabosco, a posta in luce l'Anno MDCXX,* Rome,

1684, Pl. 2 (plan). No 1620 edition of this book is known; the volume in the Biblio-theca Hertziana in Rome, which bears the date 1620 in the inscription, is without text and is probably a proof copy (I. Lavin, *Bernini and the Crossing of Saint Peter's,* New York, 1968, 45, n. 186). Plate 12 of this volume is a perspective showing the facade of the Basilica and the tower of Paul V, but it is occasionally missing from the 1684 edition.

23. See Note 20, above, on the Palace of Innocent VIII. For the later history of the tower and the clock, more below; v. especially Notes 30, 102, 197, and 204.

24. The fountain of Innocent VIII was restored and given an added ornament by Bramante in 1501 under Alexander VI; this was replaced by a larger version, designed by Maderno, at the same location but with more water drawn from the Acqua Paola. See. C. d'Onofrio, *Le fontane di Roma,* Rome, 1957, 160; H. V. Morton, *The Fountains of Rome,* New York, 1966, 205–11 (also known under the title *The Waters of Rome*); and Hibbard, *Maderno* (v. Note 37, below), 200–201.

25. Wittkower reconstructed the plan in general outline but only in verbal description (Brauer-Wittkower, 69).

26. Bibl. Vat., Chig. H II 22, fol. 97; the three objections were published in S. Fraschetti, *Il Bernini,* 314, n. 2. The text of the second objection reads as follows: "La 2da che per mettere la Guglia nel mezzo della piazza da agiustarsi per i Portici, bisognarà necessar-iam^{te} gettare à terra parte della Penitentiaria, case dei Cibi et altre adiacenti, et che quel sito, che rimarrà, sarà forsi troppo angusto per fabricarui la Canonica, che si disegna. Che però è da considerar bene che per agiustar una piazza, non resti inutile, ò si sconcerti il sito rimanente, e la strada, che è strada Penit^a, et il Palazzo dei ss^{ri} Cesi." On the plague, see Pastor, *Popes,* XXXI, 33; the *avvisi* were still discussing the plague—its ex-tinction and recurrences—as late as 1658 (e.g., Arch. Segr. Vat., Avvisi, 27, fol. 420, dated September 29, 1657). That the project is a lavish expenditure for something that is no more than a "mero ornato, e fabrica non necessaria" was a frequent objection also raised by later critics (Note 42, below) and observers (F. Haskell, *Patrons and Painters,* London, 1963, 152).

27. See the text in Note 11, above.

28. Wittkower suggested that Cardinal Pallotta might have had an unusual opportunity to examine Bernini's design in advance (Brauer-Wittkower, 69, n. 6). It might certainly be argued that the more speculative, rather than descriptive, tone of the second objection owed to the fact that the design, prepared in a brief time, was very schematic and showed only very general features. But since the cardinal's two other objections are also so obviously general, we must conclude that he was objecting to the project as such and wrote his second objection on the basis of the program rather than the design.

29. See Note 12, above.

30. Santa Caterina was pulled down in December 1659 as shown by Huelsen (rather than 1658; cf. Brauer-Wittkower, 72, n. 1); see also C. L. Frommel, "Santa Caterina alle Cavallerotte," *Palladio,* XII, 1962, 18–25. The northern colonnade began to rise that Spring (v. Note 65 below); and we can assume that the work proceeded from the central part (the cross-passage)

outward in two directions (cf. Note 70, below). The document in the Vatican that describes in detail the demolition of the "Guardia de Svizzeri" and the structures of Ferabosco and Vasanzio (Bibl. Vat., Chig. P VII 9, fol. 12; published in part in Brauer-Wittkower, 77, n. 3) is undated; but the demolition of all these was certainly in effect in 1659/60 when the final design for the northern corridor was read (Brauer-Wittkower, 93).

31. Bibl. Vat., Chig. P VII 9, fols. 40^v/41, published in Brauer-Wittkower, Pl. 189c; see *ibid.,* 67 and 97–99, and F. Fasolo, *L'opera di Hieronimo e Carlo Rainaldi,* Rome [1962], 212–17. Wittkower describes the plan as "ein Zehneck"; this surely an oversight. There is a rectangular antepiazza preceding the main piazza, but this is octagonal—not decagonal; and, in extent and general distribution of elements, it is not very different from Bernini's Piazza Obliqua. Fasolo sees in it the draftsmanship of Carlo Rainaldi before his father's death but more of the latter's ideas than Carlo's. Wittkower, on the other hand, concludes that Rainaldi must have submitted it to Alexander VII since it is found in his collection; but he speculates that it repeats a design that he had earlier prepared for Innocent X. Be that as it may, it is fairly certain that Bernini was acquainted with the design. Incorporating the upper piazza of Ferabosco and Vasanzio is economical. The idea thus suggests that it was contemporary with or preceded Bernini's trapezoidal plan; and, as Wittkower observed, Bernini's porticoes at this stage of planning resembled those of Rainaldi's project. A variant of this design by Rainaldi in the same codex (Chig. P VII 9, fol. 42) is also octagonal, but the arcades framing the main piazza have three sides rather than five. This is the version that Bonanni published in his *Numismata summorum pontificum Templi Vaticani,* Rome, 1696, Pl. 67 (with attribution to Francesco Rainaldi). Rainaldi also produced two more designs, one on a circular plan and the other on a transverse oval (Vat. Cat. 13442, fols. 28 and 29 respectively; Brauer-Wittkower, Pl. 192); these were probably conceived as alternatives to Bernini's later colonnade design. In all his projects, Rainaldi is indifferent to the pattern of the existing streets in the Borgo. Baldinucci reports that he had seen in Rainaldi's studio four different solutions for the piazza, namely, square, hexagon, circle, and longitudinal oval (*Notizie de' Professori del disegno,* Florence, 1681–1728, V. 330).

32. In particular, Bibl. Vat., Chig. P VII 9; this volume undoubtedly formed a body of reference material put together at this time for the use of the Pope, his architect, and possibly the Congregazione. Two engravings of Cosimo Morelli's proposal for the clearance of the *spina* (Figs. 91 and 92) were inserted in the volume in 1929 (Brauer-Wittkower, 97, n. 9). On Ferabosco, see Note 22, above.

33. Chantelou, *Journal,* 38 (June 25): "Il a dit qu'il [Michelangelo] était grand sculpteur et peintre, mais un divin architecte, d'autant que l'architecture consiste tout en dessin; que dans la sculpture et dans la peinture, il n'avait pas eu le talent de faire paraître les figures de chair, qu'elles n'étaient belles et considérables que pour l'anatomie. . . ." Also, 111–12 (August 22): "C'était un grand homme [Michelangelo], un grand sculpeur et architecte, que néanmoins il avait eu plus d'art que de grâce, et pour cela n'avait pas

égalé les antiques, s'étant principalement attaché à l'anatomie comme font les chirurgiens." In his own *giustificazione,* discussed below (v. Note 40, below), Bernini explains the problem of scale in designing the piazza to match the enormous facade of the Basilica by citing the Farnese Palace, the cornice of which Michelangelo, he writes, carefully and successfully proportioned to the piazza; for the text of this passage, see Brauer-Wittkower, 70, n. 1. This was, of course, another formal piazza besides the Campidoglio that Bernini could and undoubtedly did study as a model; its space extends laterally, and the arrangement of two fountains also anticipates his definitive design. On the Campidoglio, see, above all, J. S. Ackerman, *The Architecture of Michelangelo,* London and New York, 1961; and R. Bonelli, "La piazza capitolina," in *Michelangelo architetto,* ed. B. Zevi, Turin, 1964, 427–46. As obvious as it may seem, the relationship between Bernini's trapezoid plan and the Campidoglio has heretofore been overlooked.

34.   The project of Nicholas V is described in the biography of the Pope by Giannozzo Manetti (d. 1459), which was published in the third volume of L. Muratori's *Rerum Italicarum Scriptores,* Milan, 1734. Magnuson reconstructed it on the basis of Manetti's information (*Studies,* 65–97; see also the review by E. MacDougall, *Art Bulletin,* XLIV, 1962, 67f.); but with regard to the piazza, he decided Manetti's dimensions, 100 by 500 *braccia* (58 by 290 meters), incredibly narrow and long, and proposed a rectangle 125 by 297 meters. Thoenes, however, convincingly argues for Manetti's dimensions on the basis of the width of the old steps to the atrium ("Geschichte des Petersplatzes," 101–4). As Nicholas V envisioned it, the center of this circuslike piazza would be marked by the obelisk relocated from the south side of the Basilica (v. Note 36, below); three broad avenues would run through the Borgo and enter it, each avenue lined with porticoes on both sides for the protection of pedestrians from rain and heat. These porticoes, as described by Manetti, anticipate those of Bernini's trapezoidal plan: "Juxta enim variae diversorum opificum tabernae, supra vero demorum habitacula condebantur." The idea was repeated in the statement on the Bonacina Engraving (Fig. 24; v. Note 159, below). The inscription at the eastern cross-passage of the executed colonnades ("In umbraculum diei ab aestu, in securitatem a turbine et a pluvia") recorded it for all.

35.   See Note 19, above; the Via Alessandrina (later Borgo Nuovo), "che de la porta del palacio sene va a filo a la porta del Castello" (Pastor, *Popes,* XXII, 222) was possibly a realization of the second avenue of Nicholas V ("recto tramite ad portam palatinam ibatur").

36.   Thoenes, "Geschichte des Petersplatzes," 107 and n. 76 and 84, from the *avviso* of June 4, 1586 (cited by Pastor, *Popes,* XXII, 263): "N.S. disegna . . . ch'el habbia pensiero di buttare a terra tutte le case che fanno isola per mezzo borgo da ponte fino alla piazza di S. Pietro acciò in arrivando allo sboccare di Castello si vegga quella bella prospettiva della guglia, posta che sia nella piazza di S. Pietro"; see also Note 21, above. P. Lavedan suggests that Bramante had already conceived a broad avenue in the Borgo in the manner of Nicholas V's project (*Histoire de l'urbanisme: Renaissance et temps modernes,* Paris, 1959, 182); the basis of his argument, however, is a spurious Bramante sketch of a street

vista published by H. von Geymüller, who attributed it to Bramante with a question mark (*Les projets primitifs pour le basilique de Saint-Pierre de Rome,* Paris, 1875–80, Pl. 25, fig. 1).

37. Maderno's project is preserved in the plan, Uffizi, dis. arch. 263; see H. Hibbard, *Carlo Maderno and Roman Architecture 1580–1630,* University Park and London, 1971, Pl. 58a. Maderno produced an alternate project on a more modest plan (Uffizi, dis. arch. 6728; Hibbard, *Maderno,* Pl. 58b). See Thoenes, "Geschichte des Petersplatzes," 112–19, and Egger, *Madernas Projekt;* and now, Hibbard, *Maderno,* 162–63. Prior to the erection of the obelisk where it stands today, a piazza could well have been developed farther west; for, had the atrium been cleared, there would have opened an ample space 130 meters deep between Michelangelo's facade and the old steps to the atrium (Thoenes, "Geschichte des Petersplatzes," 106). Even after the obelisk had been set up, this platform, rather than the lower piazza, might have been the place of assembly; then the lower piazza, subordinated to it, would serve as a caesura between the Borgo and the platform, providing the optimum viewpoint for the dome (Thoenes, 107). Maderno's nave, however, took up half of this platform; and, moreover, in his own project for the piazza, he created a new flight of steps in front of the facade (v. Note 20, above) roughly 30 meters *west* of the old one, further reducing the upper piazza. Thus, although his main concern was the development of the platform or apron, he also enlarged the lower piazza and was to enliven it with two fountains, one around the base of the obelisk and the other a restoration of the old one from the time of Innocent VIII (v. Note 24, above); in their respective positions, they reflect the shape of the piazza and emphasize its dual role as the vestibule to both the Basilica and the Vatican (cf. Note 22, above).

38. Ehrle, "Virgilio Spada," 29 and 42; and Pl. VII: Bibl. Vat., P VII 9, fols. 56ᵛ/57. The design, submitted to the Congregazione on February 6, 1651, was conceived for the view of Michelangelo's dome–"pro maiori ac longiori prospectu templi Vaticani." There was an anonymous rectangular plan, submitted also at this time, which proposed for the same reason the clearance of the area that later became the Piazza Rusticucci (Ibid., fol. 54ᵛ/55). Needless to say, Michelangelo's dome was of concern in Spada's plan, not only in itself, but even more as a means of strengthening the character of the grand approach; used as an urban landmark, the dome would be revealed to the visitor well in advance and continuously draw him along to the Basilica. Spada died in 1662.

39. The old Benediction Loggia (v. Note 20, above) was decisive in defining the piazza as an assembly place, but it did not develop a sense of enclosure; for its construction coincided with the opening of the Borgo Nuovo (v. Note 19, above). There was a project under Pius IV (1559–65) for constructing porticoes all around the piazza (Thoenes, "Geschichtes des Petersplatzes," 107), but we know virtually nothing about its specific features. The Vatican fresco with Michelangelo's Saint Peter's in the midst (but not the center) of a vast arcaded piazza gives no clue whether the east side (front) was opened or closed; and it is moreover an ideal, or visionary, representation (Thoenes, 105). Among the seventeenth-century projects that are directional in character, besides Virgilio Spada's, Maderno's design (v. Note 37, above) and its derivative, that of Ferabosco and

Vasanzio (v. Note 22, above), the design of Papirio Bartoli, deserves mention. Bartoli, a dilettante, produced it sometime between 1614 and 1617, and it was engraved by Matthaeus Greuter in 1623 (Bibl. Vat., Chig. P VII 9, fol. 43; v. Ehrle, "Virgilio Spada," 41–42, and Wittkower, "A Counter-project," 104); like the false Bernini design (v. Note 47, below), it is infeasible because it disregards the retaining wall of Nicholas V and involves demolition or rebuilding of some of the Vatican Palaces above it. It is true that here the portico continues all around the piazza, but, according to the inscription, the portico closing the piazza on the east side is made low for assuring a long vista: "Questo Portico s'è tenuto basso de doi ordini, acciò meno impedisca la vista della facciata del Tempio." In contrast to all these projects, Rainaldi's plan (v. Note 31, above) was conspicuously an enclosure, but it still had to compete with Spada's "open-*spina*" proposal.

40. Brauer-Wittkower, 70, n. 1; the document, designated "Bericht III," is from Bibl. Vat., Chig. H II 22, fols. 107^r–109^v. The writing is in Bernini's hand and concerns in the main the course of events leading up to the adoption of the oval plan for the piazza and concludes with his reasons for this choice. On the dating of the document, see Note 112, below. The last few paragraphs of the text are crucial to our study and read as follows:

"Fù stimato assaı prudente il Bernini à far' il disegno in grande nell'istesso sito, dove doveva farsi l'opera, ma molto più avanti passò il giuditio di S. Santità, poiche conoscendo che non si può accertatamente dar giuditio dell'altezza, se prima non si vede la sua longhezza, ordinò all'Architetto che sopra molti travi dritti facesse ricorrere una traversa tanto longa quanto fosse la longhezza del Portico non comportando ne il tempo ne la spesa il farne un'intiero modello.

"Si portò N. Sig.^{re} à vedere questa dimostratione, e con ingegno più che humano, non solamente determinò l'altezza dell'opera, ma ne giudicò la forma, cosa che fece stupire l'istesso Architetto invecchiato in questa professione, imperciòche poco si fermò à vedere se voleva essere più bassa, ò più alta ma al solito di quell'ingegni, che non hanno confine, e terminano con le stelle andò ad antivedere con una sola occhiata cose grandi, e penetrò in un momento tutte le difficoltà che può suggerire una gran lunghezza di tempo, et una perfetta experienza della professione, peròche seppe (che è quello che in queste materie importa il tutto) arrivare à vedere l'effetto che haverebbe fatto la fabrica prima che fosse perfettionata.

"Antivedde subito gl'inconvenienti che s'incontravano in fare il Portico in forma quadrata, impercioche la sua altezza in quella forma haverebbe impedito al Popolo la veduta del Palazzo, et al Palazzo il prospetto della Piazza, accresciendosi l'Inconveniente mercè che solendo il Papa dalla fenestre dare la Benedittione a'i Pellegrini, e processioni che l'anno Santo vengono per ricerverla in questo modo non poteva benedirli se non in grandissima lontananza, oltre che si veniva ad impiccolire, e dividere la Piazza, lasciando fra il Palazzo, et il Portico un sito morto, quale facilmente riempito d'immonditie haverebbe trasmissi al Palazzo vapori assai dannosi.

"Havendo dunque in un'istante antiveduto S. Santità gl'inconvenienti che s'incorrevano nel far d° Portico in forma quadra con giuditio più che humano risolse farlo in forma ovata. Certo chi non sapesse l'inconvenienti sopradetti pensarebbe che à questa forma ovata si fosse S. Santità solamente appresa in risguardo del bello, essendo questa la meraviglia, che seppe unire con il bello, il proprio, et il necessario. Il bello essendo questa forma circolare più grata all'occhio, più perfetta in se stessa, e più maravigliosa à farli massime con Architravi piani sopra colonne isolate. Il proprio perche essendo la Chiesa di S. Pietro quasi matrice di tutte le altre doveva haver' un Portico che per l'appunto dimostrasse di ricevere à braccia aperte maternamente i Cattolici per confermarli nella credenza, gl'Heretici per riunirli alla Chiesa, e gl'Infedeli per illuminarli alla vera fede; e i necessario essendosi superate le sopradette difficoltà."

41. *Quadra* and *quadrata* could hardly have meant anything other than square. Baldinucci defines it as a form having "gli angoli, e le faccie eguali" (*Vocabolario toscano*, s.v.); he has a separate entry for trapezoid (*trapezzo*).

42. Wittkower's "Bericht II" (Brauer-Wittkower, 71, n. 6) from Bibl. Vat., Chig. H II 22, fol. 106. The relevant part of the text reads as follows: "Con esser uscito dalla quadra, ò piùtosto parte rellogramma [i.e., *parallelogramma* transformed by aphaeresis and subsequent dissimilation of *l* to *r*], si sono sfuggite molte cose cattive, e specialmente la perdita della vista di chi viene à Palazzo alle finestre di S. Sᵗᵃ e si sono incontrate molte cose buone, una delle quali è l'ampiezza maggiore, che si può ricevere col slagarsi; ma se in questo si eccedesse, crederei che in luogo di fare acquisto, si discapitasse." The critic then expresses his doubt whether the expenditure—"spesa così grande"—is justified and proceeds to argue that the plan is, after all, too extravagant to no advantage (cf. Note 52, below). Wittkower deduces from the text that the critic was probably a cleric (Brauer-Wittkower, 97, n. 5).

43. See Note 15, above. There were critics who submitted their observations to the Pope after the meeting (v. preceding Note and Note 53, below), but they were not members of the Congregazione.

44. We can in no way verify whether the *in situ* demonstration that Bernini describes was a fact or fiction. It is very likely that the buildings of the Swiss Guards were still standing at the time outside the walls of Nicholas V (Fig. 5), since there was no reason to clear them before the oval plan superseded the trapezoid plan (cf. Note 30, above). If this was the case, the life-size model could have still verified the drawbacks of the straight portico, but it could have hardly demonstrated in actual form the advantages to be gained from the curved portico. We are therefore tempted to speculate whether the papal intervention—invented or arranged—was not primarily a diplomatic strategy. We know, on the other hand, that three life-size models were made and tested on the site later in 1657, and another model, produced surely much earlier that year, was also life-size since it cost more than the others (v. Note 81, below). But at this cost (516 *scudi*) the model was hardly a makeshift setup that Bernini describes in the *giustificazione*. In any event, as we shall see below (Ch. II), there is evidence that the Pope and the architect conferred and agreed on the oval plan well in advance to the latter's advantage in presenting his unconventional and entirely unexpected design to the Congregazione.

45. It has been said that Bernini, complying with the recommendation of the Congregazione, produced a "Rechteck-Projekt" (Brauer-Wittkower, 70–71); but this is obviously misleading inasmuch as it was hardly a project.

46. *Templum Vaticanum,* 185 ("Forma rettiangola de i Portici nõ Practicata"); Fontana states in the text that the author of the plan is unknown. The northern portico, bent around the east side, blocks the Borgo Nuovo; and the upper piazza runs into the Vatican premises to the north. These details reveal a lack of professional knowledge in the same way as Bartoli's design (v. Note 39, above).

47. Bibl. Vat., Chig. P VII 9, fols. 32ᵛ/33; the drawing was published by Ehrle, "Virgilio Spada," 43–44, but it is also known in F. Bonanni's slightly distorted version, which was printed with attribution to Bernini (*Numismata summorum pontificum* . . . , Rome, 1696, Pl. 68. The plan combines the rectangular scheme with a circular one. They are both unrealistic; like other rectangular plans, they both disregard the fact that the Vatican premises above the retaining wall of Nicholas V cannot be disturbed. Ehrle accepted the attribution to Bernini; but questioning the practicability of the schemes, he concluded that the drawing was for demonstrating the impossible—"non proposto con serietà per essere eseguito, ma disegnato più per mostrare gli inconvenienti di coteste due forme, possibili in astratte." Wittkower, on the other hand, rejected the attribution. He argued that Bernini never planned a circular piazza because "his oval plan followed directly on the rectangular one" (v. Note 45, above). He therefore interpreted the circular plan on this drawing as a critical counterproposal (Brauer-Wittkower, 97); the argument thus implies that the rectangular plan was under criticism and was used as a foil. But we have already seen that Bernini never produced a rectangular plan. Moreover, if we examine the drawing carefully, we see that the circular plan is incomplete in outline; it looks more like an alternative to the rectangular solution. Both the rectangle and the circle must then represent a counterproposal to Bernini's "square" plan; and for one of the solutions the critic followed the recommendation of the Congregazione. The false Bernini design was reported on September 8, 1656, a few weeks after the submission of the trapezoidal plan (v. Note 13, above). The author of the drawing was apparently considering a simple unified piazza. His porticoes, in both solutions, extend westward only up to Maderno's new steps (v. Note 20, above); on the east side, they continue around, and here we find a detached closing piece like Bernini's later *terzo braccio.* This detail thus reads as a criticism of Bernini's penetrated and divided (i.e., two-part) plan, or as an answer to such a criticism. In either case, the subtlety of Bernini's first design was not understood; it may have seemed disjointed on paper, but as we have seen, the two parts were visually unified.

48. Bibl. Vat., Chig. H II 22, fol. 155ᵛ, 190 x 270 mm.

49. But, as we shall see below, this bias was not peculiar to Bernini alone but more or less prevalent in his time.

50. The term is from Lotz, "Die ovalen Kirchenräume," 55.

51. See Note 40, above, for the text. On the Renaissance idea that the circle is the most beautiful and perfect form, see Wittkower, *Architectural Principles in the Age of Hu-*

manism, London, 1952, Part I, esp. 4, 17, 21, and 25. The following incident in Paris is noteworthy in this connection. Discussing the project for the Louvre with Colbert one day, Bernini envisaged the piazza in front of it in analogy with the Piazza Obliqua; and significantly, to demonstrate his idea "pour les deux côtés de la place, il a marqué deux portions de cercle" using compasses—so relates Chantelou, *Journal,* 51–52 (July 15). Cf. Note 82, below.

52. "Bericht II" (v. Note 42, above). The critic was arguing, on the one hand, that the proposed piazza was too large and extravagant to no advantage, and yet on the other, made these three points: (1) that the arcade is too minuscule for the magnitude of the piazza and illegible unless the pilasters are doubled; (2) that the long and circuitous passage takes carriages too far away from the piazza and doubles the walking distance for pedestrians; and (3) the single-aisled porticoes make a poor shelter from sun and rain, unless it is closed on one side. It makes us wonder if he was trying to dissuade those concerned by demonstrating how unreasonably extravagant the design would have to be to make any sense at all.

53. Wittkower's "Berichte I" (Brauer-Wittkower, 71 n. 6), from Bibl. Vat., Chig. H II 22, fol. 105; the critic was probably a provincial architect (Brauer-Wittkower, 97, n. 5). The criticism suggests the Doric Order in order to keep down the height in relation to Maderno's facade. Bernini's arcade was therefore probably Ionic in proportion (v. Note 92, below). He, too, argues that simple pilasters "nella forma designata in una piazza così vasta, possino apparire meschini, e che col dupplicarsi fossero, per riuscire di maggiore magnificenza." A drawing associated with this proposal, possibly by the same critic, shows an arcade articulated with a system of Palladian motifs (Wittkower, "A Counterproject," Pl. 20d, from Bibl. Vat., H II 22, fol. 94ᵛ); the same scheme was adopted in the Counterproject of 1659 (Fig. 39; v. Note 110, below).

54. Bibl. Vat., Chig. P VII 9, fol. 34; v. Brauer-Wittkower, 72–73. The diagram on the upper half of the sheet studies various angles of the sun in different seasons, and the arcade on the left, below, tests these data to show that it is adequate in width.

55. The internal width of 20 *palmi* (4.46 meters or 14.64 feet) is not unreasonable; it is a little over that of Michelangelo's loggia on the Campidoglio. We assumed the pilaster was 6 *palmi* in width on the basis of the two-aisle arcade on this sheet. The width of the executed colonnades, 76 1/2 palmi, was verified by measurement.

56. Bibl. Vat., Chig. H II 22, fol. 136, which is a variant record of the Congregazione that met on March 17, 1657 (v. Note 15, above): "il disegno de portici nella Piazza di detta Basilica, quali nella larghezza dell'ornato abbracciano la casa del Priorato e Chiesa di S. Caterina e nella longhezza parte del Palazzo Cesis." Repeating this information, the critic emphasizes that "il disegno mostrato in Cong.ne in forma ovata non solo gionge con la longhezza di esso ovato al Palazzo Cesio, mà entra dentro di esso molte canne, si come con la larghezza non solo gionge al Priorato, mà entra anche in questo molte canne" (from "Bericht II"; v. Note 42, above).

57. The first two conditions require some explanation. First, the workshop drawing (Bibl. Vat., Chig. P VII 9, fol. 35), of which only the left half is reproduced here. Wittkower

proposed that the drawing represents a design made at a much later date than the cross-sections (Fig. 17) and outside or independent of Bernini's supervision. The arcade is taller here, and the Doric pilaster is slender (shaft 1:8) like the column of the executed colonnade (1:8.03 to 1:8.85); cf. Notes 7 and 92. The special treatment given the terminal bays (and these only) clearly presupposes a decision to pull down the tower of Paul V and replace it with a new corridor. Such a decision immediately preceded the first phase of the colonnade design (Fig. 20); but it must be pointed out, too, that the idea of providing the terminal bays with a special frame came up only in the stage of design represented on Medal IV (Fig. 23), and in our chronology outlined below, this was toward the end of 1658 at the earliest. We can, on the other hand, make a strong case for the probability that the workshop drawing represents a stage of design immediately following the cross-sections. After all, the idea of pulling down the tower of Paul V was developed in the process of reworking the arcade design. Moreover, the arcade of the elevation is higher than that of the cross-sections but substantially lower than the executed colonnade:

arcade (cross-sections)	64 *palmi* (pilaster: 42)
arcade (elevation)	69 *palmi* (pilaster: 45)
colonnade	81.5 *palmi* (column: 57.5)

One also notes that the balustrade is identical in the two drawings of the arcade: 12 *palmi*. But the crucial factor is the length of 950 *palmi;* assuming this represents the inner arc of the arcade (since the elevation facing the piazza is evidently the normal view), it is considerably more than that of the executed colonnade (795 *palmi* by algebraic computation on the basis of the large plan in the Vatican, our Fig. 6; and the adequately close 800 *palmi* according to the Bonacina Engraving, our Fig. 24, and Bibl. Vat., Chig. P VII 9, fol. 23, a workshop drawing of the colonnade elevation published in Brauer-Wittkower, Pl. 163a). An arc of this length occurs on the plan of the colonnade, not halfway as Wittkower thought (Brauer-Wittkower, 73), but only at 20 *palmi* from the outside edge. Since this dimension is too narrow as a total width for any plausible portico, we must conclude that the arcade in question had an entirely different curvature from that of the colonnade. In view of our area coverage on the one hand and the given spatial limits fixed by the wall of Nicholas V on the other, this curvature had to be more open (i.e., longer in radius); and the arcade could not have been very wide, probably no wider than 46 *palmi* like the version with a single aisle on the drawing of the cross-sections, which in our hypothesis preceded the elevation. We know that the cross-sections represent a revision of the arcade design submitted to the Congregazione, involving the idea of a wider portico (Arcade II); the elevation most likely represents the second revision by which the arcade was made taller and longer (Arcade III). The original arcade (Arcade I), as we reconstructed it, is accordingly of such length that, when widened to 46 *palmi* and properly lengthened symmetrically so that the western termination covers the corridor, it is 950 *palmi*. Given the arcade of the width of 32 *palmi* and the area coverage as specified, no conceivable alternative satisfies this condition for the total length; but the solution must, at the same time, fulfill the second condition that the minor axis of the oval piazza must be 752 *palmi.*

For the oval formed by the colonnades, the legend on the Bonacina Engraving (Fig. 24; v. Note 64, below) furnishes us the following dimensions:

> *Diametro della lunghezza del Portico nella linea esteriore palmi* 1052 1/2;
> *Diametro della linea interiore pal.* 899 1/2;
> *Diametro della larghezza del Portico nella linea esteriore pal.* 905;
> *Diametro della linea interiore pal.* 752.

Along both the major and minor axes, the difference between the internal and external dimension is 153 *palmi;* this checks with the width of the colonnade, which is 76 1/2 *palmi* (sufficiently close to 76 1/3 *palmi,* obtained by adding the widths of aisles and columns given in the same legend). But the figures in themselves are peculiar. The dimension of 899 1/2 *palmi* for the major axis of the internal oval is excessive; it should be 888 *palmi,* if we accept the radius of the colonnade, 296 *palmi,* measured off on the large workshop plan in the Vatican (Fig. 6). This, we may decide, is tolerably close. But 752 *palmi,* for the minor axis is far excessive; it should be in the vicinity of 670 *palmi* for the *ovato tondo,* the particular oval construction used in the definitive layout of the colonnades, or 680 *palmi* at the most, given the slightly augmented major axis (v. Note 6, above). In short, the legend describes an oval that is substantially stouter than that of the executed plan; these dimensions do not belong to the plan represented on the engraving. We must therefore suspect that they slipped in from an earlier source, unless we decided they are downright errors. This possibility, however, is slim. For the figure for the major axis, 899 1/2, is very precise; and it is strangely a fraction short of a round number when, given the particular oval construction, a multiple of three is expected. This dimension, on the other hand, could not have existed in the arcade design, because it is not long enough to satisfy our area requirement. The only conceivable solution, then, is that this dimension came into being when the arcade of 32 *palmi* was converted into a colonnade 76 $\frac{1}{2}$ *palmi* wide by increasing the width of the direction of the piazza. This operation gives us the major axis of the oval in our reconstruction: 899 1/2 + 2(76 1/2 − 32) = 988 1/2. A similar operation, repeated for the minor axis, does not work, however: 752 + 2(76 1/2 − 32) = 841. The result here is not acceptable, because the oval on the axes 988 1/2 and 841 *palmi* is a very round oval and would slice off the corner of the Vatican property jutting out into the site. We must therefore assume that the figure, 752, originated in the arcade design; it is adequate for our area coverage. This is consequently the minor diameter of our oval. For the pseudo-oval of the arcade design, then, the radius of the arc of the arcade (internally) was half this figure, or 376 *palmi;* the arc would have encompassed an angle in the vicinity of 120 degrees. Widened and lengthened as specified above (Arcade III), it would have had the radius of 362 *palmi* and encompassed an angle of 150 degrees (Fig. 18, heavy dashed lines); these values would yield the length $2\pi(362)(150/360) = 947$ *palmi.* Obviously, Arcade III came in conflict with the wall of Nicholas V; the colonnade, therefore, developed a curvature with a shorter radius to fit in the available space. The colonnade, however, was still wider (76 1/2 *palmi*); had it followed the curvature of the arcade, the radius would have been 332 *palmi* (as we find on the workshop drawing, our Fig. 26; cf. Note 70, below). If Arcade I had followed the band, 32 *palmi* wide, just inside the outer circumference of the future colonnade, its length (when properly extended) would have been only 920 *palmi* at the most—$2\pi(296 + 76 \ 1/2 - 32)(155/360)$; and the minor axis of the oval 760 *palmi,* which is slightly excessive.

58. The outside course may be articulated with rhythmic bays, using paired pilasters with a short entablature between arcuated bays, that is to say, a system of Palladian motifs like that attributed to one of Bernini's critics (v. Note 53, above), while retaining a system of simple pilasters on the inside course. But, obviously, this is possible only if the arcade is either very wide or describes a short radius curvature so that the outside course is substantially longer than the inside one. One example of this solution is the arcaded hemicycle in Domenichino's painting, *La probatica piscina* (Rome, Capitoline Museum, ca. 1614), illustrated in *L'ideale classico del seicento in Italia e la pittura di paesaggio: Catalogo,* Museum Civico, Bologna, 1962, 98–99, and Pl. 19. See also our Fig. 38.

59. On the first medal, see Brauer-Wittkower, 74, n. 4, where it is designated Medal I; the second version, Medal II, is a revision of the first, on the same base as evidenced by the vestige of the first fountain in front of the obelisk (*ibid.,* 74, n. 5). The inscription, taken from the Psalms, reads: "Fundamenta ejus montibus sanctis." This was Pope Alexander's imagery with a reference to the *Chigi monti* of his stemma; but Bernini was not visibly influenced by it in developing his design and *concetto.* Various trial versions for the inscription are found in Bibl. Vat., Chig. H II 22, fol. 239, of which some were published in Fagiolo dell'Arco, *Bernini,* 278. The medals give no clear evidence whether the western extensions were at this stage of design closed corridors (as eventually developed) or perhaps colonnades like the rest. The *avviso* of September 1, 1657, reported that the Pope, after visiting the church of Sant' Agostino and then Santa Maria della Pace (then being worked on), "si portò nell Piazza di S. Pietro doue fece la Cerimonia di gettare la prima pietra, e due medaglie d'oro, ed argento ne' fondamenti principiati della nuoua fabrica del Teatro de' Portici attorno d.ᵃ Piazza, e dopo udito messa nella chiesa di S. Pietro ritornò al Quirinale" (Arch. Segr. Vat., Avvisi, 105, fol. 148; printed version in Avvisi, 105, fol. 26, and Avvisi, 27 fol. 390); another manuscript *avviso,* also dated September 1, 1657, but in another hand, contains no mention of the "prima pietra" (Avvisi, 105, fol. 272), while Costantini's *avviso* (v. Note 12, above), dated August 31, 1657, gives a shorter notice as follows: "Martedì matina Il papa parti di bon'hora à piede et andò à Santa Agostino e poi alla Pace, e doppo entrò in lettica et andò a San' Pietro e gettò la pᵃ pietra nelli fondamenti con alcune medaglie d'oro, e poi entrò in chiesa e disse la messa bassa nel choro de canonici e se ne tornò al Quirinale" (Avvisi, 105, fol. 270). Shortly before the laying of the foundation stone, Bernini's fees were settled (Arch. Fabb. S.P., I Piano, Arm., vol. 314, fol. 116, and I Piano, ser. 1. vol. 6, No. 20; v. also Fraschetti, *Il Bernini,* 315, n. 2; and Ehrle, "Virgilio Spada," 35, n. 158.

60. See Note 52, above; doubling the pilaster was also proposed by Critic I (v. Note 53, above). For paired columns on a curve, see also our Fig. 47.

61. Brauer-Wittkower, 78, n. 1, designated Medal III.

62. Precision in layout naturally is not expected on these medals; but a few details indicate that some of the crucial points were probably provisional. If a straight line is drawn connecting the two terminations of the colonnade and extended westward, it touches the corner of Maderno's facade, not inside of it as it should, while one recognizes a conspicuous gap between this corner and the wall of the corridor. The axis of the corridor, extended eastward, almost touches the corner of the eastern termination of the colonnade, while in the executed layout this line keeps clear of it.

63. Brauer-Wittkower, 83, n. 4, designated Medal IV.

64. A copy of the engraving exists in the Vatican Library; v. Note 154, below. On the dating of the print and the preparatory drawing for it, see below, Ch. III, and Note 155. The publicity purpose of the engraving is stated on the engraving in Latin and Italian (v. Note 159, below). G. B. Falda's print (Fig. 36) was based on the information provided by this source (v. Note 105, below).

65. Bibl. Vat., Chig. II 22, fol. 162. Of the remaining seven columns then standing, six were in the second course and one in the third. The document, however, contains errors. In its entry of the total number, it claims that there were altogether 128 columns, which would be thirty-two quadruples, while the breakdown lists eight additional columns "nell'ornato dell tre porti"; it is not clear which eight this refers to, but more likely those inside and outside the central cross-passage (cf. Note 154, below). The documents also conclude that there would be 42 pilasters altogether; the two framing the opening to the corridor may have been considered a part of the corridor and discounted. The documents lists, in addition, that the entablature and parapet would be 826 *palmi* in length internally, and 966 *palmi* externally; this is a slight overestimation (cf. Note 57, above). Wittkower reported erroneously that the colonnade began to rise in March 1659, repeating Fraschetti's error (v. Note 15, above). By a very rough estimate, the first column probably rose late in 1658. The *avviso* of March 2, 1658, reported the Pope's visit of the site, which was still at the foundation level: ". . . ieri passò Nostro Signore à S. Pietro alla deuozione del Crocifisso con caualcata, e passeggio numeroso di principi, e Prelati, ritornando poi a Monte cauallo, doppo vedute le prime fondamenta, e getti della nuoua fabbrica de portici del Vaticano" (Arch. Segr. Vat., Avvisi, 107, fol. 106; printed version, 28, fol. 128).

66. In virtually all published plans, including the Bonacina Engraving, the layout is inaccurate with regard to both the curvature of the colonnade and the alignment of columns, more on which below (Ch. III). So far as the colonnades go, only the Vatican Plan, to my knowledge, agrees with the actual construction in every detail and idiosyncrasy. There are two exceptions, however; the *terzo braccio* was never built, nor were the paired columns that frame the outside facade of the middle cross-passage. These columns appear also on the Bonacina Engraving and the Falda Print (Figs. 24 and 36); they were eliminated when shortly after this time the idea of developing a new pilgrim's road on this axis proved economically unfeasible; Brauer-Wittkower, 83. See also Note 70, below. Cf. Note 153, below.

67. See Note 81, below.

68. Most were published by Wittkower (Brauer-Wittkower, Pls. 56–68, 161–64); of these, twenty-two concern the piazza, out of which twelve are from this phase of design, eight are later, and two earlier.

69. See Note 115, below.

70. Bibl. Vat., Lat. 13442, fol. 27. The workshop drawing represents the middle cross-passage. But the plan differs from the executed version in two ways: double columns, rather than twin pilasters, frame the passage, and columns are uniform in size throughout (6 1/2 *palmi,* inscribed but hatched over in the two middle columns along the cross-passage) and not progressively augmented toward the outside course. The layout is otherwise remarkably close to the definitive state, and the drawing is also of interest for what it reveals about the method of design. First of all, control units in the layout are column bases, not column diameters, as we might expect in this stage of design; Wittkower misinterpreted the inscribed dimensions between the bases, in spite of the arrows, as intercolumnar dimensions (Brauer-Wittkower, 79, n. 2). Study also shows that the inscribed dimensions do not always agree with the actual dimensions used in the plan. But wherever they deviate, they correspond with actual executed values; in short, they represent revisions. The innermost course was executed with bases of 9 1/6 *palmi* (and columns of 6 1/2 *palmi*) at intervals of 10 *palmi*—all as drawn and inscribed here; the aisles of 10 1/4 *palmi* and 21 1/2 *palmi* (between the bases) were also executed exactly as established here. On the outmost course, however, the bases are spaced at 15 *palmi,* while the inscriptions read 14; the execution followed the inscribed dimension. By this revision, then, these bases should be larger by 2 *palmi* than they are represented to be; they are actually not 9 1/6 but 11 1/6 *palmi.* The cross-passage, the central axis of which is designated *mezza,* is misrepresented; it is shown to be twice as wide as the inscribed dimension, 19 1/4 *palmi;* again, the inscribed value is the actual width. The error led Wittkower to conclude that the drawing was abandoned because of it. Rather than a discard, however, the drawing represents two phases of design that lead directly to the Vatican Plan (Fig. 6). In fact, a square representing a pilaster is tried out over the circle of the two outer columns adjacent to the cross-passage. Finally, the plan demonstrates that the layout proceeded from the middle cross-passage in both directions by first marking out bases and intervals cumulatively on the innermost course and then completing the remaining courses radially. The additive method, which contrasts with that based on the division of the given arc into a convenient number of unit bays, seems awkward but assures that the interval dimensions (for the extreme courses, at least) are expressible in whole numbers; it was undoubtedly followed not only in drawing up the Vatican Plan but also, to advantage, in the actual construction. The dotted lines to the right of the last set of columns, together with the inscribed figures, are additions in another hand. The two sets of figures (12, 13 1/2, 16 1/2, and 18, and their halves, 6, 6 3/4, 8 1/4, and 9) stand for the dimensions of the intervals and supports, according to which the augmentation is altogether excessive. The ratio of increment in each set was no doubt, but erroneously, derived from the fact that in the original plan the inter-

vals increased from 10 to 15 with uniform bases of 9 1/6. Notwithstanding the error, the proposal was further developed in a plan to the left, representing four columns that augment on one axis only, that is, into ovals. The quadruplet is drawn at the scale five times that of the principal plan, and the widths of the columns correspond with the figures in the second set. The oval cross-sections are suggestive of the split circle; but we cannot know for certain whether the proposal represents a transitory effort under Bernini's supervision or the result, instead, of a later tampering by a lesser assistant. The lines of the radii on this plan do not converge consistently; and the center of the arc is at least 330 *palmi* from the inner columns rather than 296 *palmi* (cf. Note 6, above). This indicates conclusively that the oval of the Vatican Plan was not yet established at this stage of design. It also supports our reconstruction of the arcade plan (cf. Note 57, above).

71. Brauer-Wittkower, 78–81 and esp. Pl. 58b (Paris, Bibl. Natl., Ital. 2082, fol. 91ᵛ). The figure 22 on this sketch plan of the eastern termination is evidently the width of the cross-passage (pilaster to pilaster); in actual measurement it is 22.4 *palmi*.

72. This is, however, more true outside Italy; we read of "Il Colonnato di piazza San Pietro" in Fagiolo dell'Arco, *Bernini*, 151–54 *et passim*.

73. *Vocabolario toscano,* s.v. Earlier, in Manetti's description of the project of Nicholas V, we read of the "amplissima & ornatissima area, & ut Graeci expressius dicunt, platea" (Magnuson, *Studies*, 80; v. Note 34, above). Our piazza is designated "Forum S. Petri" on Bufalini's 1551 Plan of Rome, "Platea S. Petri" on those of Cartaro (1576), Du Pérac-Lafréry (1577), and Tempesta (1593), and subsequently in its Italian equivalent "Piazza di San Pietro." See Ehrle and Egger, *Piante e vedute di Roma* for these maps of Rome (v. Note 20, above).

74. See Note 40, above, for the *giustificazione;* for the minutes of the Congregazione in which this expression occurs, see Note 15, above.

75. See Note 14, above. But none surpassed Carlo Fontana in precision; he calls Bernini's piazza the "famosissimo Teatro con suoi Portici che recingono la Piazza Vaticana, auanti il Tempio" (*Templum Vaticanum*, 179).

76. See Note 82, below, for Alveri's text; Baldinucci's definition is in his *Vocaborario toscano* where *teatro* is an "edificio rotondo doue si rappresentano gli spettacoli."

77. A rectangular piazza surrounded by porticoes may be figuratively called *teatro* to capitalize the scenographic character of the space; after all, there was nearby the "Theatro di Beluedere" (Fig. 8). But with Bernini's piazza, the analogy is unquestionably more than a figure of speech.

78. See Note 14, above. In September the project is still called "portici" (v. Note 13, above). Subsequently, the term *teatro* also appears in the writings of Bernini and Alexander VII (Bibl. Vat., Chig. H II 22, fols. 239 and 223, respectively, as noted by Fagiolo dell'Arco, *Bernini*, 278) as well as in accounts (e.g., Bibl. Vat., Chig. H II 22, fol. 148; *ibid.*, fol. 142; and Arch. Fabb. S.P., I Piano, Arm., vol. 313, fols. 336f.; v. Note 81, below) and descriptions (v. Note 82, below). On G. B. Falda's Map of Rome of 1676, the piazza is inscribed: "Piazza e Teatro di S. Pietro." See also Note 234, below.

79. See Notes 12 and 13, above.

80. In subsequent *avvisi,* the idea is sometimes emphasized with "già disegnato."

81. Bibl. Vat., Chig. H II 22, fol. 142 (another copy in Arch. Fabb. S.P., I Piano, Arm., vol. 314a, fasc. 4): "Si notano le spese del Teatro nella Piazza di S. Pietro cominciando dalli 8 di Nov^re 1656 che cominciò l'opera per tutto decembre 1657," under which there follow these entries:

Manuali per giornate per liste	s.	8508
Modelli per il primi Archi del Teatro quali fece Cosmo Carcano	s.	516
Modelli del Teatro fatti da Gio. Maria Giorgietti	s.	373
Modelli sud.^i fatti da Ant.° Chichari	s.	420
Modelli sud.^i fatti Cosimo Carcani	s.	356

The rest of the account concerns purchase and transport of various building materials, e.g., *pozzolana, tufo, calce,* and *travertini.* The initial date in the heading of the account marks the beginning of payment for the piazza project; cf. Arch. Fabb. S.P., I Piano, ser. 1, vol. 9, No. 2 (*ristretto*) and *ibid.,* ser. 4, vol. 33, fasc. 7 (*riscontro*). The possibility that the first model by Carcani might have been for the trapezoid plan is ruled out; for, returned for rework, this design was surely already shelved away by November. The remaining models are described in detail in the carpenter's accounts, Arch. Fabb. S.P., I Piano, Arm., vol. 313, fols. 344–46 (Giorgetti), 340–42 (Chicari), and 336–38 (Carcani); the first two are dated November 6, 1657, the third November 10, 1657. They are all life-size models ("il Modello nuovo posto sul la Piazza di S. Pietro d'ordine del Sig. Cavalier Bernini"); there is no mention of arches. By chronology, the three models are best associated with the colonnades of 1657, represented on Medals I–III; there is a reference in each case, however, to "li Capitelli delle doi colonne con la sua Campana," which makes one think of the Corinthian Order. An *avviso* reported on November 10, 1657 (Arch. Segr. Vat., Avvisi, 105, fol, 34; printed), that the Pope "si compiacque di vedere il modello del nuouo Teatro da farsi attorno quella Piazza, di già cominciato da fondamenti." A huge model, measuring 25 *palmi,* or 5.58 m., was made by Lazzaro Morelli between April 1, 1659 and January 31, 1660, but its present whereabouts is unknown (Brauer-Wittkower, 81, n. 6). Finally, as late as April 25, 1659, another life-size model was ordered by the Pope ("Confectione Columnarum et Pilastrorum": Arch. Fabb. S.P., I Piano, ser. 3, vol. 163, fol. 168, Minutes of the Congregazione). A month later, the Congregazione reported the Pope's intention "quod perficiantur integraliter quatuor arcus Porticus, qui construitur in Platea S. Petri cum eorum totali perfectione, ut esse debent, quando Porticus erit totaliter terminata" (Arch. Fabb. S.P., I Piano, ser. 3, vol. 163, fol. 173^v, dated May 30, 1659). If this refers to the same model, *quatuor arcus* does not make any sense unless it simply meant four bays; on the other hand, no construction with four arches is known in the area of the Piazza. Moreover, one wonders about the use of a life-size model at this date, when the construction was already well advanced (v. Note 65, above).

82. G. Alveri, *Della Roma in ogni stato,* II, Rome, 1664, 153–54; "Hebbe anticamente

dall'occaso il Cerchio di Nerone, ò come altri vogliono di Caiu, il quale haueua il suo Principio, e la sua entrata doue hora è la Chiesa di S. Marta alle falde del colle, e finiua à gli vltimi scalini delle scale antiche di S. Pietro; longo palmi 720 largo 400, cinto di tre ordini di muri alti da terra palmi 41 grossi palmi 14, che sosteneuano le volte, e sedili per i spettatori, rinchiudendo nel loro giro una piazza doue si faceuano i giuochi, larga palmi 230. Hoggi è cinto da vn magnifico portico, che lo rende in forma di Teatro, opera del Caualier Bernino famoso, & insigne ingegnero, fatto d'ordine di Nostro Signore Alessandro Settimo. . . . Il Teatro, como diceu è di forma ouale, che è la più perfetta, essendo composto di dui cerchi, non continuato. . . ." The subject of the second sentence, "Hoggi è cinto . . . ," can only be either "una piazza" or, indefinitely, "thereabout"; on the other hand, the author correctly locates the circus on the south side of the Basilica. Unconsciously or deliberately, he is ambiguous; and the two monuments merge in the reader's mind. One must remember, in fact, that the circus witnessed the slaughter of Christians under Nero and was by tradition the site of Peter's martyrdom; see also Note 21, above.

83. *Templum Vaticanum,* 178–79 (Book IV, ch. 2: "Il Paragone degl' Antichi romani edifizij col Tempio Vaticano, e suoi Portici").

84. In Paris Bernini told a story about a painter who came to see the Colosseum, only because he had heard time and again about the beauty and magnificence of the monument, but seeing it in ruin upon approaching Rome, as he was from Naples (where "l'on n'aime que les bagatelles et les dorures"), he could hardly believe how anyone could seriously admire such a hideous thing and immediately turned back without entering Rome; v. Chantelou, *Journal,* 23 (June 8). The story was a retort to M. le Nonce, who remarked that the Pope should restore such a monument from Antiquity instead of pouring his funds on extravagant new projects. See also following Note.

85. As he described it, "une espèce d'amphithéâtre à l'imitation du Colisee et du théâtre de Marcellus; lequel étant double aurait une de ses faces vers le Louvre, et l'autre vers le palais des Tuileries, dans chacune desquelles il y aurait a y placer jusques à dix mille personnes de la noblesse" (Chantelou, *Journal,* 96 [August 13]).

86. R. Bernheimer, "Theatrum Mundi," *Art Bulletin,* XXXVIII, 1956, 225–47, esp. 242f.; see also Fagiolo dell'Arco, *Bernini,* Cat. No. 85. The play is also known as *Due Covielli.* The most complete account of the play is that of Massimiliano Montecuculi (quoted in full by Bernheimer), which was written in 1637 and addressed to the Duke of Modena; but there is also Bernini's own version told to Chantelou (v. following Note). On Bernini in the theater, see also G. L. Bernini, *Fontana di Trevi, Commedia inedita,* ed. Cesare d'Onofrio, Rome, 1963, and the review by I. Lavin, *Art Bulletin,* XLVI, 1964, 568–72; and Fagiolo dell'Arco, *Bernini,* ch. 8 (177–95). On the seventeenth-century theater in Italy, see A. Ademollo, *I teatri di Roma nel secolo decimosettimo,* Rome, 1888; A. Saviotti, "Feste e spettacoli nel seicento," *Giornale storico della letteratura italiana,* XLI, 1903, 42–77; and H. Leclerc, *Les origines italiennes de l'architecture théâtrale moderne,* Paris, 1946, esp. 167–72 (on Bernini).

87. Chantelou, *Journal*, 68 (July 26): "L'on vit un grand clair de lune, la représentation de la place de devant Saint-Pierre, une quantité de cavaliers, les uns à cheval, les autres en carosse et à pied, lesquels passaient et se retournaient par cette place, plusieurs flambeaux dont les uns paraissaient gros, les autres moyens, d'autres plus petits en enfin quelques-uns menus comme un filet, accommodés à la dimunition que la perspective fait dans le vrai, et qu'il avait aussi par art fait diminuer les lumières de grosseur et par affaiblissement de clarté." A *veduta* like this might have been an established convention; an *avviso* of February 5, 1659, in describing an opera, isolates the scene showing "il Palazzo Vaticano, la facciata, e Cuppola di S. Pietro, Borgo nuovo, e Castel S. Angelo ripieno de'-Lumi" (Arch. Segr. Vat., Avvisi, 103, fol. 101v). The piazza, nevertheless, might have been mentioned in Montecuculi's account, had it been actually featured in the 1637 production; still one might argue that the detail could have been omitted simply as being inessential. On the other hand, while Bernini's account is generally less detailed, this particular scene, as he describes it, is very concrete. To him, therefore, the setting showing the piazza, whether remembered or imagined, was undoubtedly important. And in recounting it, Bernini would have found it difficult to visualize the site without completing it with the colonnades, on which he had been working for almost a decade.

88. Literally, of course, the amphitheater is two theaters: it was "due Theatri congiunti insieme con le fronti loro" according to Barbaro (W. Lotz, "Die ovalen Kirchenräume," 15–16). Cf. Note 85, above.

89. Of Bernini's piety, F. Baldinucci wrote that since his marriage in his fortieth year "he began to behave more like a cleric than a layman" with such sincerity "that he might have been worthy of the admiration of the most perfect monastic" (*Vita di Gran Lorenzo Bernini,* Florence, 1682; *The Life of Bernini,* trans. C. Enggass, University Park and London, 1966, 68).

90. Bernini's scenography will be discussed below in another context (Ch. IV). There exist two anonymous plans of the piazza illustrating the problem of visibility with visual lines (Wittkower, "A Counter-project," 101, n. 2); see also Bernini's drawing for the church in Ariccia (Brauer-Wittkower, Pl. 94, and Kitao, "Bernini's Church Facades"; v. Note 180, below).

91. Once this fact is recognized, it is clearly an unrewarding, if not unnecessary, pursuit to try to find prototypes specifically for the colonnade that is free-standing and circular, as does Thoenes ("Geschichte des Petersplatzes," 124–25), who proposes several prototypes, among which is Ligorio's illustration of an aviarium (based on Varro's description).

92. D. S. Robertson observes that there is no sufficient ground for labeling the columns of the lowest story of the Colosseum Tuscan rather than Doric (*A Handbook of Greek and Roman Architecture,* Cambridge, 1954, 285). They are certainly more slender than standard Tuscan columns. Moreover, the entablature features a plain frieze, the architrave is divided into three faciae, and the cornice has base moldings of three parts; these are some of the characteristics of the Ionic entablature according to W. B. Dinsmoor (*En-*

cyclopaedia Britannica, s.v. "Order"). In the executed colonnade, the column is 57 1/2 *palmi* in height, including base and capital; the column diameter varies from 6 1/2 to 7 1/6 *palmi* according to the legend on the Bonacina Engraving (on which see Note 64, above). Accordingly, the outer column (1:8.03) is Doric, but the inner column (1:8.85) is more Ionic in proportion. Since the inner course is more basic and represented as the norm in elevations, Carlo Fontana is accurate in describing the columns as consisting of Doric capital and Ionic shaft (*Templum Vaticanum,* 187); the arcade must have been this way, too (cf. Note 53, above). Thoenes observes that Bernini's choice of slender columns reveals his concern for harmonizing the colonnades with Maderna's facade ("Geschichte des Petersplatzes," 123, esp. n. 158). On the Order in Bernini's arcade design, see Note 53, above.

93. Wittkower, who calls this combination unorthodox observes that Bernini was anticipated by Pietro da Cortona in his portico for Santa Maria della Pace, begun 1656 (*Art and Architecture,* 127 and 160). But as Wittkower remarks in a footnote, Pietro was unorthodox in the Doric column as well as in the Ionic entablature; the shaft is conspicuously slender, the basis is Ionic, and the entablature features a plain frieze and characteristic faciae (v. Note 92, above), but lacks dentils at the cornice, as is the case for that matter with Bramante's Ionic in the cloister of the same church (best illustrations for these in P. Portoghesi, "S. Maria della Pace di Pietro da Cortona," *Architettura,* VII, 1962, 830–51). The same mixture appears earlier in Pietro's painting, *Xenophon's Sacrifice to Diana* (Wittkower, *Art and Architecture,* Pl. 88B). The "mixed" Order like Pietro's and Bernini's was adopted earlier in such notable works as Peruzzi's Palazzo Massimi (1535) and Vasari's Uffizi (1560). It is more frequent in church facades: e.g., San Crisogono (1626, G. B. Soria), Sant' Anastasia (1636), and San Stanislao dei Polacchi (1580), all in Rome; in these, the frieze provides space for an inscription (as in Santa Maria della Pace). Bernini used it in his church facades at Castelgandolfo and Ariccia (with dentils in the campanile of the latter church); it appears also in Domenchino's painted arcade (v. Note 58, above). Some of these examples may appear Tuscan; but the Tuscan entablature has a simple architrave, for example, the facade of the Villa Giulia and the upper story of the Palazzo Vidoni Caffarelli, in Rome.

94. Bernheimer, "Thetatrum Mundi," 243 (v. Note 86, above); also A. M. Nagler, *Theater Festivals of the Medici, 1539–1637,* New Haven, 1964, for description of various *intermezzi.*

95. Bernheimer, "Theatrum Mundi" *passim.* The idea of reversing the auditorium and the stage during the play was first realized in the performance in the Palazzo Vecchio in Florence for the wedding of Don Francesco de' Medici with Giovanna d'Austria in 1565; Vasari, who described the event, was himself in charge of the stage design (Bernheimer, 233–35). The auditorium and stage were merged into one amphitheater for the first time in 1589 on the occasion of the wedding of Ferdinando de' Medici and Christine de Lorraine; Buontalenti directed and designed the performance. It was described by B. de Rossi (Bernheimer, 236–37): "S'appresentò agli occhi di giascheduno tutta la

sala una amfiteatro perfetto (perciochè la Prospettiva che era in faccia con la sua architettura Corintia si congiungeva con l'apparato)." Buontalenti produced an *intermezzo* of similar design again in 1600 for the marriage of Maria de' Medici with Henry IV of France (Bernheimer, 238–40).

96. In the celebration of 1589. Christine of Lorraine was actually led to a "theater" at the city gate on her entry into Florence and was crowned Archduchess of Tuscany after the image of the Coronation of the Virgin (Bernheimer, "Theatrum Mundi," 238); on the idea of the sky as the theater, see Bernheimer, 235–36. Besides Raphael's *Disputa,* we can call to our mind any number of various Renaissance representations of the Coronation of the Virgin, Assumption, and similar subjects; but in these examples the amphitheater is suggested, not architecturally, but only compositionally.

97. Our illustration is the "Reign of Love" designed by Giulio Parigi for the final scene of *La Liberazione di Tireno e d'Arnea;* the occasion was the wedding of Ferdinando Gonzaga and Catherine de' Medici, which took place during the Carnival of 1617. For this and other examples, see Nagler, *Theater Festivals,* 131f., also Pls. 107 and 125. A thorough study of the relation between Bernini's architecture and the theater and festival decorations of the time is much needed.

98. That is, "ultima et reccide il filo di tutte le comedie"; v. Fagiolo dell'Arco, *Bernini,* Cat. No. 85.

99. The arcade design already featured statues all around the balustrade (Figs. 17 and 19). Speaking of the executed colonnades, Fontana called the statues befitting components to the "Macchina Teatrale," as though in analogy with the Teatro Olimpico in Vicenza or the Amphitheater of the Boboli Gardens in Florence. We have no evidence other than formal analogies that Bernini knew Palladio's theater; but see Wittkower, "Palladio e Bernini" (v. Note 222, below). On Palladio's drawing (London, RIBA, vol. X, fol. 3), see G. Zorzi, *Le ville e i teatri di Andrea Palladio,* Venice, 1969, 232–42. For balustrades with statues Bernini could turn to Michelangelo's Campidoglio; and, after all, colonnades, arcades, statues, and fountains were also stock props in the Florentine *intermezzi.*

100. See Note 227, below.

101. Cf. A. Muñoz, who already described the piazza as the "smisurato teatro in cui tutto il mondo è chiamato al sacro spettacolo della chiesa trionfante" (*G. L. Bernini, architetto e decoratore,* Rome, 1925, 30); v. also Mariani, *Significato* and Fagiolo dell' Arco, *Bernini,* 278.

102. The drawing is Bibl. Vat., Chig. a I 19, fol. 26. Wittkower misinterpreted the plan to the right as follows (Brauer-Wittkower, 74–75). The northern portico, as earlier, terminates clear of the axis of the entrance to the Vatican located in the tower of Paul V, which would properly function as the focus of a vista only with the extravagant rerouting (two parallel lines) of the Borgo Nuovo; it was decided, therefore, to sacrifice the tower, extend the western termination (four short strokes), and develop it as a new gateway (elevation) which would appear fully on the axis of the Borgo Nuovo as it is,

which runs obliquely and therefore keeps clear of the symmetrically positioned eastern termination; the double columns of the tetrastyle, finally, emerged as the basic motif of the design on the first medal.

There are several difficulties to this interpretation, however. The suggestion that the removal of the tower was introduced as an alternative to the reconstruction of the Borgo is intriguing; but if this is the point of the plan, it is strange that there is no indication of the tower in any form anywhere. The new gate at the new location implies an oblique line for the corridor, and while this is crucial in the argument, it is not indicated on the plan either. The idea of making the western termination serve as a gateway was briefly tried out in the arcade design (Fig. 19), but the colonnade design left it out for some time; it was not yet present at the time of Medal III. In fact, in these early medals I/II and III), there is no attempt to match the last bay of the colonnade with the axis of the corridor. Then, the dots to the right and left of the obelisk suggest two fountains, while the encircled dot is too far up to be Maderno's fountain in its original location; and the tetrastyle elevation is definitely later in style (v. Note 104, below). Finally, the sequence of strokes in completing the plan clearly suggests that the four short strokes were corrected by the darker strokes at their right rather than vice versa.

In this connection, the following should be noted. In a sketch plan like this one, lines tend to be darker when what they represent requires emphasis or clarification (e.g., the cornice profile in the elevation) and also when they represent a correction. The very light curve (Fig. 35, element 3) was superseded by the darker one (5) that defines a taller oval, and the only explanation for this correction is to bring the oval closer to the two lines at right angles (2), which were consequently there first. The four short strokes (6), representing the tetrastyle, should have come in early but only after the two elements they bind; for, carefully positioned at right-angled corner, they presuppose it. The plan had a false start (1); perhaps there was a fleeting thought of showing the northern half only because of the tight space. When the colonnades came to be defined, it was clear that the initial oval left too little space both left and right as well as between it and the corner above, where we see some fudging. Symmetry suggests that the short ends of the colonnades on the east side were introduced all at once. The street (12) should have followed, rather than preceded, this operation, as it is controlled on the right side by the east end of the northern colonnade (11). The short strokes at the end of the street (13) do not represent the terminating edge of the colonnade; single lines serve that purpose elsewhere in the drawing. They also make up the most emphatic element; therefore, they can only be a revision of the four lines to the left made only to correct a technical error. Why the already existing dot was not encircled for the fountain cannot be determined.

103. The idea of developing the area to serve as a vestibule to both the Basilica and the Vatican was anticipated in the steps of Pius II (v. Note 20, above) as well as in the positioning of Maderno's fountain (v. Note 37, above).

104. The clock, too, is surmounted with the papal tiara and keys (shown in outline only) as are those that decorate the facade of the Basilica today; the cornice carries a parapet rather than balustrade in the sketch as well as Bonacina's elevation. The choice of a

parapet in place of balustrade was apparently a decision made only after the development of the colonnade with simple columns and dropped soon after the publication of the Bonacina Engraving. The arcade had a balustrade (Fig. 17). The colonnades of paired columns carried an attic above the cornice, and a balustrade above it, according to the drawing of a *terzo braccio* in the Palazzo Chigi, Ariccia (Wittkower, "Il terzo braccio," Fig. 2). There is one drawing by Bernini that postdates Medal III, on which a balustrade (in cross-section) is recognized (Bibl. Vat., Chig. a I 19, fol. 50; Brauer-Wittkower, Pl. 59). The document of July 30, 1659 (v. Note 65, above) mentions only "il basamento e cimasa del finimento della facciata," which probably refers to the parapet, since it is called "Imbasamento sopra la cornice" on the Bonacina Engraving; one other elevation, a shop drawing, repeats this detail (Bibl. Vat., Chig. P VII 9, fol. 23; Brauer-Wittkower, Pl. 163a). On Falda's print (Fig. 36), the colonnade already features a balustrade rather than a parapet, as executed.

105. *Il Nuouo teatro delle fabriche et edificii in prospettiva di Roma moderna,* Rome, 1665, I, Pl. 3; cf. Note 64, above.

106. See Note 59, above. Needless to say, the two fountains may suggest but are not identical with the foci of the ellipse of which the oval of the plan is an approximation (Fig. 52, center).

107. R. Bernheimer, "Theatrum Mundi" (v. Note 86, above), 232. See also Lotz, "Die ovalen Kirchenräume," 15–16, where Alberti's idea of the amphitheater as a circular structure is discussed and examples in the treatises of Filarete and Francesco di Giorgio are mentioned. For the Vitruvian theater, see also G. Zorzi (v. Note 99, above).

108. *Perspectiva pictorum et architectorum,* II, Rome, 1700, Pl. 44; Francesco di Giorgio's amphitheaters, see A. Chastel, *The Age of Humanism,* New York, 1963, pl. 223. See also preceding Note.

109. R. Wittkower, *Architectural Principles,* 1–32.

110. Some of these twenty-five drawings (now in the Vatican Library, according to Fagiolo dell'Arco, *Bernini,* 269) were first published by A. Busiri-Vici, *La Piazza di San Pietro nei secoli III, XIV, XVII,* Rome, 1893, and were almost invariably attributed to Bernini before Wittkower defined them as a counterproject initially in 1931 (Brauer-Wittkower, 98–101). Subsequently, he published and discussed all the twenty-five drawings of the set in his study, "A Counter-project," in which he also attributed them to a nephew of Papirio Bartoli (cf. Note 39, above) and characterized them as "a last and powerful appeal to the Congregazione before construction of the piazza was started in the Spring of 1659" ("A Counter-project," 99). He proposed this dating on the following basis: (1) the critic knew not only Bernini's design of the colonnade with single columns but also the plan for a new pilgrim's road which Bernini entertained briefly in the spring of 1659 when the Bonacina Engraving was in preparation as is evidenced by the existence on the engraving (but not on the preparatory drawing for it) of the framing columns on the outside facade of the middle cross-passage (Figs. 24 and 36) which were omitted in execution (Figs. 2 and 28b); and (2) a proposal involving such drastic changes from Bernini's design would not have made sense unless it was produced before the beginning

of the actual construction, which was certainly underway in the spring of 1659 (v. Note 65, above). Cf. Note 112, below.

111. Mainly on the basis of Durandus and the Psalmist (xviii, 5); Wittkower, "A Counter-project," 89–91, 96–97, and 104; and Pls. 16a, 16b, 19a, and 19b.

112. Wittkower concluded in his earlier study (1931) that Bernini's *giustificazione* followed the Counterproject of 1659 on the belief that "dieses klug berechnende Schriftstück scheint eine Antwort Berninis auf die gegen sein Projekt gerichteten Angriffe zu sein" (Brauer-Wittkower, 100), and proposed the bracket date 1659–60 for it (*ibid.,* 70, n. 1); the statement was not repeated in the later study. A comparison of these two sources, suggests, however, that the *giustificazione* came first. The Counterproject proposed a circular piazza; the basis of the argument was an elaborate emblematic (but not necessarily "mediaevalizing") symbolism, against which Bernini's oval was censured. The *giustificazione* is hardly an answer to this particular issue; for it expounds the formal, functional, and iconographical merits of the oval plan against the "square" plan. The Counterproject, on the other hand, almost certainly presupposes Bernini's argument. Against the assertion that the oval plan successfully solves the problem of visibility, the critic points out that it still has blind spots which the circular plan would completely eliminate (Drawing 4, "A Counter-project," Pl. 16b). To the explanation that the colonnades symbolize the arms of the Church, he replies that the arms will be deformed unless the piazza is perfectly circular all around (Drawings Nos. 1 and 2; our Fig. 40). For the simple assumption that the oval is essentially a variant of the circle, the critic substitutes an elaborate system of symbols; and in so doing, he insists that an oval is *not* a circle. Finally, Bernini's use of the papal sanction is tactful and effective as an anticipatory defense, a preventive measure; but it sounds like an awkward subterfuge as an answer to the direct attack on the oval plan. We are therefore forced to conclude that the *giustificazione* was written *before* the preparation of the Counterproject but after the completion of the definitive plan of the piazza and the colonnades: the very beginning of 1659, or, more likely, the end of 1658. Cf. Note 65, above.

113. Wittkower, "A Counter-project," 103; Bernini's . . . comparisons are no more than similes, meant in a metaphorical sense. . . . The critic on the other hand is completely absorbed in mediaeval symbolism which implied that the arrangement of his plan is dependent on an external correspondence between the symbolical idea and the architectural form." In the critic's *concetto,* it must be emphasized, the correspondence has partial bearing only on certain selected abstract qualities as that in a metaphor.

114. Cf. Note 8, above.

115. Bibl. Vat. Chig. a I 19, fol. 28; the castle to the left is by another hand. The sketch plan, treating the colonnade and corridor as a single arm, is in contrast to the preceding drawing (Fig. 34). Three cross-passages are shown; the western passage, initially indicated by four lines as the eastern counterpart, is scrawled over by two darker slanting lines. There are two likely interpretations for this detail. On the one hand, it may mean that the cross-passage at this point, when adjusted on the axis of the corridor, falls out of the radial pattern of the rest of the colonnade, and calls for a special solution involving de-

tachment of some of the twin pilasters here (Brauer-Wittkower, 80); on the other hand, and more likely, it may be simply that the cross-passage, laid out on the axis of the Borgo Nuovo as specified in the previous drawing, will be oblique and will create, as were eventually developed, rhombic pilasters (Fig. 6). In either case, the joint gains importance as a link between the two elements. The sketch of the Basilica above may be a reference to the *contrapposti*—a calculated contrast in height—between the facade and colonnades (on which, more in Ch. IV, below).

116. A further implication of this change is discussed below (Ch. IV).

117. The geometrical construction of this oval proceeds as follows. Two circles are first described, interlocked in such a way that the center of one circle falls on the circumference of the other; these circles describe the two smaller arcs of the oval. Two larger arcs with their centers at the intersection points of the initial circles complete the figure. Cf. Notes 5 and 6, above.

118. *Il primo libro d'architettura*, Paris, 1545, 13–14. The particular construction was accurately described by Wittkower (Brauer-Wittkower, 76–77) and illustrated by Pamela Askew ("The Relation of Bernini's Architecture to the Architecture of the High Renaissance and of Michelangelo," *Marsyas*, V, 1947–49, 39–61, esp. 51), but neither referred to Serlio. See Note 5, above.

119. The designation was introduced in G. Troili (or Trogli) da Spinlamberto, *detto* Paradosso, *Paradossi per practicare la prospettiva senza saperla*, Bologna, 1683 (but written before 1672), 10–11, where Serlio's four ovals are all illustrated. The currency of the term in Italy is uncertain, but it is adopted here for lack of a better term; it must be pointed out, on the other hand, that Troili's term appeared earlier in French equivalent in J. Dubreuil, *La perspective pratique*, I, Paris, 1642, of which the Italian treatise was essentially a copy. The term *ovato tondo* was also adopted by Ferdinando Galli Bibiena, *Architettura civile*, Parma, 1711.

120. W. Lotz, "Die ovalen Kirchenräume des Cinquecento," 11–13. The statement applies only to the oval as a two-dimensional figure. The ellipse was known to Dürer as a conic section; v. Appendix, 1.

121. The major axis, of course, is 3R, where R. is the radius of the initial circles; the minor axis is (Fig. 3)

$$(pq + p'q') - pp' = (2R + 2R) - \sqrt{(2R)^2 - R^2} = 4R - \sqrt{3R^2} = (4 - \sqrt{3})R,$$

or 2.268R. The ratio x/y for the *ovato tondo* is consequently 0.756, which should be compared with 0.707 and 0.757 of Serlio's second and third oval, respectively. Cf. Note 6, above.

122. See Note 119, above, for the source of these terms.

123. Uffizi, dis. arch. 531, first published by Lotz, "Die ovalen Kirchenräume," 11–12.

124. A mason could describe an elliptical arch very quickly by using strings and applying the general principle of Serlio's first oval (Fig. 46), and this Serlio knew and discussed elsewhere; v. Appendix, 1.

125. W. Dinsmoor, "The Literary Remains of Sebastiano Serlio," *Art Bulletin,* XXIV, 1942, 74, n. 92.

126. For the survey, Lotz's study (v. Note 120, above) is essential. In addition, the following are useful: J. H. Müller, *Das regulierte Oval,* Bremen, 1967; M. Zocca, *La cupola di S. Giacomo in Augusta e le cupola ellittiche in Roma,* Rome, 1945; and Furio Fasolo, *L'opera di Hieronimo e Carlo Rainaldi,* Rome, 1962. The *ovato tondo* may be recognized on an architectural plan by the characteristic "haunches" and the ratio of the axes, $x/y = 0.756$. But it can be verified only by reading compass marks: four centers forming a diamond of two equilateral triangles, two of them at the thirds of the major axis. The *ovato tondo* appears certainly or almost certainly on the following plans: Peruzzi's projects in his Uffizi drawing, dis. arch. 453 (Villa Trivulzio; Lotz, Fig. 4), 577 (San Giacomo degli Incurabili; Lotz, Fig. 11) and 4137 (our Fig. 47); Serlio's oval church plan in his Fifth Book (Fig. 48); Il Campidoglio, oval pavement; Francesco da Volterra's San Giacomo degli Incurabili (Lotz, Fig. 38; also Maderno's Albertina, our Fig. 49); Negri's project for the sanctuary at Mondovì (Lotz, Fig. 51); Ricchino's project for a crypt (Lotz, Fig. 63); the drawing, Albertina 166, once associated with San Carlo alle Quattro Fontane (Hempel, *Francesco Borromini,* Vienna, 1924, Fig. 7); Borromini's Palazzo Carpegna (Albertina 1019); Carlo Rainaldi's oval project for Santa Maria in Campitelli (Fasolo, Pls. 52 and 55), Santa Maria di Monte Santo (Fasolo, Fig. 39), and three of his oval church projects in the Vatican (Bibl. Vat., Chig. P VII 10, fols. 127, 128, and 130, Fasolo, Figs. 35, 32, and 33, respectively, of which fol. 130 is our Fig. 50); the Trinità dei Spagnuoli in Via Condotti by Manoel Rodrigues dos Santos (Zocca, Pl. VI). In Vignola's two churches, Sant' Andrea in Via Flaminia and Sant' Anna dei Palafrenieri (Lotz, Figs. 19 and 28), the oval is close enough to the *ovato tondo* that we could accept it as one. One critic, however, interpreted it as a slightly varied form (Müller, Figs. 13b and 15b).

127. *Ovato tondo* does not appear on the plans of the eighteenth-century churches, Santa Maria dell'Orazione e Morte and Santi Celso e Giuliano; see, respectively, G. Matthiae, *Ferdinando Fuga,* Rome, ca. 1951, Fig. 1, and Segui, Thoenes, and Mortari, *Ss. Celso e Giuliano,* Rome, 1966, Fig. 11. For Bernini's Sant' Andrea, there are several plans that survive from the seventeenth century, but none of them shows the *ovato tondo* (Fig. 76); F. Borsi's analysis of what he calls "tracciati regolatori" demonstrates conclusively that the plan evolved internally as well as externally either with a geometrical web so intricate that it hardly qualifies as a regulatory system, or, as is more likely, with no clear geometrical system (*La chiesa di S. Andrea al Quirinale,* Rome, 1967, 46–51). P. Askew's diagram reproduced in Fagiolo dell'Arco, *Bernini,* Fig. 45, is obviously inaccurate; she shows an *ovato tondo* for the external outline, but no existing plan records compass marks that support her analysis. One of Carlo Rainaldi's oval projects (Bibl. Vat., Chig. P VII 10, fol. 129; Fasolo, *Rainaldi,* Fig. 34) is an oval based on two circles at a closer distance to each other than the case of the *ovato tondo.* Aleotti's plan for San Carlo, Ferrara, follows Serlio's first oval; even though three inscribed circles makes it look like his second oval at first sight, the secondary centers of the oval are determined

by equilateral triangles (D. R. Coffin, "Some Architectural Drawings of Giovan Battista Aleotti," *Journal of the Society of Architectural Historians,* XXI 1962, 123, Fig. 13). An oval identical to this appears on Borromini's plan of San Carlo alle Quatro Fontane (Albertina 173; P. Portoghesi, *Borromini nella cultura europea,* Rome, 1964, frontispiece). See also the following Note.

128. The oval of Vignola's project "Parma 17" (Lotz, "Die ovalen Kirchenräume," Fig. 24) is considerably slimmer than the *ovato tondo.* The compass marks on the drawing suggest an oval of somewhat irregular construction (Müller, *Das regulierte Oval,* Fig. 14b); but the plan is apparently drawn loosely. When it is correctly redrawn to the inscribed dimensions, 50 and 75, it shows that the underlying oval (as Lotz described on p. 42, n. 15, and p. 72, n. 4) was based on two circles tangent to each other, and its major and minor axes were related to each other in *diapente* or *sesquialtera* (i.e., 2:3). If this is the case, we find here an oval that surpassed the *ovato tondo* in rational structure. The diamond core is composed of Pythagorean triangles (3:4:5); each large arc is therefore described from the center located on its counterpart opposite it, and the radii as well as the axes are expressible in whole numbers. The oval possesses that perfect "corrispondenza et proportione de' numeri insieme" (Vignola, *Regola delli Cinque Ordini,* Venice, 1562, Preface), that the architect aspired to achieve in all his work. Vignola, in fact, used this commensurable oval—or, rather, a half of it—as early as 1547 for the design of the projected bridge over the Samoggia (M. Walcher Casotti, *Il Vignola,* Trieste, 1960, Fig. 77). The oval of Mascherino's Santo Spirito dei Napoletani (Lotz, Fig. 46) is probably of the same kind (but cf. Müller, Fig. 24b). Guarini's oval construction is original but needlessly complicated (*Architettura civile,* Turin, 1737, 59).

129. See Appendix, 1.

130. "In Ellipsi foci duo sunt, aequaliter a centro figurae remoti," according to Kepler (*Vitellionem Paralipomena,* Frankfurt, 1604, cited by W. Lotz, "Die ovalen Kirchenräume," 94). Strictly speaking, the oval has four centers because it consists of four circular segments. But the two on the minor axis are peripheral. Those on the major axis therefore stand out and are also associated with the foci of the corresponding ellipse, with which, however, they are obviously not identical (Fig. 52, center). This bifocal image is further strengthened by the general idea that the oval is a circle elongated by doubling it: *tŏdo bisŭgo* (i.e., *tondon bislungo*) in Baldinucci's definition (*Vocabolorio toscano dell'arte del disegno,* Florence, 1681, s.v. "ovale"). On the knowledge of the ellipse among architects of the seventeenth century, see Appendix, 1.

131. In common speech, ellipse and oval are interchangeable, but we draw a distinction between them for the purpose of this study, reserving the latter term for the approximate form composed of circular segments. Cf. Appendix, 1.

132. G. B. Passeri objected to the transverse oval precisely for its bifocalism, which he thought disruptive of and opposed to unity. See Appendix, 2.

133. This is true, as we shall see below, even in a longitudinal oval church with a centralizing counteraxis.

134. See Notes 126 and 127, above, for a list of major oval buildings and projects in Italy. Fornovo's plan of the Annunziata in Parma (begun in 1566) was transverse in scheme; but, rather than a real oval, it was a "pseudo-oval," consisting of two full semicircles joined by straight lines so that its circumference is not a continuous curve and the figure reads more as a composite form. Moreover, the design was presumably inspired by Michelozzo's circular choir of the same name in Florence (Lotz, "Die ovalen Kirchenräume," 57). It is therefore truer to say that the Annunziata was conceived as a variant of the circular plan than as an oval plan. Ligorio's Casino of Pius IV in the Vatican (begun in 1558) likewise used a "pseudo-oval." Transverse ovals could be found in lesser projects, however. There were halls, stairs, and fountains (e.g., Palazzo Barberini, Caprarola, and Villa d' Este in Tivoli); and there were chapels, too, which were often shallow and wide rather than narrow and deep, regardless of their shape, whether for lack of space or in conformity with their subordinate role within the total scheme of the church, which was often perpendicular to them in axis. More private than churches and rarely self-contained, these projects were also modest in stature and generally in scale as well and therefore less substantial in influence than the few major oval churches.

135. See Note 130, above.

136. For other example, see Notes 126 and 127, above.

137. R. Wittkower, "Carlo Rainaldi and the Roman Architecture of the Full Baroque," *Art Bulletin,* XIX 1937, 242–313, esp. 267f.

138. Lotz, "Die ovalen Kirchenräume," 35–54 and 94–97.

139. M. J. Lewine, "Vignola's Church of Sant' Anna de' Palafrenieri in Rome," *Art Bulletin,* XLVII, 1965, 199–229.

140. Wittkower, "Carlo Rainaldi," 267f.

141. Wittkower ("Carlo Rainaldi," 268), to whom we owe this expression, applied it specifically to the oval space in which the circle is subordinated to the axial direction.

142. Or, in Lotz's own words, a "durch Fassade und Altar richtungsbestimmten, in der Querachse ausgewieteten Raum" ("Die ovalen Kirchenräume," 55).

143. Lotz, "Die ovalen Kirchenräume," 67–68.

144. Wittkower, "Carlo Rainaldi," 267.

145. Borromini's originality in the design of his San Carlo alle Quattro Fontane was, by contrast, to have transformed the oval so completely that the plan was no longer oval but basically cruciform instead.

146. See Appendix, 2.

147. Brauer-Wittkower, 76–78; see also Ch. 1, above.

148. Carlo Rainaldi's project, probably submitted under Innocent X before Bernini's appointment, was a polygonal plan (Brauer-Wittkower, 67 and 97–99; Fasolo, *Rainaldi,* 212–17; also Note 31, above). In general distribution of architectural elements, Bernini's final design comes close to his predecessor's; but it differs vastly in formal character. The general resemblance undoubtedly owes much to the closely defined program and tight topographical condition.

149. For Fontana's discussion of this problem, see Appendix, 2. Bernini himself discussed it in his memorandum to the Pope (*giustificazione*) as though visibility determined the form of the piazza (v. Note 40, above; and Brauer-Wittkower, 70). One must be cautious here, however; the architect's decision, as discussed in his memorandum, was not a matter of finding a suitable form but, rather, one of choosing between two possible solutions, "square" and oval, as we have seen above (Ch. I).

150. See Ch. I and Note 48, above.

151. See Note 9, above.

152. The remaining two sets (d and e), framing the cross-passage, are all but parallel with each other and fall outside the system; v. Note 162, below.

153. The axis of these pilasters, as well as that of the last set of columns, appear slightly turned counterclockwise. In the view from the secondary center (p), they are turned very slightly clockwise; the shift, however, is ever so slight here and not clearly recognizable. That the terminal bays differ from the rest, on the other hand, can be verified by measuring, even with a string, the intercolumniations in this segment (i.e., 14–15, 15–16, and 16-c). The Piazza Obliqua is obviously too vast for accurate tape measurements, and since the colonnades are curvilinear, they provide few reliable co-ordinates for sighting. That the actual piazza describes an *ovato tondo,* and the colon-nades in consequence a composite curve, can be quickly ascertained, however, in the following four ways. (1) The straight edge that terminates the northern colonnade at the east, when extended or sighted against the facade of the Basilica, marks a point immediately inside the outermost pilaster (Fig. 22, A, T-T″); in the layout of our third solution, this line reaches a point near the center of the facade. (2) The straight line drawn (or sighted on the east side of the piazza between the two col-onnades from the outer corner of one to the inner corner of the other (Fig. 22, A, s) intersects the minor axis of the oval immediately inside its circumference, which is marked out in the pavement design; the corresponding point would fall outside the circumference in our third solution. (3) The straight line connecting the inner corners of the colonnades and the arc of the oval between the same corners (legible on the pavement) are distant from each other at the center about 40 *palmi* (9 meters or 30 feet); this distance is only about 22 *palmi* (5 meters or 16 feet) in our third solu-tion. (4) The pilasters framing the cross-passage at the western end are conspicuously diamond-shaped in distortion rather than moderately off-square, their obtuse corners averaging more or less 106 degrees.

154. There exists a copy of the engraving in the Vatican Library (Chig. P VII 9, fol. 19ᵛ/20 535 x 833 mm.). The drawing, British Museum, Payne Knight Oo 3–5, is identical with the engraving except for the following details: (a) absence of some of the written ma-terial; (b) absence of the four columns framing the central cross-passage on the outside on both the large plan and the accompanying small plan (upper left); and (c) wording of the inscription over the central cross-passage in the elevation, which includes the year. Since the arc is a single circular segment, the pilasters framing the western cross-passage are not as diamond-shaped as expected (v. preceding Note); and pilasters and column bases

at the eastern end show distortion. The radius of the arc is in close agreement with the measurement on the Vatican Plan (which is 296 *palmi*). The center is located at the inscribed frieze of the elevation in the engraving and near the top of the parapet in the preparatory drawing. But in both plans the convergence point of the quadruple columns lies unaccountably 20 to 30 *palmi* farther south. The ratio of the axes (x/y), graphically obtained, is 0.704 instead of 0.756 of the *ovato tondo;* the minor axis would therefore be 625.15 *palmi* (cf. Note 6, above).

155. Brauer-Wittkower, 81; the drawing furnishes the date "A.V.," that is, the fifth reigning year of Pope Alexander VII, which began on April 7, 1659; this was omitted from the engraving. On September 6 of that year two copies of the engraving were sent to the Inquisitor of Malta (v. also Paster, *Popes,* XXXI, 294, n. 2).

156. See Note 65, above.

157. This estimate was arrived at by interpolating very roughly the data furnished, in particular, by the condition in July 1659 and the *avviso* of March 2, 1658 (for both of these, v. Note 65, above), as well as the distribution of the documents connected with the construction work and the *avvisi* reporting the visit of the site (both concentrated after 1659; v. Note 188, below).

158. The design of the corridor, included on the small supplementary plan, is characterized by seventeen rather than thirteen bays; this represents an earlier phase of design than that on the Vatican Plan (Brauer-Wittkower, 90). But there is no reason why the Vatican Plan was not executed in two installments; the upper part could well have been completed at a later date, that is, following the publication of the Bonacina Engraving (cf. Brauer-Wittkower, 89–90). The *ovato tondo* of the small plan by Bonacina can be verified by sight as well as by the rules discussed in Note 153, above.

159. This purpose is announced in the statement on the engraving in both Latin and Italian. The Italian text reads as follows: "Conoscendo molti Sommi Pontefici che il frequentare la Chiesa di S. Pietro, e le funtioni del Palazzo Pontificio era di grande scommodo per esser l'Estate la Piazza dominata dal Sole, e l'Inuerno impraticabile per le pioggie, hebbero in animo di fare vn Portico per il quale rimediasse à questi inconuenienti. Hora la Sta di N. Sig.^re PAPA ALESSANDRO VII, mosso dal Medesimo zelo del ben publico, come anco per accrescere magnificenza al Tempio, e spicco alla facciata di S. Pietro ha inalzato il presente Portico con treplicate corsie diuise da quattro ordini di Colonne per maggior commodità de Pedoni, come delle Carozze. E perche molti di lontani paesi desiderano vedere il disegno di quest' opera così famosa si è stimato bene per sodisfare alla loro curiosità di mandarlo alle stampe." Cf. Note 34 above.

160. Chantelou, *Journal,* 18 (June 6): "Il a dit autre chose plus extraordinaire encore: c'est que, quelquefois, dans un portrait de marbre, il faut, pour bien imiter le naturel, faire ce qui n'est pas dans le naturel." And he added that the effect of the livid area around an eye is achieved by a cavity that creates a shadow there.

161. *Templum Vaticanum,* 181 (Fig. 62), 185 (Fig. 54), 205, and 211, among others. Fontana's plans are sometimes very crude; the two eastern terminations are misshapen

on p. 185, and they end with four pilasters (instead of two columns and two pilasters) on p. 181. But the circularity of the colonnades is clearly noticeable; and the pilasters at the western cross-passage are accordingly more nearly square than they are expected to be (cf. Notes 42 and 43, above). See also Appendix, 2.

162. Fontana, in fact, never grasped the exact configuration of the oval piazza. On one of his plates (*Templum Vaticanum,* 181; our Fig. 29), he enters the dimensions of the external oval along the two axes; but they are 1050 and 780 *palmi.* By subtracting the width of the two colonnades (76 ¾ from his own data on p. 185, our Fig 54) twice, we obtain 896 ½ and 626 ½ *palmi* for the two axes of the internal oval; needless to say, this is a significant deviation from the correct values (v. Note 6, above). The ratio of the axes, then, is 0.699, which is much closer to that of the oval of our third solution (0.704) than of the *ovato tondo* (0.756). The plan itself, to which these inscribed dimensions refer, moreover, contradict them; it is drawn to the axes of 1030 and 790 *palmi,* which yield the ratio of the axes, 0.726, internally. That Fontana did not examine the Vatican Plan for the preparation of these plates for his book is almost incredible, but that was evidently the case. Fontana, instead, relied solely on the Bonacina Engraving. We now notice that Fontana's section elevation of the colonnade on p. 185 (Fig. 54) is similar to that on the engraving, but the two halves are reversed. His detail plan of the eastern cross-passage on the same page is that of the southern, rather than northern, colonnade; it is the mirror reversal of that portion of the large plan from the engraving. It is as though Fontana had these details copied on his plates for the book directly from the engraving. This does not prove but strongly suggests that Fontana used the Bonacina Engraving as his model. Moreover, we now understand why Fontana is unsure about the oval of the piazza. The engraving lacks a large plan of the entire piazza; information is therefore incomplete with regard to the exact configuration of the oval plan. The legend gives the dimensions of the axes: 899 ½ and 752 *palmi.* But they are obviously incorrect as it has been shown elsewhere (Note 57, above). Finally, there is one more point to remember. The plan of the colonnade from the engraving was cut out and pasted on the lower part of a large drawing in the Vatican, attributed to Fontana, showing the development of a new pilgrim's road north of the piazza (Wittkower, "A Counter-project," 94 and 99; Lewine, "Sant' Anna de' Palafrenieri," Fig. 12). If this work is really Fontana's, we can be sure he knew the engraving intimately. The Bonacina Engraving was certainly more informative than the Vatican Plan; but to Fontana it was surely the only major graphic source.

163. The eastern cross-passage tapers in intercolumnar width from 5.34 to 5.00 meters (23.92 to 22.40 *palmi*), and the central cross-passage, from 5.25 to 4.93 meters (23.52 to 22.08 *palmi*) according to the author's measurements. The cross-passage is parallel at the western termination, where it is coordinated with the corridor; it is 4.90 meters (22 *palmi*) in width.

164. P. M. Letarouilly, *Le Vatican,* Paris, 1882, II, "Place St. Pierre," Pl. 3. The central and eastern cross-passages are even more tapered than in Fontana's plan, because the

straight eastern end of the colonnade is also lined up with the center of the arc of the colonnade (o); cf. Note 42, above. Though the primary centers (o, o') are correctly located at the thirds of the major axis of the oval, this measures here 201.5 meters, or 903 *palmi,* which makes the radius slightly more than the true value found on the Vatican Plan and the Bonacina Engraving (i.e., 296 *palmi*). The minor axis is 142 meters (636 *palmi*); the ratio of the axes is consequently 0.704 (cf. Note 43, above).

165. On those maps of Rome, on which the configuration of the oval can be more or less accurately determined, the plan of the Piazza Obliqua features as a rule perfectly circular colonnades and more often than not comes closer to Letarouilly's layout with prominently tapered eastern cross-passages than to Fontana's. This is the case with the Nolli Plan, Angelo Uggeri's map of 1826 (A. P. Frutaz, *Le Piante di Roma,* III, 1962, Pl. 480), and that of the Direzione Generale del Censo, 1829 (Frutaz, Pl. 490). Uggeri, however, adopted in 1800 a version closer to Fontana's (Frutaz, Pl. 455); and so did A. C. d'Aviler in his large plan of Saint Peter's and the colonnades, 1679 (University of St. Thomas, Houston, Texas, *Builders and Humanists: Exhibition Catalogue,* 1966, 192), while F. Bonanni published a plan like Letarouilly's in his book, but with the two centers slightly closer together than for an *ovato tondo* (Numismata summorum pontificum . . . , Rome, 1696, Pl. 71). But on the plan of the piazza by an unknown Frenchman (Fig. 80), the colonnades trace a composite curve; the plan is nevertheless inaccurate since the secondary centers are located closer to each other than they should be so that the arc of each colonnade is more conspicuously composite. The oval, in consequence, gives an impression that it might be more accurately a true ellipse. Among the published plans of the Piazza Obliqua in modern literature on the subject, the single *almost* correct layout is T. A. Polazzo's in his plan for the redevelopment of the *spina* in the Borgo (*Da Castel S. Angelo alla Basilica di San Pietro,* Rome, 1948, Pl. 80). Unaware of the subtle irregularity in the columnar alignment at the eastern termination, he assumed that all the columns, including the last set (but not the pilasters behind it), converged at the primary center (o, o').

166. See Note 102, above.

167. See Note 70, above.

168. On Galileo, see E. Panofsky, *Galileo as a Critic of the Arts,* The Hague, 1954, 25.

169. In contrast to Bernini's contemporaries, who seem to have thought ovals significantly different from the circle, Serlio introduced his own oval church plan (Fig. 48) by saying that "appresso la rotondità perfetta, le forme ouali sono più vicine a quella" (*Quinto Libro,* 204). In his memorandum (*giustificazione*) to the Pope (Brauer-Wittkower, 70, n. 1), Bernini himself wrote of the beauty of the *forma ovata* in these words: "Il bello essendo questa forma circolare più grata all' occhio, più perfetta in se stessa, e più meravigliosa à farli massime con Architravi piani sopra colonne isolate" (v. Ch. I and Notes 40 and 51, above). It is noteworthy that the expressions

used here are the traditional epithets of the circle. In modern conception, of course, the circle is but a special case of the ellipse (i.e., when x = y).

170. Notwithstanding the Colosseum, the amphitheater was understood to be circular by definition, as we have already seen above (Ch. II; also Notes 76, 88, and 99).

171. Fagiolo dell'Arco, *Bernini,* 151–52; there is no evidence that Bernini held such a *concetto,* even though there was a project under Innocent XI (1676–89), proposed by a Dutch engineer, Cornelis Meijer, of a cosmological design for the pavement introducing Tycho Brahe's scheme against Copernicus's (Kruft, "Symbolik in der Architektur Bernini's"; v. Note 1, above).

172. The fact that the position of the fountains in the executed design roughly coincides with that of the foci of the comparable true ellipse (Fig. 52, center) is a mere coincidence. Cf. following Note. See also Note 106, above.

173. In this plan by Rainaldi, the components of the triad are so far apart from one another that the effect of the whole is actually monofocal. This is true of his circular plan with two fountains; his transverse oval plan, on the other hand, features only one fountain in front of the obelisk like the design on the first foundation medal. See Note 31, above.

174. On this and subsequent medals, each fountain appears well within the embracing arc of the colonnade; the arc, in consequence, gives an impression of being a full semicircle. A position on the axis of the Borgo Nuovo was tested out in the chalk drawing (Fig. 34), as we have seen; but on the Bonacina Engraving, each fountain lies on the chord that joins the two terminal cross-passages of the colonnade, perhaps still reflecting the idea from the sketch plan. On the Vatican Plan, it is farther out from the obelisk, the one to the south even farther than its counterpart; evidently this was still a provisional arrangement. In execution, the fountains are on the line that connects the pilasters next to the last column at the ends of the colonnade. The exact position of the fountains was not determined, therefore, until much later. But while the form of the colonnade and even the character of the oval changed subsequently, the triad remained as established on Medal II.

175. See Note 115, above.

176. The steps still appear in the bird's-eye view on the Bonacina Engraving, but this is more likely an anachronism like the narrow corridors (v. Note 158, above), the dimensions of the oval entered in the legend (v. Note 57, above), and the position of the two fountains (v. Note 174, above).

177. See Note 154, above.

178. See Ch. III, and Note 158, above.

179. The colonnades were free-standing and physically penetrable, but their allegiance was to the space of the piazza rather than the "outside," no less than in such cases as Michelangelo's loggias on the Campidoglio and the "unilateral" arcades of the Piazza San Marco in Venice and the Piazza della SS. Annunziata in Florence. Cf. Note 231, below. It is true that statues decorate both the outer and inner balustrades according

to the medals and prints of the time; in these representations, however, the colonnades are unrealistically isolated from the proper urban setting, of which Bernini was undoubtedly aware. In execution, statues were omitted from the outer balustrades, partly, one conjectures, for economic reasons.

180. The principle of frontality is equally essential in Bernini's conception of church facades; but this particular case is especially comparable to the plan of Sant' Andrea al Quirinale on the Vatican chirograph (Bibl. Vat., Chig. P VII 13, fols. 40ᵛ/41), dated October 26, 1658, on which an aedicular facade, attached to the rotonda, frontalizes it. See Kitao, "Bernini's Church Facades: Method of Design and the *Contrapposti*," *Journal of the Society of Architectural Historians,* XXIV, 1965, 263–84, esp. 264–67 and Figs. 6 and 22.

181. The idea that the Piazza Obliqua is the new atrium was already suggested by D. Gnoli in 1889 ("Nuovo accesso," v. Note 257, below; also Gnoli, *Have Roma,* Rome, 1909, 187). Many writers, especially Italians, have repeated it since then.

182. The *concetto* of maternal arms, explained in the architect's own words in his *giustificazione,* has adequately been treated by modern critics. Although the image of embrace may suggest enclosure, the open arms are basically a penetrated form; and the *concetto* has been associated with the two inscriptions put up by the Pope (Pastor, *Popes,* XXXI, 297): "Venite, procidamus ante Dominum in templo Sancto ejus et nomen Domini invocemus; Venite, ascendamus in montem Domini, adoremus in templo Sancto ejus" (Come, let us prostrate ourselves before the Lord in His holy temple, and let us call upon the name of the Lord; Come, let us go up to the mountain of the Lord, let us worship in His holy temple). The image of the open arms is therefore linked with the idea of the atrium. Though the colonnades are perforated—the point perhaps overemphasized by Thoenes ("Geschichte des Petersplatzes," 125)— there is no doubt that the piazza is a secluded place like an atrium and yet, open and penetrated, it is unmistakably a vestibule in character.

183. Brauer-Wittkower, 83, and Wittkower, "Counter-project," 94 and 99; see also Note 162. The project was apparently still in effect in 1661 according to the medal of that year; see Note 189, below.

184. The drawing in Ariccia, Palazzo Chigi; published by Brauer-Wittkower, 83 and Pl. 63b.

185. Brauer-Wittkower, 84; Bernini studied the portico in both frontal elevation and section profile (Bibl. Vat., Chig. a I 19, fol. 32; Brauer-Wittkower, Pl. 61). Cf. Michelangelo's tetrastyle portico recorded on a Vatican fresco (Thoenes, "Geschichte des Petersplatzes," Fig. 8).

186. See Note 65, above.

187. See Note 105, above.

188. Of the documents on the piazza preserved in the Archivio della Reverenda Fabbrica di San Pietro, those that concern the actual construction work date in the major part from the years between 1659 and 1663. It is noteworthy, too, that while the two volumes of documents that deal with the transportation of travertine (I Piano, Armadi, vols. 316 and 317) cover the period from the fall of 1657 to the spring of 1660, the

massive "Diario dei lavori" of one Benedetto Drei, who supervised the work, extends from the fall of 1659 to the winter of 1662/63 (I Piano, ser. 4, vol. 29). Correspondingly, the Pope's visits to the construction site, according to the *avvisi* that reported them (Arch. Segr. Vat., Avvisi, vols. 108–13), were concentrated in the years from 1659 to 1663 as follows:

October 4, 1659 (Avvisi 108, fol. 244)

September 11, 1660 (Avvisi 109, fol. 226)
December 18, 1660 (Avvisi 109, fol. 304)

February 26, 1661 (Avvisi 110, fol. 50)
June 18, 1661 (Avvisi 110, fol. 136)
August 20, 1661 (Avvisi 110, fol. 172)
October 8, 1661 (Avvisi 110, fol. 200)

March 11, 1662 (Avvisi 111, fol. 36)
June 24, 1662 (Avvisi 111, fol. 96)
September 9, 1662 (Avvisi 111, fol. 140)
November 18, 1662 (Avvisi 111, fol. 180)

April 17, 1666 (Avvisi 113, fol. 272)
October 9, 1666 (Avvisi 113, fol. 373)

189. Brauer-Wittkower, 83, n. 5; two versions designated Medal V (Fig. 66, dated in the exergue) and Medal VI (similar in design, but with Alexander VII's motto—*Fundamenta eius in montibus sanctis*—in the exergue and undated; v. Note 59, above). The columnar embellishment is still shown on Falda's print of 1665 (Fig. 36; v. Note 105, above). The reliability of the plan on the medal is undermined, however, by the fact that projecting columns are missing from the eastern cross-passages on the outside and also from the *terzo braccio* altogether, that is, inside and outside. The columnar embellishment in question appears as late as 1668 on the plan of Rome by Matteo Gregorio De Rossi (Frutaz, *Le Piante di Roma*, III, Pl. 355); but this surely an anachronism.

190. Arch. Segr. Vat., Avviso, 110, fol. 172, dated Rome, August 20, 1661 (Pastor, *Popes*, XXXI, 294), which reads in part: "il Pontificie . . . andò a S. Pietro a far oratione e doppo si compiacque di dare una uista alli nuoui fondam.^{ti} di quel Teatro, cominciati dall'altra parte. . . ."

191. Brauer-Wittkower, 88–96.

192. Arch. Segr. Vat., Avvisi, 113, fol. 272, dated Rome, April 17, 1666 (Pastor, *Popes*, XXXI, 295), which reported that "essendo hormai perfectionato il Teatro di S. Pietro si demoliscono li Palazzi, e Case che restano fra mezzo di esso." Since the *teatro*

could only mean the Piazza Obliqua, we can be sure that there were now standing the two colonnades plus the northern corridor. The palaces for demolition probably refer to the Priorato block, although this was not razed until much later (cf. following Note). The *avviso* of March 19, 1667 (Arch. Segr. Vat., Avvisi, 114, fol. 48; *Popes,* XXXI, 295), announced that "si termina il braccio, che unisce il Teatro col Portico di S. Pietro con dimolirsi il Palazzo del Priorato, et altri per far le poca parti di mezzo, che manca per terminarlo. . . . ," using the same term *mezzo* again; the *"braccio"* can only mean here the southern corridor. See also Note 234, below.

193. Arch. Fabb. S.P., I Piano, ser 3, vol. 164, fol. 510 (Ehrle, "Virgilio Spada," 62–63): "Capitoli, patti e conventioni da osservarsi da Giuseppe Buccimazzi nel getto del Priorato e case annesse nella Piazza di San Pietro et altre case verso Borgo Vecchio sino al fine del Palazzo detto di Raffaello." The demolition, projected at this time, therefore seems to have covered not only the first block with the Priorato Palace but at least a half of the first of the second oblong block, beyond it, that closed the Piazza Scossacavalli; the "Palazzo detto di Raffaello" refers to the Palazzo Spinola, later dei Convertendi, that terminated the block. On this, see now A. Bruschi, *Bramante architetto,* Bari, 1969, 1040–46. In another version of the minutes (Bibl. Vat., Chig. H II 22, fol. 238), it is simply reported that "si è stabilito il gettito del Priorato." When the demolition finally took place, only the first block was cleared (Fig. 64).

194. Bibl. Vat., Chig H II 22, fol. 238, entitled "Ragguaglio della Cong^ne Piccola della Fabrica tenuta li 19 Febraro 1667"; the third paragraph reads: "Si è considerato il modello dell'Orologio da farsi sulla piazza di S. Pietro, et unitamente tutti hanno riuerito il pensiero di Sua Santità, il quale è che si sollecitino per hora le guide e le selciata della piazza, e che di poi con le douute considerazioni si pigliara risolutione." See also Brauer-Wittkower, 85–86, and Wittkower, "Il terzo braccio." Although tabled, the proposed revision was actually submitted and considered by the Congregazione; this fact demonstrates Bernini's seriousness with regard to this design and disproves the theory that the architect himself probably decided to abandon it for aesthetic reasons (G. C. Argan, *L'architettura barocca in Italia,* Milan, 1957, 95, later elaborated on by L. Quaroni, *Immagine di Roma,* Bari, 1969, 257).

195. At the stage of design represented by Medal I, there was an attempt to distinguish the *terzo braccio* by surmounting it with a papal coat of arms as it was eventually done in the elaboration phase of design; this is recorded on a workshop drawing, now in the Chigi Collection in Ariccia (v. Note 104, above). Apparently, the idea was quickly dropped. On Medal III, curiously, the *terzo braccio* has eight (even number) bays so that one set of columns stands on the central axis of the structure (Fig. 22); if the detail had been from negligence, it still is in conformity with the increased emphasis on the loop—the continuous circumference. On the Vatican Plan, the *terzo braccio* has only three bays on each side of the middle passage; but the number was increased to four on the preparatory drawing for the Bonacina Engraving (Fig. 27). Here, as well as on the Vatican Plan, the terminal set consists of columns and pilasters

matching the terminal set of the main colonnade across the opening, creating a smooth transition and reinforcing the loop. Falda gives a spurious variation consisting of twin pilasters in one of his prints (dated 1662, reproduced by E. Strong, "The Approach to St. Peter's, Rome," Pl. 1; v. Note 259, below; also in Fraschetti, *Il Bernini*, 316).

196. Bibl. Vat., J VI 205, fol. 33ᵛ; v. Brauer-Wittkower, 85, and Wittkower, "Il terzo braccio." Note the similarity in the design of the ornamental frame for the clock between this drawing and its source (Fig 34). The clock is, however, overscaled in relation to the tetrastyle; this was interpreted to mean that the drawing represents the superstructure to surmount the propylaeum.

197. The tower of Paul V was torn down in 1659 (v. Note 30, above). The tetrastyle support for the clock is concave in the drawing. This has been interpreted to mean that the colonnade it surmounts is still curved. But it does not follow from this that Bernini at one point *projected* a clock tower on the *terzo braccio* in its original location on the oval outline of the Piazza Obliqua, nor that he conceived the structure, still curved, out in the antepiazza which he was planning to create (on which see below). Evidence for the latter possibility is slim; v. Note 204, below. The fact that the new structure is a two-story monument argues against the latter; it demands independence. The sketch was hardly a solution; it was only a tentative idea. The architect was undoubtedly thinking of the curved *terzo braccio* on the oval outline—but only provisionally; he was very likely entertaining an antepiazza in his mind but uncertain as to how the lower structure would look like or where it would be. The curve of the tetrastyle raises one other problem; the sketch suggests that the clock was to face the Basilica rather than the Borgo. The inward orientation complies with the general introvert character of the colonnades (v. Note 179, above), if this two-story structure were to stand on the oval outline; but it conflicts with the conception of the structure as a gateway and landmark and contradicts the architect's strong preference for frontality in general (v. Note 180, above, and 213, below). We must therefore assume, considering the tentative character of the sketch, that the clock would have been replicated for the outside facade in correspondence with the columnar frame which until this time would have appeared on both the inside and outside facade of the central passage as we have seen above (Fig. 6). It must be pointed out, however, that one of Bernini's earlier critics regarded the principal view of the piazza to be "quella, che si havrà nell'uscire della Basilica" (Critic II; v. Note 42, above); and the Counterproject created a fully developed backdrop on the east side, as represented in a view of the Borgo from the portico of the Basilica (Wittkower, "A Counter-project," Pl. 17c and 19d; v. Note 110, above). Moreover, a later pavement study shows the propylaeum unilaterally facing the Basilica (Fig. 73); see Note 234, below. These cases, needless to say, hardly represent Bernini's conception and fail to support Fagiolo dell'Arco's proposition that the propylaeum (or *terzo braccio*) was conceived as a picturesque backdrop by which to "ornare e addobbare scenograficamente le povere casupole dei Borghi" (*Bernini,* 154). Bernini's own decoration of the Porta del Popolo

for the entry of Christina of Sweden (1665) was applied only on the inner facade; in this instance the gate was the backdrop for the queen's entry, the audience those receiving her inside. See also Note 204, below.

198. Bibl. Vat., Chig. a I 19, fol. 63ᵛ; Brauer-Wittkower, 85–86, and Wittkower, "Il terzo braccio," 131. The double columns that framed the central passage in the *terzo braccio* design now disappeared. The entablature nevertheless still protrudes above the four central columns; and since the central bay is slightly wider, this middle section echoes the tetrastyle of Maderno's facade more accurately than before (cf. our Figs. 36 and 65). Contrary to Wittkower's observation (Brauer-Wittkower, 86), the intercolumniation does not seem to have been changed from that of the colonnades, which varied from two column-diameters to two and a quarter (cf. Note 70, above); see Note 203, below, for our calculations. The superstructure seems octagonal. The clock is not shown; but note the resemblance of this upper part to that of the tower of Paul V. Cf. our Fig. 83.

199. Bibl. Vat., Chig. J VI 205, fol. 36ʳ; the sheet also shows a sketch plan of the church at Castelgandolfo with the indication of the terrace toward the lake (Brauer-Wittkower, 119, n. 3).

200. Bibl. Vat., Chig J VI 205, fol. 36ᵛ. The bird's-eye view of the Piazza Obliqua is superimposed on a lightly drawn tentative plan of the oval piazza. The portion of the Borgo represented includes the block of the Priorato (initially, not the hatched rectangle but a lightly drawn elongated trapezoid which lies a little lower than this in the sketch), another block below it (i.e., the block with the Palazzo Spinola, later dei Convertendi, and the two Borgo streets. The crux of the drawing is evidently the two sets of *visuali*. In each of them, the view in question is the southwestern portion of the piazza with the viewpoint located on the Borgo Nuovo; in each case, too, the left arm of the V is drawn emphatically, and we are reminded of the diagonal line in the earlier study (Fig. 34). With the first *visuali,* Bernini probably wanted to demonsrtate that, when the block of the Priorato is cleared, the visitor will see from the corner of the second block a portion of the piazza, which will exclude the midpoint of the colonnade (the line to the left cuts the southern colonnade). He then explains with the second *visuali* that only from a point farther up the street one can see the colonnade up to the midpoint, as well as more of the facade of the Basilica. The heavy horizontal stroke to the left of this point therefore indicates that the antepiazza should preferably stop here, or more specifically, that the new propylaeum should rise here. The study thus made it clear that the whole Priorato block should be first cleared; the block was then redrawn (right over the previous sketch out of relation to it for some reason) with some indication of the Palazzo del Priorato and hatched to signify that this was staked for demolition. The drawing is vaguely anthropomorphic; Wittkower saw in it a schema of the human figure with open arms and related it to the *concetto* of the embracing arms of the Church on the one hand and with the drawing in the Counterproject of 1659, on the other, which similarly identified the Basilica with the human form but more specifically with the figure of Saint Peter

(Fig. 40; Brauer-Wittkower, 85 and 100, and Wittkower, "A Counter-project," 103). The idea of combining the Basilica and the colonnades in the visitor's first view of the piazza apparently prompted the eventual position of the propylaeum and also explains the peculiar anthropomorphism as we shall see below.

201. Bibl. Vat., Chig. a I 19, fol. 68. The plan of the Priorato block with the indication of the palace (now in greater detail) is clearly derived from the previous drawing.

202. Bibl. Vat., Chig. P VII 9, fol. 15. The drawing was published in a grossly distorted form by F. Bonanni, *Numismata summorum pontificum* . . . , Rome, 1696, Pl. 70.

203. These are the dimensions taken on the pavement study at the stylobate; Wittkower reported them erroneously as 90 x 230 *palmi* (Brauer-Wittkower, 86, n. 2). He also observed incorrectly ("Il terzo braccio," 131) that the propylaeum on this plan is about 40 *palmi* longer than what the *terzo braccio* was supposed to be on the Bonacina Engraving. The nine-bay *terzo braccio* of the engraving is illustrated only in small scale; but since the seven-bay structure on the Vatican Plan measures 75 x 180 *palmi*, median, we can deduce from this the dimensions 75 x 220 *palmi* for the Bonacina version. The new propylaeum, represented in Bernini's sketch (Fig. 68), differs, however, in the arrangement of columns. If we assume for this structure, taking the median, columns of 7-*palmo* diameter placed at 2-1/6 column-diameter intervals with the central passage one column-diameter wider than the intercolumniation, we obtain the length 213 1/2 *palmi*, which is close enough for the stylobate of the pavement plan.

204. Bibl. Vat., Ottob. lat. 3154, between fol. 347 and 348. Wittkower ("Il terzo braccio," 131) thought that the print represented a design that preceded the first ideation of the clock tower (Fig. 67). He had two reasons for this conclusion. First, the propylaeum of the Conclave design is like the *terzo braccio* of the Bonacina Engraving and the Falda Print (Figs. 24 and 36); and it is still curved rather than straight in plan. We must keep in mind, however, that this is a seven-bay structure. Secondly, Wittkower thought that the propylaeum, removed from the oval outline, was not positioned quite as far into the Piazza Rusticucci as it eventually was; this position, however, agrees with that established in the drawing by Bernini (Fig. 72). It seems, therefore, that the author of the Conclave Print took the *terzo braccio* of the Vatican Plan and placed it as stipulated in Bernini's sketch plan. In this connection, Wittkower also observed that the first clock tower design (Fig. 67) was incorporated in Falda's map of Rome of 1667 ("la piccola pianta"; see Frutaz, *Le Piante di Roma*, III, Pl. 347), and the position of the propylaeum in this representation is similar to what he read in the Conclave Print. But accuracy in positioning is hardly expected at this scale; and as for the clock tower, the design could as well be Bernini's second design (Fig. 68) or even Falda's own interpolation from incomplete data. The clock tower was repeated on the map of Matteo Gregorio De Rossi, 1668 (Frutaz, III, Pl. 355). It must also be noted here that the clock of Innocent VIII was eventually mounted on the narrow end of the short wedge-shaped wing protruding from the corner of Raphael's loggia and remained there until the end of the nineteenth century (Fig. 27, dated 1870; cf. Fig. 1 and Frontispiece).

205. "S'aggiungeva che il formare un Portico, non solo apportava maggior belezza e decoro al Tempio mà veniva à coprire molte imperfettioni di quello, essendo che la facciata che per se stessa è di forma quatta havrebbe spiccata, et in certo modo si sarebbe sollevata sopra se stessa. . . ."; v. Note 40, above). *Spiccare* could mean "to detach and isolate"; the passage, in that case, suggests that the corridors, acting as a break (or better, as a flexible joint), make the colonnades appear to squeeze the facade outward and upward. But in conjunction with *sollevarsi,* the word should mean in this context no more than "to set off by contrast." The passages from Chantelou's diary (v. following Note) confirm this reading.

206. Chantelou, *Journal,* 42, 52, and 114: "Il a dit qu'il n'avait eu ces égards qu'à l'église de Saint-Pierre de Rome dont le portail paraissait bas, au jugement de tout le monde; il avait trouvé pour remède et conseillé au pape de faire faire deux ailes de colonnades qui faisaient paraître ce portail plus haut, quoiqu'il ne le fût pas; en a montré l'effet avec le crayon, et fait voir que c'était comme deux bras à une tête; a dit qu'il en serait de même des deux galeries, au respect de cette façade, et que l'architecture consistait en proportion tirée du corps de l'homme" (July 1); "Le Cavalier a dit que ce pourrait être comme à la place Saint-Pierre dont il a esquissé le portail, et a dit que, comme du temps de Paul V il n'a pas été exécuté suivant le dessin de Michel-Ange, le portail a toujours été trouvé trop bas, eu égard à sa largeur; ce qui a été cause qu'on a proposé diverses fois de l'abattre, et qu'Urbain VIII en avait eu la pensée et Innocent X après lui; mais que, comme les papes ordinairement n'arrivent au pontificat que vieux, cela a empêché qu'ils n'aient osé entreprendre ce grand ouvrage qu'il fallait commencer par abbattre; que le pape d'à présent lui en ayant demandé son avis, il avait étudié et trouvé qu'en faisant des loges plus basses de côté et d'autre de ce portail, cela le ferait paraître plus haut et en corrigerait le défaut" (July 15); "Il a allégué encore après à ce sujet le portail de l'église de Saint-Pierre de Rome et les loges qu'il a faites de part et d' autre, afin de le faire paraître plus haut par l'opposition de ces corps beaucoup moins élevés que ce portail, et a dit que cela avait réussi, comme il l'avait imaginé" (August 23). For the first two passages, the context of the discussion was the Louvre design; the third passage follows the explanation of the *contrapposti* (v. Note 208, below).

207. The alleged optical illusion was a popular issue in the early decades of this century. It was undoubtedly stimulated by the passages (cited in the preceding Note) from Chantelou's diary, which was published in 1885 after having been serialized in the *Gazette des Beaux-Arts;* it was introduced by the pioneering critics of Baroque art— C. Gurlitt in 1887 (*Geschichte des Barockstiles in Italien,* Stuttgart, 408–13), A. Schmarsow in 1897 (*Barock und Rokoko,* Leipzig, 243–47), and M. Reymond (*Le Bernin,* Paris, [1911], 114), and was set forth in a systematic form by A. Riegl, ed., *Filippo Baldinuccis Vita des Gio. Lorenzo Bernini,* Vienna, 1912, 170–76. According to Riegl, Bernini's design works as an optical corrective to Maderno's facade in three ways. First, the ground of the Piazza Retta rises toward the facade, but the eye understands it to be level; in compensation, the piazza appears deeper than it actually is,

and in consequence, the facade appears farther away and higher. Secondly, the corridors framing the Piazza Retta converge toward its open side (i.e., diverge toward the facade); but since the eye does not recognize the convergence, the facade appears only as wide as the opening to the piazza and correspondingly slimmer and taller. Finally, since the colonnades are circular the oval of the Piazza Obliqua, disposed transversely, appears as a foreshortened circle, and the eye tends to overestimate its depth; the facade, remoter in appearance, is consequently slimmer and higher. The theory obviously suffers from the flaw that it jumbles up the perspective phenomenon with the Gestalt theory of perception. Moreover, it is test proof; for it leads us ultimately to the insoluble question whether the facade *actually* appears higher than it actually is or only *appears* to appear so, and thus confuses the issue instead of clarifying it. But the problem of the optical illusion received a full measure of attention within the next decade from E. Panofsky ("Die Scala Regia im Vatikan und die Kunstanschauungen Berninis," *Jahrbuch der preussischen Kunstsammlungen*, XL, 1919, 241–78, esp. 266–70), H. Voss ("Bernini als Architekt an der Scala Regia und an der Kolonnaden von S. Pietro," the same *Jahrbuch*, XLIII, 1922, 2–30, esp. 19–26), and H. Sedlmayr ("Divergenz der Wände am Petersplatz in Rom," *Belvedere*, Forum V, XXIII, 1924, 133–35). The thesis was revived in a modified form more recently by D. Gioseffi, *La cupola vaticana, un' ipotesi michelangiolesca*, Trieste, 1960, 82–84. In view of Bernini's own articulate and insistent testimony, on the other hand, Thones's total rejection of illusionism in the design of the piazza is entirely unwarranted ("Geschichte des Petersplatzes," 122–23). Thoenes goe so far as to argue that Bernini's objection was not the squat facade at all but the whole nave, for which Maderno was responsible, and claims that the wide facade was at the time generally regarded a merit; but this proposition, based on an opinion of 1612, hardly disproves Bernini's dissatisfaction with the facade (in its truncated form without the projected towers). After all, Bernini himself voiced it in his *giustificazione,* as we have seen, as well as to Chantelou. See also the following Note.

208. Chantelou, *Journal,* 114 (August 23). The subject came up when Bernini was discussing the difficulty of the art of architecture with one Vigarani, himself architect and scenographer. In the course of this discussion, when Vigarani remarked that geometry and perspective are indispensable to architects, Bernini immediately retorted "qu'un des points les plus importants était d'avoir un bon oeil pour bien juger des *i contrapposti; que les choses nous paraissent non seulement ce qu'elles sont, mais eu égard à ce qui est dans leur voisinage, qui change leur apparence.*" After this general statement, Bernini went on to illustrate with specific examples what he meant by the Italian term. He described, for example, how the head of a statue may appear smaller than it would be otherwise, when it is seen in *contrapposti* with a drapery on the shoulder; and this calls for an adjustment in the proportion of the head to the body. He also observed that a figure dressed in one color appears larger than another in different colors, and that a mile on the ocean seems longer than a mile on land. In this context Bernini brought up the optical illusion in the design of the piazza for the third time (v. Note

206, above). As a general principle, then, two elements in juxtaposition may influence each other subtly or forcefully; the elements may be in contrast or in harmony. The relationship always exists; and the artist, Bernini implies, is free to exploit this phenomenon. For the *contrapposti* in Bernini's architecture, see Kitao, "Bernini's Church Facades," 281–84. Thoenes, while rejecting illusionism in Bernini's design (v. preceding Note), correctly recognizes "ein rein quantitativen Gegensatz" in which Maderno's facade is treated as a closed block to be seen in isolation; the idea is analogous to that of Bernini's project of restoring the rotonda and the temple front of the Pantheon (represented as closed blocks in his drawings) to their pristine form (v. Note 9, above).

209. The angle of vision, established according to Bernini's sketch is about 81 degrees within the framing temple fronts. The single eye takes in comfortably up to about 50 to 60 degrees; a lens with the focal length of 28 mm. can embrace 76 degrees. The normal vision, however, is bifocal, and cannot normally remain perfectly stationary; it can, therefore, encompass the whole piazza and marginally include even the temple fronts that frame the view. Piranesi could capture the sweep in his print (Frontispiece) as no photographer could ever do.

210. The improvement in the visibility of Michelangelo's dome is quantitatively small. Still it is significant. From the oval outline, *less* than half of the drum is visible; from the new propylaeum, one can see more than half. But for the whole drum, one must retreat all the way back—almost the full stretch of the *spina* to the bank of the Tiber.

211. See Note 209, above.

212. See the analogy of this composition, in particular, with the prospect of the church at Ariccia, 1662–64; see Kitao, "Bernini's Church Facades," 279–81. On the use of the word scenography as applied to Bernini's architecture, see Note 222, below.

213. For this idea, see R. Wittkower, *Art and Architecture,* 102–3; the phrase is from Hibbard, *Bernini,* 134, where it is applied in particular to the Cornaro Chapel. The statue housed in a niche is, as an ensemble, a relief by definition, that is, "a three-dimensional picture," insofar as the niche, by framing the statue, establishes a reference plane and also frontalizes the composition as a whole. Donatello's Saint George, in this respect, is not unlike Bernini's niche statues like Santa Bibiana and Saint Longinus. Bernini applied the principle of relief to projects of all scales, however; this problem in relation to Bernini's churches will be dealt with in a study currently in preparation. But see the Postscript, below.

214. The elements crucial to the purpose of the drawing were the midpoint of each colonnade, the *visuali,* and the propylaeum; they were all duly (if also crudely) emphasized, and it is also evident that they were drawn in this order. Sighting could not have taken place on the site since the Priorato block was certainly still standing in February, when the revision was proposed to the Congregazione (v. Note 193, above); by April 1, the demolition was complete (Arch. Fabb. S.P., I Piano, Arm. vol. 354).

215. The illustration is from Vignola, *Le due regole della prospettiva practica,* Rome, 1583, 91; Egnatio Danti's commentary accompanying the diagram is entitled, "Del

Modo che si tiene nel disegnare le prospettive delle Scene, acciò il finto della parete accordi con quello, che si dipigne nelle case vere, che di rilieuo si fanno sopra il palco." A similar method was discussed also in N. Sabbatini, *Practica di fabricar scene,* Pesaro, 1637/38. For perspective in Renaissance and Baroque scenography, see T. K. Kitao, "Prejudice in Perspective: A Study of Vignola's Perspective Treatise," *Art Bulletin,* XLIV, 1962, 173–94, esp. 186–89.

216. See Note 86, above, for general bibliography; also, Fagiolo dell'Arco, *Bernini,* 177–95, and Catalogue, *passim,* in particular. Not a single stage set designed by Bernini is known at first hand; cf. Note 219, below.

217. On the prevalence of one-point perspective in Baroque scenography, see Kitao, "Prejudice in Perspective," 188.

218. Chantelou, *Journal,* 68–69 (June 26); following the description of the *Due Teatri* (v. Note 87, above), we read that Bernini "a dit que cette représentation avait trompé tout le monde, et a ajouté qu'aux perspectives des chandelles il ne fallait pas que le lieu eût au plus que vingt-quatre pieds de profondeur; que cet espace suffisait pour faire voire élognements infinis, en ménageant bien les lumières; qu'il fallait éviter de faire de ces représentations qui veulent n'être vues que d'un seul point." Bernini, then, discusses Annibale's ceiling. As he relates it, Annibale first entrusted the decorative scheme to his brother, Agostino, who came up with "un dessin d'une belle entente et magnifique, où tout concourait régulièrement à un point de vue qu'il avait même tout tracé sur le lieu"; but Annibale immediately saw and indicated to his brother the shortcoming of the design that it shows "un mauvais effet" unless one glued himself to the designated spot to see it, and as Agostino felt insulted and left, Annibale had to redo it himself, "le composant de compartements à la voûte, de termes et autres ornements qu'on peut voir de quelque place où l'on se mette. . . ." The earliest sketch for the ceiling decoration (J. R. Martin, *The Farnese Gallery,* Princeton, N. J., 1965, 192 and Figs. 148–51) was, in fact, more clearly a *quadratura,* reminiscent of Tibaldi's Ulysses Cycle in Bologna; but the executed design, though free of major distortions, is obviously still a perspective with one vanishing point. Clearly, Bernini had in mind neither *la scena per angolo,* later adopted by the Bibienas nor a system with several or shifting vanishing points. On the distinction between the vanishing point of a perspective system and the point of sight, see Kitao, "Prejudice in Perspective," 184.

219. Bernini has sometimes been credited for the scenes of *Sant' Alessio* (produced in 1634 at the Teatro Barberini); but the attribution, unlikely for this reason (they are mostly straight street vistas), has also been rejected on documentary ground by I. Lavin (v. Note 86, above). The last scene of the *Due Teatri* achieved its effect, significantly, not by perspective of orthogonal lines, but by the use of light that diminished in size and intensity (v. preceding Note).

220. See Wittkower's discussion (*Art and Architecture,* 100–3) that in looking at Bernini's sculptural compositions, "once the beholder relinquishes the principal aspect, new views may appear in his field of vision, yet they are always partial ones," and "the climax of an action can be wholly revealed from one point alone." This is, of

course, in conformity with the ideal of a three-dimensional picture and of architecture conceived as a relief or scenography (cf. Notes 213, above, and 222, below).

221.   Wittkower, *Art and Architecture,* 128; and Chantelou, *Journal,* 33 (June 14): "Il leur a dit encore qu'il serait bon qu'il y eût quelque partie qui avançât sur le devant, parce que les églises qui sont rondes tout à fait, quand on y entre, on fait ordinairement sept à huit pas, ce qui empêche qu'on puisse pas bien voir la forme." Spoken in 1665, the statement undoubtedly alludes to the design of Sant' Andrea al Quirinale and the Assunta in Ariccia; the passage follows, in fact, a discussion on the phenomenon that an interior always looks larger when it is roofed than it does before it is covered, and Bernini cites his church at Castelgandolfo before and after it was vaulted. In 1665, all these three churches were his latest architectural achievements. On entering a church of this scale, then, seven or eight steps would carry the visitor well into the interior, perhaps a fourth or a third of the depth of the church, unless a vestibule is provided. If, allowing for this, a vestibule is provided, the visitor, after a few steps on entering the portal (since it is assumed that he would not pause there), would find himself at or near the circumference of the interior proper; this, in other words, is the position from which the visitor is expected to embrace the form of the interior in its entirety. The position that is analogous to this in the Piazza Obliqua, is, then, the position of the *terzo braccio* of the Bonacina Engraving, not that of the new propylaeum. The compactness of the space should make it possible to survey the contour of the church from its circumference, and the dome is certainly better in view from here than from the portal preceding the vestibule. The Piazza Obliqua, by contrast, is hypaethral and, more importantly, urban in scale; it is also more a transitional rather than terminal space in the sense that there is another vast space, the Piazza Retta, beyond it which has to be traversed. At this scale, then, the visitor can embrace the form as a whole only from the propylaeum at the location the architect designated in 1667. In this connection, Passeri's argument against the transverse oval (Appendix, 2) is noteworthy.

222.   This is not to exclude a "cinematic" vision, of course. We may enjoy shifting views we might absorb in motion; we may take pans and closeups. The piazza is a three-dimensional scene, and nothing prevents us from walking into it and experiencing it three-dimensionally. But views one has from within the space of the piazza are fragmentary because of its enormous scale; assembled in memory, they add up to a sum of fragments, better understood as a whole only after an exposure to the comprehensive view from the propylaeum. Palladio's villas, too, frequently combined the central pavilion with straight or quadrant wings in *contrapposti* in such a way that the ensemble extended horizontally and demanded a distant, frontal view. The stylistic relation between Bernini and Palladio has not been adequately studied, although similarities have been recognized by Mariani (v. Note 1, above) and Wittkower ("Palladio e Bernini," *Bollettino del Centro Internazionale di Studi d'Architettura A. Palladio,* VIII, 1966, 13–25). Wittkower used the term "scenographic" to characterize the late Baroque in general in contrast to the "dynamic" High Baroque and, more specifically, to distinguish Carlo Fontana's design (on which see below) from Bernini's; he ob-

served that in the former "the near and far ends of the arms of the colonnades would have appeared in his [the beholder's] field of vision like isolated wings on a stage" (*Art and Architecture*, 194 and 245). It is perhaps more accurate to say that both designs are scenographic, but, while Fontana achieves a scenographic effect at the expense of architectural unity, Bernini uses a scenographic effect to achieve an architectural unity which would not otherwise be possible. In this connection, it is significant that Palladio, as demonstrated by Wittkower, created a unity of disparate parts in his design of the church, Il Redentore, by scenographic means (*Architectural Principles*, 87–88); for a fuller discussion of the tradition of Palladio's "scenography," see Wittkower, "Santa Maria della Salute," *Saggi e Memorie di Storia dell'arte*, III, Venice, 1963, 33–54, which in an earlier and shorter version was entitled, "S. Maria della Salute: Scenographic Architecture and the Venetian Baroque" (*Journal of the Society of Architectural Historians*, XVI, 1957, 3–10). It must be pointed out, however, that both in the Redentore and Longhena's church the unity relies heavily on the longitudinal axis the visitor is expected to trace, whereas in Bernini's scenography the stationary point is strongly emphasized.

223. This is more a psychological "trick" than a purely optical one. Cf. Note 243, below.

224. Conditioning like this is not inconceivable. In his classical bias, Burckhardt described Vignola's Sant' Andrea in Via Flaminia—of all places, in his *Cicerone*—as "die bekannteste, quadratischer Unterbau, runder Oberau mit niedriger Kuppel" (Lotz, "Die ovalen Kirchenräume," 35).

225. See Note 2, above.

226. See, especially, Panofsky and Voss (v. Note 207, above).

227. The obelisk, needless to say, was the well-established symbol of the sun. See, for example, Michele Mercati, *De gli obelischi di Roma,* Rome, 1589, 282, writing of the Circus Maximus, explains that "il Cerchio rappresentava il mondo, & l'Obelisco i raggi del sole, & secondo che il sole è uno, non conveniva in un Cerchio esser più di uno Obelisco, & quello nel mezzo, secondo che il sole era tenuto principal dominatore del mondo"; see N. Huse, *Gianlorenzo Berninis Vierströmebrunnen,* Munich, 1966, 23–24, and n. 40. Note, too, that an exegesis was attempted to read the Piazza Obliqua as an enormous sundial (Bibl. Vat., Chig. H II 22, fols. 251–53: Explicatio Horoscopij Vaticani); see Fagiolo dell'Arco, *Bernini,* 278, where A. Kircher's epigram from this source is quoted. Cf. Note 171, above.

228. Bibl. Vat., Chig. P VII 9, fol. 16. The first pavement study (Fig. 73), by contrast, seems to be an attempt in reverse, that is, to play down both the circularity and the penetrating axis of the space; the design is obviously unsatisfactory since the obelisk and the fountains (not shown) block the pathways.

229. The axis from the propylaeum to the facade of the Basilica is about one and a half times the long (transverse) axis of the oval; but this length is duly foreshortened in perspective. The horizontal extension of the colonnades, moreover, accentuates the lateral expansion of the oval piazza, and the obelisk at the intersection of the two axes endorses the cruciform organization.

230. There is also a suggestion of Saint Andrew's cross in the chiastic arrangement of the chapels in the plan of Sant'Andrea al Quirinale. Bernini also planned such a cross as a crowning motif above the lantern of this church, instead of the conventional cross and orb, as evidenced in his autograph sketches (Brauer-Wittkower, 111–12).

231. The colonnades are free-standing, open, and physically penetrable, but four columns abreast, normally overlap in view and create a strong sense of enclosure (cf. Note 179, above). The obelisk at the center, organizing the space centripetally, contributes to the introvert character of the piazza in no small measure. This type of *insular* piazza was common in Italy, not only in the Middle Ages and the Renaissance but also earlier; the Imperial Fora constitute the prototype. Following examples might be added to the list: the Campo in Siena; the piazza in Pienza; the Piazza dei Signori in Verona; and in Rome, the Campo dei Fiori and the Piazza Navona. There is, however, a second type of piazza, which is characteristically more *nodal* than insular: Piazza delle Erbe in Verona, Piazza del Santo in Padua, and in Rome, Piazza del Monte Cavallo (Quirinale) and Piazza di Spagna. Such a piazza is integrated with the flow system—that is, with the organization of thoroughfares—rather than isolated from it. It is a space that suggests convergence and dispersal—that is, flow—rather than collection and containment, and as a rule they are expanded streets or intersections; the Campidoglio, for example, is therefore more in the second category even though the piazza itself is enclosed on three sides.

232. Falda left a large open space in front of the *terzo braccio* in his representation (Fig. 36), but this seems to owe largely to graphic expediency. One important clue is the program for demolition, recorded in the minutes of the Congregazione of February 19 (v. Note 193, above), which suggests that the architect intended as much space outside the propylaeum as inside, that is, a piazza preceding the gateway.

233. Uffizi, dis. arch. 266, first published by Wittkower ("Il terzo braccio," Fig. 9). The propylaeum has been elaborated; and the piazza in which it is set has been made deeper than that of the first pavement study. The oval of the piazza, moreover, is not an *ovato tondo;* note the distortion in the eastern cross-passage. See also Note 162, above. The plan is unclear regarding the kind of buildings which were to enclose the piazza around the propylaeum.

234. The pavement studies deal with the pavement; and they represented rejected solutions at that. Therefore, they are not to be trusted for details. The propylaeum on the first pavement plan, for example, face the Basilica; this is in itself implausible (v. Note 197, above). Contradicting this detail, the eastern cross-passages are two-faced, while this very detail is incorrectly represented on the second pavement study. The stairs to the portals of the Basilica are completely different from the executed version; the stairs on Bernini's sketch plan (Fig. 72), on the other hand, are like those on the Vatican Plan and come close to the executed version (Fig. 63) in outline and proportions. The *avviso* of January 22, 1667 (Arch. Segr. Vat., Avvisi, 114, 16; Pastor, *Popes,* XXXI, 295) reported that "si è dato principio a fare la scalinata, et al braccio, che

unisce il Teatro col Portico com'anco al fondamente della fontana simile all'altra e di là della guglia." In the context of the development, *scalinata* can only be the stairs to the portals of the Basilica (i.e., what Fontana calls "Piazza Pensile"; v. Note 2, above). In fact, other references to the stairs appear in the documents dated January 1 and 14, 1667 ("la scalinata della Chiesa e del Teatro"; Bibl. Vat., Chig. H II 22, fols. 227 and 228); there is also an "istrumento" on the "scalini tutto intorno al Portico," dated January 1, 1667 (Arch. Fabb. S.P., I Piano, ser. 3, vol. 164, fol. 495). Note, too, that the southern corridor (*braccio*), reported to have been started in this *avviso*, could not have been completed in two months; the phrase "si termina" in the *avviso* of March 19 (v. Note 192, above) must therefore indicate progress only.

235. J. S. Ackerman, *The Architecture of Michelangelo,* London and New York, 1961, ch. 10 (114–22). Visually, however, the propylaeum would be less penetrable on account of the columns placed four abreast in depth; there would be no vista extending beyond it.

236. See Ch. I, above; and Appendix, 2.

237. Typically, Wittkower, *Art and Architecture,* 128; but usually more harshly by many Italians, for example, Argan, *L'architettura barocca in Italia,* Milan, 1957, 18: "La grande strada rettilinea è stata sciaguratamente aperta alcuni anni or sono: distruggendo vandalicamente i Borghi, sfigurando irrimediabilmente un insieme che poteva considerarsi il frutto della collaborazione, a distanza d'un secolo, di Michelangelo e del Bernini." See also Note 268, below.

238. Wittkower described in similar words the columned screen between the high altar chapel and the main oval space of Sant' Andrea al Quirinale, and, furthermore, related the motif to the scenographic device in Palladio's church, Il Redentore (*Art and Architecture,* 120, and *Architectural Principles,* 87–88). In these two instances, the link is essentially visual; the visitor is not invited to physically enter the realm beyond. The propylaeum is a barrier and link, of course, as the doorway is by definition; it stands in our way but we are expected to pass through it. Cf. Note 222, above.

239. Kitao, "Bernini's Church Facades," 281–84.

240. A similar combination of continuity and contrast has been observed between the facade and the interior of Sant' Andrea al Quirinale (Wittkower, *Art and Architecture,* 121). In the church design, however, the break is inherent in the inside-outside dichotomy; moreover, one is covered and the other is open. The two forms, the facade and the interior elevation, are therefore only analogous. In the design of the piazza, on the other hand, the two spaces are both outdoor spaces; they are fundamentally different in form and expression, and instead of merely adjoining each other, they actually run into each other. The two parts are forcefully set in *contrapposti.*

241. Drawing by Israel Silvestre, 33.5 x 113.4 cm., in the Fogg Museum, Harvard University; published by H. A. Millon, "Notes on Old and Modern Drawings: An Early Seventeenth Century Drawing of the Piazza San Pietro," *Art Quarterly,* XXV, 1962, 229–41.

242. *La fiera di farfa;* v. Fagiolo dell'Arco, *Bernini,* Cat. No. 98, and for other examples, *ibid.,* Cat. Nos. 85 and 86. See also Bernini, *Fontana di Trevi* and Lavin's review (v. Note 86, above).

243. Lavin's review, cited in Note 86, above, where the importance of the psychological (rather than visual) factor in Bernini's dramatic scenography is discussed.

244. F. Truffaut, *Hitchcock,* New York, 1967, 51–52; the director, defining suspense as "the stretching out of an anticipation," explains that, while a sudden explosion on the screen is a mere surprise, had the audience been informed in advance of the explosion that had been planned to happen at a certain hour and had it been, moreover, warned of the approaching catastrophe from time to time (as by being shown a closeup of the clock), it will experience suspense for an extended time rather than a surprise which lasts only a few seconds. This kind of psychological maneuver, at which Hitchcock is a master, is also eminently Bernini's specialty.

245. One is tempted to speculate that Bernini decision in 1667 to enlarge the project far beyond the scope envisioned by the Congregazione or the Pope might have been motivated in part by his personal vision of restoring in art the rapidly declining power of the Papacy. His trip to France, which he made in 1665, as it turned out, was only one of the maneuvers of Louis XIV to humiliate the Pope (F. Haskell, *Patrons and Painters,* London, 1963, 153); and the Louvre, which he proposed to make "grander and more magnificent than the palaces of the emperors and the popes" (Chantelou, 15), was beginning to look like a project in perpetual revision by this time. In the spring of 1666 Bernini sent his assistant, Matthia de' Rossi, to Paris to supervise the execution, but little was accomplished; in the spring of 1667 the king decided to abandon Bernini's plans. By the beginning of that year, Bernini was psychologically ready for a Grand Design for his Pope. On the Louvre projects, see Brauer-Wittkower, 129–33, and Fagiolo dell'Arco, *Bernini,* Cat. No. 203.

246. It is true that the equestrian statue of Marcus Aurelius rises like a ship on the horizon as we walk up the ramp, but the revelation nevertheless comes suddenly at the summit because going up a slope the body necessarily tilts forward and our vision *tends* to be lower on the path and remain so until we reach the level ground, where we spontaneously look up to take in the new vista; until then the depth of the piazza looks deceptively shallow because of the oblique lines of the lateral palaces, and so both the trapezoid and the oval come as a surprise. Cf. Ackerman, *The Architecture of Michelangelo,* London, 1961, I, 57 and 60. The tapered form of the Cordonata was, to be sure, introduced by Della Porta "to avoid blocking the access to the Aracoeli steps" (Ackerman, II, 57–58), but it is a part of the complex in this form and was undoubtedly considered Michelangelesque in Bernini's Rome.

247. Rome, 1694, Book VI, Chs. 9–12, and Book V, ch. 1.

248. *Templum Vaticanum,* 221 and 211, respectively; the plan is entitled: "Pianta proposta da noi qvale dimostra la gionta de bracci ò corritori verso la città per ottenerne meglior dispositione e perfetta figvra et ingrandimento della piazza." The exit point of the propylaeum is marked S and is explained in the legend as the "luogo per ottenere

miglior contorno del Tempio, quando non uenisse effectuato l'altro più proprio sop.ª il Ponte S. Angelo."

249. The drum still is not completely in view from this point, but Fontana's concern with this problem is evident in the legend on the plan, cited in the preceding Note. With regard to the symmetry about the obelisk, the architect draws on the authority of Vitruvius (Bk. I, ch. 3, in Fontana's citation); on this, see *Templum Vaticanum*, 208–9, where one also reads of the propylaeum as a "magnifica Mole ad vso d'Orologio, e Campanile in luogo di quello demolito . . ."

250. On the "true ellipse" see Appendix, 2. In this connection, the phrase "perfetta figura" in the title of the plan is noteworthy; but Fontana speaks in the text, in fact, of Bernini's closing structure, which was planned, according to the latter's drawings and medals, "dentro la linea, che circonscriue questa non perfetta Ellipse"—the phrase used in the early discussion. See *Templum Vaticanum*, 208.

251. *Templum Vaticanum*, 420–21; the hemicycle with niches does not appear on the previous plan, but it is indicated by P ("Teatro Semicircolare") and discussed in the text (p. 209). In the legend, moreover, the two streets, marked Q, are specified as the "strade, che da ponte uerrebbero ad imboccare nell'ambito della Piazza."

252. *Templum Vaticanum*, 231; the plan also shows a vast piazza behind the Basilica. Ambitious and uncompromising, the second design is hardly an alternative to the first; rather, it is a design in the nature of a master plan or ideal plan without prospect of immediate execution. Fontana writes, in fact, as follows (p. 229): "Ne abbiamo perciò esposta l'inuenzione, e modo nella seguente Pianta, per appagare la curiosità, essendone lontana l'effettuazione." The phrase "quando non uenisse effettuato l'altro" in the legend on the first plan, cited in Note 248, above, reflects this statement.

253. The idea of the commercial mall, of course, goes back to the project of Nicholas V; Fontana argues that there is a need for a commercial zone but emphasizes that a separation between the sacred and secular functions is essential (*Templum Vaticanum*, 229), but he was no less interested in the view of the dome as the title of his Chapter 11 indicates: "Viste mirabili da ottenersi dal Ponte al Tempio Vaticano" (p. 228).

254. *Templum Vaticanum*, 245; the plan reads like a site plan for the second design, demonstrating the area for demolition, but the change of the designation from Piazza di Mercato to *stradone* clearly indicates that it represents a new, more developed conception. Moreover, given the argument, more emphatic than before, that "è tale la grandezza di questo Tempio, che non potendo essere ben compreso dall'occhio, se non in gran distanza, abbiam . . . trovato che non in altro luogo possa meglio riceuersi la veduta di questo Edifizio, che di doue termina Ponte di Castel S. Angelo . . .," the third design is better understood as an improvement on the second. But Fontana, in fact, proposes in the text (p. 243) that "si potrebbero dal principio de' lati del Borgo, fino all'imbocco della Piazza, fra li due Bracci circolari del nuouo Portico, fabbricare altri Portici," primarily for the procession of the Corpus Domini; in conjunction with the accompanying plan, the proposed porticoes cannot be the corridors of the first and second plans. The account of the Corpus Domini in 1658 is in this connection relevant

(Arch. Segr. Vat., Avvisi, 28, fol. 325): "Mercoledi per la vigilia della festiuità del Corpus Domini S. Santità tenne il vespro al Quirinale, e la mattina seguente si trasferì al Vaticano, di doue proceduta processionalmente dal Clero Regolare e Secolare, nobiltà, Vescoui, Arciuescoui, Patriarchi, e Sig. Cardinali tutti vestiti alla Pontificale, con mitrie in testa, e torcie in mano, portò il Santissimo inginocchioni per Borgo nuovo, e vecchio (riccamente apparate) nella Basilica di S. Pietro, e la sera S. Beatitudine con nobile caualcata se ne ritornò al Quirinale."

255. Bibl. Vat. Chig. P VII 9, fols. 21 and 22, respectively. The perspective view is inaccurate; the line of the buildings on the left swings out too far, making the avenue appear more symmetrical than it would be. Morelli also proposes the elimination of the outermost bays of Maderno's facade (illustrated only on the south side) to improve its proportion.

256. Tournon's prefecture lasted from 1809 to 1814. In June 1811 he outlined his program for the urban development of Rome, including the *spina* clearance, and reported it to the Minister of the Interior; for the letter, see J. Moulard, *Le Comte Camille de Tournon,* II, Paris, 1930, 319–23 (also published, in Italian translation, in L. Quaroni, *Immagine di Roma,* Bari, 1969, 282–91). The substance of the letter was carried into Napoleon's decree of August 9, 1811 (A. La Padula, *Roma 1809–1814: Contributo alla storia dell'urbanistica,* Rome, 1958, 38–46, with documents in Rome, especially those in the Archivo di Stato di Roma). Tournon later published the project in his *Etudes statistiques sur Rome,* Paris, 1831. See also P. Lavedan, *Histoire de l'urbanisme: époque contemporaine,* Paris, 1952, 43–51, on Tournon's Rome in general; on the Borgo development, in particular, see La Padula, *Roma 1809–1814,* 77–79. Valadier produced a drawing in 1812 illustrating a project of raising two Roman commemorative columns at the opening to the new avenue (Rome, Biblioteca di Archeologia e Storia dell'Arte, Collez. Lanciani, Roma, XI, 100/2, 119; La Padula, *Roma 1809–1814,* pl. XXX); see also P. Marconi, *Giuseppe Valadier,* Rome, 1964, 175–76.

257. D. Gnoli, "Nuovo Accesso alla Piazza di San Pietro in Roma," *Archivio storico dell'arte,* II, 1889, 138–52, esp. 142–43; the Napoleonic project interested the Republic of 1849, whose effort to carry out the *spina* clearance resulted only in the creation of the Piazza Pia at the fork of the two Borgo streets, carried out in 1856 under Pius IX. On the Piano Regolatore of 1873, see I. Insolera, *Roma moderna, un secolo di storia urbanistica,* Turin, 1962 and 1971; and, now, L. Benevolo, *Roma da ieri a domani,* Bari, 1971.

258. The *spina* clearance, incorporated in the 1881 Plan, was however rejected in 1882 and removed from the 1883 Plan; see Ehrle, "Virgilio Spada," 31–32, and n. 147. See also M. Zocca, "Roma capitale d'Italia," *Topografia e urbanistica di Roma,* in *Storia di Roma,* XXII, Bologna, 1958, 698–700; and Insolera, *Roma moderna,* 46–59.

259. Gnoli, in fact, wrote his article to protest against the *spina* clearance included in the 1887 Plan ("Nuovo Accesso," 138–39). Of the proposals made in the first decades of this century, the best known are the projects of Gugler, Brasini, and Budden. Eric Gugler, a student of the American Academy in Rome, presented to the Società fra

Cultori ed Amatori dell' Architettura in 1915, and subsequently to the Pope, an open-avenue projects in the tradition of those of Morelli and Tournon; the proposal, in typescript, with accompanying plates, is preserved in the Library of the American Academy and carries the title, "Accesso alla Piazza di San Pietro." To Lionel Budden, Gugler's plan was a poor compromise; and he proposed, instead, that the approach must be perfectly axial with the nave of Saint Peter's and symmetrical in itself. The proposal, published in the *Town Planning Review*, VII, 1917–18, 98–103 ("The Approach to St. Peter's, Rome"), was immediately criticized by Eugénie Strong in the same review "The Approach to St. Peter's Rome," *Town Planning Review*, VII, 1917–18, 195–202), who stated her preference for Brasini's design. Armando Brasini, noted for his Piranesian transformation of the historical center of Rome (Zocca, "Roma capitale d'Italia," pl. CLVIII), produced a grandiose design of opening an axial and symmetrical avenue and filling the center with a monumental colonnaded gallery from the Piazza Pia to the Piazza Rusticucci; first published in 1916 in P. Orano, *L'Urbe Massima: L'architettura e la decorazione di A. Brasini,* Rome, n.d., the project is illustrated in Strong's article. The projects of Gugler and Brasini are also discussed in Ehrle, "Virgilio Spada," 32–33.

260. Typically, Gnoli and Strong, cited in Notes 257 and 259, respectively. Fraschetti, who assumed in his monograph on Bernini (1900; v. Note 1, above) that the 1659 design was the final scheme, was undoubtedly influential. But in this connection, the crucial publication was Busiri-Vici's (1893; v. Note 110, above), in which the drawings of the Counterproject of 1659, then in his possession, were made public for the first time with attribution to Bernini; the drawings argued vehemently for a closed piazza. Even after Wittkower's study (Brauer-Wittkower, 84–87, and 98), Italian writers continued to publish them as Bernini's: for example, G. Tardini, *Basilica Vaticana e Borghi* in *Illustrazione Vaticana*, VII, Rome, 1936, and L. Tombolini Barzotti, *La Basilica di S. Pietro in Vaticano nei simboli e negli elementi architettonici di Gianlorenzo Bernini,* Rome, 1937. Busiri-Vici himself proposed in 1886 a project for the Borgo, and it was significantly an avenue with an "interropimento" (*Architettura*, 1936, 33; v. Note 262, below); the projects of 1915–17, however, reasserted the tradition.

261. The history of the Piacentini-Spaccarelli project is a complex matter that requires a separate volume, for it must take into account Mussolini's plan of Rome and the socio-political history of the decade. Only a barest outline is presented here. The proponents and opponents of the *spina* clearance cannot be grouped into architects and art historians, especially because architectural historians were often architects; but historically oriented architects tended to oppose the clearance (e.g., Giovannoni). The factional line, in any case, was not a political one between Fascists and non-Fascists.

262. See the article signed O. S., "La sistemazione dei Borghi per l'accesso a S. Pietro: architetti Marcello Piacentini and Attilio Spaccarelli," *Architettura: Revista del Sindacato nazionale fascista architetti,* 1936, fascicolo speciale (Urbanistica della Roma Mussoliniana), 21–53, in which the architects' various plans were published; also F. L. Berra and G. B. Rosso, "La sistemazione dei Borghi e il Cavalier Gian Lorenzo

Bernini," *Arte cristiana,* XXVI, 1938, 57–82, esp. 67f., with the architects' plans and perspective views. These articles and various newspaper clippings relevant to the Piacentini-Spaccarelli project, collected by Chester Holme Aldrich, are preserved in the Library of the American Academy in Rome under his authorship. The architects themselves later published their account in M. Piacentini and A. Spaccarelli, *Memoria sugli studi e sui lavori per l'accesso a San Pietro,* Rome, 1944 (also in English translation).

263. See G. A. Andriulli, "La Grande Strada da Castel S. Angelo alla Basilica Vaticana," *Il Messaggero,* June 30, 1936, and the architect's statement accompanying the article. Previous to their appointment, the two architects had already been working on the project independently, although the Piano Regolatore of 1931 did not include the development of the Borgo. Piacentini's plan, submitted to the city but rejected by the effort of Gustavo Giavannoni, was an axial and symmetrical open avenue like Fontana's third design; it was published in 1934 (*Il Messaggero,* November 21 and 23, cited by Berra and Rosso, 66). See also *Architettura,* 1936, 21; G. Giovannoni, *Vecchie città ed edilizia nuova,* Turin, 1932; and M. Piacentini, *Le vicende edilizie di Roma dal 1870 ad oggi,* Rome, 1952, 167. Spaccarelli's plan, on the other hand, was a modest scheme consisting only of the clearance of the two blocks of the *spina* from the Piazza Pia to the Piazza Scossacavalli halfway up the Borgo (*La Tribuna,* November 28, 1934, cited by Berra and Rosso, 66); his argument was apparently that an open avenue would require parallel sides in order to frame Maderno's facade for a proper optical effect (*Architettura,* 1936, 21).

264. There is a fundamental difference, of course, that the portico in the modern version is only a visual screen and not a landmark; the two areas are visually treated as a single unit. The portico, it was indeed said, "non vuole essere una 'chiusura,' sibbene un 'segno di separazione,' e, nello stesso tempo, di 'collegamento' fra i due ambienti . . ." (*Architettura,* 1936, 21). The argument for the zonal distinction, however, is directly from Fontana (v. Note 253, above), who owed it to Bernini's design and eventually abandoned it in his third and final design. The official publication (*Architettura,* 1936, 28–31) illustrated, in fact, not only all three of Fontana's designs but also Bernini's drawing illustrating the relocation of the propylaeum as well as the pavement study that followed it (our Figs. 72 and 73).

265. G. A. Andriulli, who reported on the 1936 project (v. Note 263, above), immediately responded with a devastating criticism ("La sistemazione dei Borghi: Aperta o chiusa la strada per San Pietro?," *Il Messaggero,* July 4, 1936). The criticism is inconsistent but deserves a summary. Andriulli considered the design derivative of Fontana's and objected to this fact because the argument for the zonal separation does not hold any longer inasmuch as merchants are not likely to spill into the piazza as the case might have been in the seventeenth century; moreover, the piazza, in contrast to the Basilica itself, should be liturgically the merging place of civic life and religion. The portico, he also observed, is too much like a "colossale viadotto ferroviario"; and it ineffectively separates Michelangelo's dome from Maderno's facade in the view up the avenue

as though the latter did not exist, while the two parts are inevitably displayed in the view from the portico as an integral whole (v. Note 270, below). Finally, the critic protested that the project involves too many historical buildings in dismantling and reconstruction (on which, see the following Note). The 1936 design also stimulated alternative proposals, the three best known of which were all open-avenue designs. Luigi Kambo proposed a design with large planted areas to isolate the Basilica ("Il problema della spaziosità e la sistemazione dei Borghi," *Il Messaggero,* October 14 and 26, 1937); Oreste Zunica provided three arteries in the Borgo that converged toward the piazza and articulated the central avenue with the redeveloped Piazza Scossacavalli (*La piazza di San Pietro e i Borghi,* Tivoli, 1937); and, earlier than the other two, Nino Bertoletti's project anticipated the revision of Piacentini and Spaccarelli with a tapered avenue that terminated with a bottleneck preceding the Piazza Rusticucci (*Il Tevere,* August 30, 1936). All the three projects are illustrated and briefly described in Berra and Rosso, "La sistemazione dei Borghi," 79–82.

266. P. Scarpa, "L'allineamento degli edifici: verso Piazza Rusticucci e la prova dell'interrompimento," *Il Messaggero,* June 17, 1937. In proposing a tapered avenue in 1936, Piacentini and Spaccarelli were apparently convinced that for a perfectly symmetrical alignment it would be simpler to rearrange the buildings on the former Borgo Vecchio to match those on the Borgo Nuovo, which form a straight line (Fig. 64), and come up with a tapered avenue than to realign both sides to produce a parallel avenue (*Architettura,* 1936, 21). At that time, however, they had considered a more economical solution, too, which they eventually discarded; and that was to rework only on the blocks nearest the Piazza Rusticucci and leave the rest essentially untouched, and the result was two lines of building facades that were somewhat irregular but approximately parallel with each other and with the axis of the Basilica. Readopted in 1937, then, the plan left intact the three most important buildings on the old Borgo Vecchio: Palazzo dei Penitenzieri, which originally faced the Piazza Scossacavalli and whose facade is parallel with the axis of the Basilica, and the two palaces that follow this one toward the Piazza Obliqua—Palazzo Serristori and Palazzo Cesi. On the opposite side, an oblique line extending from Santa Maria in Transpontina to the Palazzo Giraud-Torlonia (which also faced the Piazza Scossacavalli) was left unchanged; the block west of this was cleared, and on a line matching that across the avenue there were reconstructed three palaces from the area—Palazzo dei Convertendi (which adjoined the Piazza Scossacavalli), Palazzo Rusticucci, and the house of Leo X's physician, Giacomo di Bartolomeo da Brescia (which in reconstruction was placed on the side street, Via Rusticucci). On the major palaces cited here, see Gnoli, "Nuovo accesso," 145–52.

267. C. Broggi, "La decisione sui Borghi: Niente interrompimento," *Il Giornale d'Italia,* May 21, 1938. For a thoughtful and well-documented criticism of this plan, see Berra and Rosso, "La sistemazione dei Borghi," 69–79; their preference for the 1936 design, however, is based on the familiar argument that Bernini conceived his piazza as a closed "amphitheater."

268. The following passage from E. A. Gutkind, *Urban Development in Southern Europe: Italy and Greece,* New York, 1969, 174, summarizes the assessment of the Piacentini-Spaccarelli project as expressed in the literature of the past few decades: "Today a wide avenue, the Via della Conciliazione, leads to the Piazza. This bombastic monstrosity is lined by buildings five or six stories high in a modernistic insurance-company style and was begun under the *régime* of Mussolini. The motif of the obelisk has been degraded to lampposts with stable lanterns on top instead of the cross of Christ that crowns the original obelisk in the Piazza. This truly great demonstration of modern barbarism pretends to revive an old idea of Carlo Fontana. Unfortunately the main point of his scheme was overlooked. Fontana's plan provided for a low arcade connecting the two arms of the Piazza Rusticucci which would have retained the scale and the unity of the Piazza di San Pietro . . ."; see also L. Benevolo, *Storia dell'architettura del Rinascimento,* Bari, 1968, II, 834; L. Quaroni, *Immagine di Roma,* Bari, 1969, 255–56; and A. Cederno, *Mirabilia Urbis,* Turin, 1965,189 ("obbrobrioso squarcio littorio detto di poi via della Conciliazione"), among contemporary Italian critics. A more balanced view is presented by M. Zocca, "Roma capitale d' Italia," 674–75 (v. Note 258, above). In an effort to correct the "disaster," T. A. Polazzo proposed after the war a project of filling the avenue with an arcaded gallery like Brasini's (v. Note 259, above), but simpler and more modest in scale (*Da Castel S. Angelo alla Basilica di San Pietro,* Rome, 1948). On Piacentini's fascism, see H. A. Millon, "The Role of History of Architecture in Fascist Italy," *Journal of the Society of Architectural Historians, XXIV,* 1965, 53–59. See also Note 237, above.

269. On the Vatican Plan, where the *terzo braccio* is shorter, the gap is just about 135 *palmi.* The Via della Conciliazione is 50 meters wide for the rest.

270. Cf. Andriulli's criticism (v. Note 265, above); also Gnoli on the 1881 Piano Regolatore ("Nuovo accesso," 144). The distinction whether the focus of the vista is or should be Michelangelo's dome by itself (including the drum) or the total mass comprising the dome and the facade of the Basilica is spurious. If the earlier proponents of the open avenue were ambiguous on this point, it was because they assumed rightly that bringing the dome into view would improve the total composition and also because the issue was by and large the vista in itself rather than its focus. The masking of the squat facade, however, is effective.

271. See Note 205, above.

272. In contrast to Fontana's design, in which a trapezoidal space was repeated, there is a decisive contrast between the corridorlike avenue and the laterally expansive Piazza Obliqua. In this connection, the ill-criticized obelisk-lampposts (v. Note 268, above), which ingeniously conceal the irregularity of the lines of the buildings, also contribute to the axiality of the avenue; they create an impression that the central section they define is the avenue, to which the peripheral sections are as aisles are to the nave.

273. To isolate architecture from nonarchitecture in Bernini's *oeuvre* is not easy; and one is tempted to question the usefulness of such an attempt. Architecture and sculpture are inseparably combined in his altars, tombs, fountains, chapels, and churches, not to speak

of the Baldacchino and the Cathedra Petri; or they defy such a distinction. Still there is no doubt that the three churches and the Piazza Obliqua constitute the whole of the artists' works from his mature period that can be said to be strictly architectural, complete in themselves, fully or nearly fully executed, and essentially unaltered.

274. The orthography of this church is given this way in the letterhead and adopted by most Italian writers; it should be accepted as the standard form. Wittkower, however, used another, S. Tomaso di Villanova, in his *Art and Architecture in Italy;* the first edition of the *T.C.I. Guida d'Italia:* Roma, Milan, 1925, gave this orthography. The sixth edition (1962) of this guide, however, changed it to S. Tomaso da Villanova, while T.C.I.'s own *L'Italia in automobile: Lazio,* Milan, 1953, changed it to S. Tommaso di Villanova.

275. On these churches, see Brauer-Wittkower, 115–19, 110–13, and 122–26; Wittkower, *Art and Architecture,* 114–21; and Kitao, "Bernini's Church Facades."

276. See Note 9, above.

277. This theme will be dealt with in the author's study on Sant'Andrea now in preparation; but see Bordini, "Bernini e il Pantheon" (v. Note 9, above).

278. *Memorie degli architetti antichi e moderni,* Bassano, 1785, 4th ed., II, 169–89. Milizia calls Sant' Andrea "l'elegantissima Chiesa del Noviziato de' Gesuiti" (p. 179) and summarized Bernini's architecture as follows (p. 185): "Siccome il carattere del Bernini nella Scultura è il morbido ed il tenero, così nell'Architettura la gentilezza, la leggiadria, la sveltezza spiccano in tutti i suoi edifizj cosicchè piaciono subito anche agl'ignoranti. Egli intese assai bene la Meccanica, e la condotta delle forze moventi. Seppe ben adattarsi ai siti obbligati ed angusti, e trarne vantaggi. In tutt'insieme nelle fabbriche è buono ed armonioso: graziosa la sua maniera di profilare, e vaghi i suoi ornamenti, benchè talvolta alquanto profusi." This is, of course, an extravagant compliment next to what he had to say about Borromini's "frenesia architettonica" (pp. 157–62). See also A. C. Quatremère de Quincy's tribute, *Dictionnaire historique d'architecture,* Paris, 1832, s.v.

279. *De Architectura,* Lib. I, 2.

280. Begun in the spring of 1658, San Tommaso da Villanova was complete except for the dome in the autumn of 1659; the papal chirograph for Sant' Andrea was signed on October 26, 1658, and the revised plan, which is essentially like the executed design, appears on a copy of the chirograph, now in the Archivio di Stato di Roma (Fig. 76). See Kitao, "Bernini's Church Facades," 264, 271, and 277.

281. See Note 221, above.

282. Panofsky, *Galileo as a Critic of the Arts,* 7–11.

283. See Note 222, above, on Wittkower's use of the term.

284. Wittkower, *Art and Architecture,* 119: "Obviously, Bernini saw no contradiction between classical architecture and Baroque sculpture—a contradiction usually emphasized by modern critics who fail to understand the subjective and particular quality with which seemingly objective and timeless classical forms have been endowed." Wittkower, however, attributed the subjective quality to the decoration rather than to the

architecture itself: "the architecture is no more and no less than the setting for a stirring mystery revealed to the faithful by sculptural decoration."

285. I. Lavin, *Bernini and the Crossing of Saint Peter's,* New York, 1968, 39: "Bernini treats a volume of real space as the site of a dramatic action, in which the observer is involved physically as well as psychologically. The drama takes place in an environment that is not an extension of the realworld, but is coextensive with it. And because the statues act as witnesses, the observer is associated with them and hence, inevitably, becomes a participant in the event." In other words, Bernini's art is not that kind of illusionism that is so thorough in deception that the observer is transported away from the real world into the fictional world; and this was true even of his theater like the *Due Teatri.*

Bibliography

Asterisks indicate major sources.

ACCOLTI, PIETRO. *Lo inganno degl'occhi,* Florence, 1625.

ACKERMAN, JAMES S. *The Architecture of Michelangelo,* London and New York, 1961.

ADEMOLLO, ALESSANDRO. *I teatri di Roma nel secolo decimosettimo,* Rome, 1888 (also 1969).

*ALDRICH, CHESTER H. Materials on Plans for Borghi and Piazza San Pietro, collected by Chester Holme Aldrich and deposited in the Library of the American Academy in Rome, ca. 1938.

*ALVERI, GASPARO. *Della Roma in Ogni Stato,* 2 vols., Rome, 1664.

*ANDRIULLI, GIUSEPPE A. "La grande strada da Castel S. Angelo alla Basilica Vaticana," *Il Messaggero,* June 30, 1936.

*————. "Aperta o Chiusa: la strada per San Pietro," *Messaggero,* July 4, 1936.

ARGAN, GIULIO CARLO. *L'architettura barocca in Italia,* Milan, 1957 (also 1960).

ASHBY, THOMAS. "Lievin Cruyl e le sue vedute di Roma (1664–70)," *Atti della Pontificia Accademia Romana di Archaeologia,* Series III, Memoria I, i, 1923.

ASKEW, PAMELA. "The Relation of Bernini's Architecture to the Architecture of the High Renaissance and of Michelangelo," *Marsyas,* V (New York, 1950), 39–61.

BALDINUCCI, FILIPPO. *Notizie de' professori del disegno da Cimahue in qua,* Florence, 1681–1728 (also 1702, 1769, and Milan, 1812).

————. *The Life of Bernini,* tr. C. Enggass, University Park and London, 1966.

*————. *Vita di Giovanni Lorenzo Bernini,* Florence, 1682; ed. Sergio Semek Ludovici, Milan, 1948.

*————. *Vocabolario toscano dell'arte del disegno,* Florence, 1681.

BALTRUSAITIS, JURGIS. *Anamorphoses ou perspectives curieuses,* Paris, 1955; rev. ed. 1969.

BARBARO, DANIELLO, tr. *I dieci libri dell'architettura* by Vitruvius, Venice, 1567.

BAROZZI, FRANCESCO. *Admirandum illud geometricum problema,* Venice, 1586.

BARTON, ELEANOR DODGE. "The Problem of Bernini's Theory of Art, entitled *Anamorphoses, ou magie artificielle des effets merveilleux,*" *Marsyas,* IV, 1945–47 (New York, 1948), 81–112.

BELLORI, GIOVANNI PIETRO. *Le vite de'pittori, scultori, ed architetti moderni,* Rome, 1672 (also 1728).

BELTRAMI, G. "Martino Ferabosco, architetto," *Arte,* XXIX, 1926, 23–37.

BENEVOLO, LEONARDO. *Roma da ieri a domani,* Bari, 1971.

———. *Storia dell'architettura del Rinascimento,* 2 vols., Bari, 1968.

BERGNER, HEINRICH. *Das Barocke Rom,* Leipzig, 1914.

*BERNHEIMER, RICHARD. "Theatrum Mundi," *Art Bulletin,* XXXVIII, 1956, 225–47.

BERNINI, DOMENICO. *Vita del Cavalier Giovanni Lorenzo Bernino,* Rome, 1713.

*BERNINI, GIAN LORENZO. *Fontana di Trevi, Commedia inedita,* ed. C. d'Onofrio, Rome, 1963.

*BERRA, F. L. and G. B. ROSSO. "La sistemazione dei Borghi e il Cavalier Gian Lorenzo Bernini," *Arte Cristiana,* XXVI, 1938, 57–82.

BIBIENA, FERDINANDO GALLI. *Architettura Civile,* Parma, 1711.

BLUNT, ANTHONY. "Palazzo Barberini: The Contributions of Maderno, Bernini and Pietro da Cortona," *Journal of the Warburg and Courtauld Institutes,* XXI, 1958, 256–80.

BOEHN, MAX VON. *Lorenzo Bernini, seine Zeit, sein Leben, sein Werk,* Leipzig, 1912 (also 1927).

BOLOGNA, MUSEO CIVICO. *L'ideale classico del seicento in Italia e la pittura di paesaggio: Catalogo,* Bologna, 1962.

BONANNI, F. See BUONANNI, below.

BONELLI, RENATO. "La piazza capitolina," in *Michelangelo architetto,* ed. B. Zevi, Turin, 1964, 427–46.

*BORDINI, S. "Bernini e il Pantheon: note sul classicismo berniniano," *Quaderni dell'Istituto di storia dell' architettura,* ser. XIV, fasc. 79–84, 1967 (Rome, 1968), 53–84.

BORSI, FRANCO. *La Chiesa di S. Andrea al Quirinale,* Rome, 1967.

*BRAUER, HEINRICH, and RUDOLPH WITTKOWER. *Die Zeichnungen des Gianlorenzo Bernini,* 2 vols., Römische Forschungen der Bibliotheca Hertziana, IX and X, Berlin, 1931.

BRINCKMANN, ALBERT E. *Die Baukunst des 17. und 18. Jahrhunderts, I: In den romanischen Ländern,* Berlin, 1915.

———. *Platz und Monument.* Berlin, 1908 (also 1923).

———. *Stadtbaukunst,* Berlin, 1920.

*BROGGI, CARLO. "La decisione sui Borghi: Niente interrompimento, la mirabile visione dal Ponte Elio a San Pietro," *Il Giornale d'Italia,* May 21, 1938.

BRUHNS, LEO. *Die Kunst der Stadt Rom,* Vienna, 1951.

BRUSCHI, ARNALDO. *Bramante architetto,* Bari, 1969.

BUDDEN, LIONEL B. "The Approach to St. Peter's, Rome," *The Town Planning Review,* VII, 1917, 98–103.

*BUONANNI (or BONANNI) FILIPPO. *Numismata summorum pontificum Templi Vaticani Fabricam Indicantia,* Rome, 1696 (also 1715).

*BUSIRI-VICI, ANDREA. *La Piazza di San Pietro nei secoli* III, XIV, XVII, Rome, 1893.

CAFLISCH, NINA. *Carlo Maderno,* Munich, 1934.

CECCARELLI, GIUSEPPE (pseud. Ceccarius). *La "spina" dei Borghi,* Rome, 1938.

CEDERNA, ANTONIO. *Mirabilia Urbis,* Turin, 1965.

*CHANTELOU, M. DE. *Journal du voyage du Cavalier Bernin en France,* ed. L. Lalanne, Paris, 1885.

CHASTEL, ANDRE. *The Age of Humanism,* New York, 1963.

CLEMENTI, FILIPPO. *Il Carnevale romano,* Città di Castello, 1938–39.

COFFIN, DAVID R. "Some Architectural Drawings of Giovanni Battista Aleotti," *Journal of the Society of Architectural Historians,* XXI, 1962, 116–28.

COSTAGUTI, GIOVANNI BATTISTA. *Architettura della Basilica di S. Pietro in Vaticano,* Rome, 1684. See FERABOSCO, below.

COUDENHOVE-ERTHAL, E. *Carlo Fontana und die Architektur des römischen Spätbarock,* Vienna, 1930.

DEL RE, NICCOLO. "La Sacra Congregazione della Reverenda Fabrica di S. Pietro," *Studi romani,* XVII, 1969.

DINSMOOR, WILLIAM BELL. "The Literary Remains of Sebastiano Serlio," *Art Bulletin,* XXIV, 1942, 55–91 and 115–54.

———. "Order," s.v. *Encyclopaedia Britannica.*

DONATI, UGO. *Artisti ticinesi a Roma,* Bellinzona, 1942.

———. *Carlo Maderno,* Lugano, 1957.

*D'ONOFRIO, CESARE. *Le fontane di Roma,* Rome, 1957 (also 1962).

*———. *Gli obelischi di Roma,* Rome, 1965 (also 1967).

*———. "Gli 'Avvisi' di Roma dal 1554 al 1605 conservati in biblioteche ed archivi romani," *Studi romani,* X, 1962, 529–48.

DUBREUIL, JEAN. *La Perspective pratique,* 3 vols., I, Paris, 1642.

DÜRER, ALBRECHT. *Underweysung der Messung mit dem Zirckel vnd richtscheyt in Linien ebnen vund Gantzen Corporen durch Albrecht Dürer zusamen getzoge etc.,* Nuremberg, 1525 (also 1603).

*EGGER, HERMANN. *Carlo Madernas Projekt für den Vorplatz von San Pietro in Vaticano,* Römische Forschungen der Bibliotheca Herziana, VI, Leipzig, 1928.

———. "Das päpstliche Kanzleigebäude im 15. Jahrhundert," *Festschrift zur Feier des Zweihundertjahrigen Bestandes des Haus- Hof- und Staatsarchivs* (Mitteilungen des Österreichischen Staatsarchivs Ergänzungsband, III), II, Vienna, 1951, 487–500.

———. *Römische Veduten,* Vienna and Leipzig, 1911–31.

———. "Der Uhrturm Pauls V," *Mededeelingen van het Nederlandsch Historisch Instituut te Rome,* IX (1929), 71f.

———. "Quadriporticus Sancti Petri in Vaticano," *Papers of the British School at Rome,* XVIII, 1950, 101–3.

*——— and Franz Ehrle. *Piante e vedute di Roma e del Vaticano del 1300 al 1676,* Vatican, 1956.

———— and C. Huelsen. *Die römischen Skizzenbücher von Marten van Heemskerck im Königlichen Kupferstichkabinett zu Berlin*, 2 vols., Berlin, 1916.

*EHRLE, FRANCESCO. "Dalle carte e dai disegni di Virgilio Spada (1662): Codd. Vaticani Lat. 11257 e 11258," *Atti della Pontificia Accademia Romana di Archeologia*, Serie III, Memorie II, 1928, 1–98.

EVERS, H. G. "Zur 'Scala Regia' des Vatikans," *Atti della Pontificia Accademia Romana di Archeologia*, Rendiconti 39, 1966–67, 189–215.

*FAGIOLO DELL'ARCO, MAURIZIO and MARCELLO. *Bernini: una introduzione al gran teatro del barocco*, Rome, 1967.

FALDA, GIOVANNI BATTISTA. *Il nuouo teatro delle fabriche, et edificii in prospettiva di Roma moderna*, Rome, 1665 (also 1699).

FASOLO, FURIO. *L'opera di Hieronimo e Carlo Rainaldi*, Rome, n.d. [1962].

FASOLO, VINCENZO. "Sistemi ellittici nell'architettura," *Architettura e arti decorative*, X, 7, 1931, 311f.

*FERABOSCO (or FERRABOSCO), MARTINO. *Architettura della Basilica di S. Pietro . . . posta in luce l'anno MDCXX. Di nuovo dato alle stampe da Mons. Gio. Battista Costaguti . . .* , Rome, 1684.

FLORENCE, ACCADEMICI DELLA CRUSCA. *Vocabolario degli accademici della Crusca*, Verona, 1806.

FOKKER, T. H. *Roman Baroque Art: The History of a Style*, London, 1938.

*FONTANA, CARLO. *Templum Vaticanum (Il Tempio Vaticano e sua origine con gl'Edifitii piu cospicui antichi, e moderni fatti dentro, e fuori di Esso)*, Rome, 1694.

FONTANA, DOMENICO. *Della Trasportatione dell'obelisco vaticano et delle fabriche di nostro signore Papa Sisto V*, Rome, 1590.

*FRASCHETTI, STANISLAO. *Il Bernini: la sua vita, le sue opere, il suo tempo*, Milan, 1900.

FREY, DAGOBERT. "Berninis Entwürfe für die Glockentürme von St. Peter in Rom," *Jahrbuch der kunsthistorischen Sammlungen in Wien*, N.F. XII, 1938, 203–26.

FROMMEL, C. F. "Santa Caterina alle Cavallerotte," *Palladio*, XII, 1962, 18-25.

*FRUTAZ, AMATO P. *Le piante di Roma*, 3 vols., Rome, 1962.

GARDNER, HELEN. *Art Through the Ages*, 4th Ed., New York, 1959.

GEYMÜLLER, H. VON. *Les projets primitifs pour la basilique de Saint-Pierre de Rome*, Paris, 1875–80.

GIACHI, GUALBERTO, and G. MATTHIAE. *S. Andrea al Quirinale* (Le Chiese di Roma Illustrate, 107), Rome, 1969.

GIEDION, SIGFRIED. *Space, Time, and Architecture*, Cambridge, Mass., 1941 (also 1954).

GIGLI, GIACINTO. *Diario romano*, ed. Giuseppe Ricciotti, Rome, 1958.

*GIOSEFFI, DECIO. *La Cupola Vaticano, Un'ipotesi michelangiolesca*, Università degli studi di Trieste, Istituto di storia dell'arte antica e moderna, No. 10, Trieste, 1960.

GIOVANNONI, GUSTAVO. *Vecchie città ed edilizia nuova*, Turin, 1932.

*————. "Roma dal Rinascimento al 1870," *Topografia e urbanistica di Roma*, in *Storia di Roma*, XXII, Bologna, 1958, 442–50 and 524–32.

GNOLI, DOMENICO. *Have Roma*, Rome, 1909.

*————. "Nuovo accesso alla Piazza di San Pietro in Roma," *Archivio storico dell'arte,* II, 1889, 138–52.

GOMBRICH, E. H. *Art and Illusion: A Study in the Psychology of Pictorial Representation,* New York, 1960.

GUARINI, GUARINO. *Architettura Civile,* Turin, 1737.

GUGLER, ERIC. Acceesso alla Piazza di San Pietro (with a volume of plates and at the end of that volume three supplements), typescript, bound, numbered 23753, and noted "presented by Mr. G. P. Stevens, February 1926"; deposited in the Library of the American Academy in Rome.

GURLITT, CORNELIUS. *Geschichte des Barockstiles in Italien,* in *Geschichte der neueren Baukunst,* V:1, 408-13.

GUTKIND, E. A. *Urban Development in Southern Europe: Italy and Greece,* New York, 1969.

*HASKELL, FRANCIS. *Patrons and Painters,* London, 1963.

HEMPEL, EBERHARD. *Francesco Borromini,* Vienna, 1924.

————. *Carlo Rainaldi, Ein Beitrag zur Geschichte des römischen Barocks,* Munich, 1916.

*HIBBARD, HOWARD. *Bernini,* Harmondsworth and Baltimore, 1965.

*————. *Carlo Maderno and Roman Architecture 1580–1630,* University Park and London, 1971.

HOFFMANN, LUCIA. *I Borghi,* n.p. and n.d.

HOFMANN, THEOBALD. *Raffael in seiner Bedeutung als Architekt,* 4 vols., Zittau, 1900–1911.

HUELSEN, CHRISTIAN. *Le chiese di Roma nel medio evo,* Florence, 1927.

*HUSE, NORBERT. *Gianlorenzo Berninis Vierströmebrunnen,* Munich, 1966.

INSOLERA, ITALO. *Roma moderna, un secolo di storia urbanistica.* Turin, 1962 (also 1971).

*IVERSEN, ERIK. *Obelisks in Exile, I: The Obelisks of Rome,* Copenhagen, 1968.

KAMBO, LUIGI. "Il problema della spaziosità e la sistemazione dei Borghi," *Il Messaggero,* October 14, 1937.

————. "Il sistemazione dei Borghi e il problema della spaziosità," *Il Messaggero,* October 26, 1937.

KEPLER, JOHANNES. *Ad Vitellionem Paralipomena,* Frankfurt, 1604.

KERNODLE, GEORGE R. *From Art to Theatre,* Chicago, 1944.

*KITAO, TIMOTHY KAORI. "Bernini's Church Facades: Method of Design and the *Contrapposti,*" *Journal of the Society of Architectural Historians,* XXIV, 1965, 263–84.

————. "Prejudice in Perspective: A Study of Vignola's Perspective Treatise," *Art Bulletin,* XLIV, 1962, 173–94.

KRUFT, HANNO-WALTER. "Symbolik in der Architektur Berninis," *Neue Zurcher Zeitung,* 267, June 11, 1972, 51–52.

KURZ, OTTO. "Dürer, Leonardo and the Invention of the Ellipsograph," *Raccolta Vinciana,* XVIII, Milan, 1960, 15–25.

*LA PADULA, ATTILIO. *Roma 1809–1814—Contributo alla storia dell'urbanistica,* Rome, 1958.

LAVEDAN, PIERRE. *Historie de l'urbanisme: époque contemporaine,* Paris, 1952.

————. *Histoire de l'urbanisme: Renaissance et temps modernes*, Paris, 1941 (also 1959).

*LAVIN, IRVING. Review of G. L. Bernini, *Fontana di Trevi* (ed. C. d'Onofrio), *Art Bulletin*, XLVI, 1964, 568–72.

————. *Bernini and the Crossing of Saint Peter's*, New York, 1968.

————. "Lettres de Parmes et Débuts du Théâtre baroque," *Le lieu théâtral à la Renaissance*, Paris, 1964, 105–58.

LECLERC, HÉLÈNE. *Les origines italiennes de l'architecture théâtrale moderne: l'evolution des formes en Italie de la renaissance au XVIIᵉ siecle*, Paris, 1946.

LETAROUILLY, PAUL M. *Edifices de Rome moderne*, 6 vols., Paris, 1840–57.

————. *Le Vatican et la Basilique de Saint-Pierre de Rome*, 2 vols., Paris, 1882.

*LEWINE, MILTON J. "Vignola's Church of Sant'Anna de' Palafrenieri in Rome," *Art bulletin*, XLVII, 1965, 199–229.

*LOTZ, WOLFGANG. "Die Ovalen Kirchenräume des Cinquecento," *Römisches Jahrbuch für Kunstgeschichte*, VII, 1955, 5–99.

LYNCH, K. *The Image of the City*, Cambridge, Mass., 1960.

MacDOUGALL, ELIZABETH. Review of Magnuson, *Studies in Roman Quattrocento Architecture*, *Art Bulletin*, XLIV, 1962, 67–75.

MAGNUSON, TORGIL. "The Project of Nicholas V for Rebuilding the Borgo Leonino in Rome," *Art Bulletin*, XXXVI, 1954, 89–115.

*————. *Studies in Roman Quattrocento Architecture* in *Figura*, IX, Stockholm, 1958.

MARCONI, PAOLO. *Giuseppe Valadier*, Rome, 1964.

*MARIANI, VALERIO. *Significato del Portico berniniano di San Pietro: Prolusione*, Rome, 1935.

————. *Storia della scenografia italiana*, Florence, 1930.

MARTIN, JOHN R. *The Farnese Gallery*, Princeton, N.J., 1965.

MARTINELLI, VALENTINO. *Bernini*, Milan, 1953.

MATTHIAE, GUGLIEMO. *Ferdinando Fuga*, Rome, 1951.

MERCATI, MICHELE. *De gli obelischi di Roma*, Rome, 1589.

*MILIZIA, FRANCESCO. *Memorie degli architetti antichi e moderni*, 4th ed., 2 vols., Bassano, 1785.

*MILLON, HENRY A. "Notes on Old and Modern Drawings—An Early Seventeenth Century Drawing of the Piazza San Pietro," *Art Quarterly*, XXV, 1962, 229–41.

————. "The Role of History of Architecture in Fascist Italy," *Journal of the Society of Architectural Historians*, XXIV, 1965, 53–59.

MONTE, GUIDO UBALDO, MARCHESE DEL (or Guidobaldo dal). *Planisphaeriorum universalium theorica*, Pesaro, 1579.

MORTON, H. V. *The Fountains of Rome* (also entitled *The Waters of Rome*), New York, 1966.

MOULARD, J. *Le Comte Camille de Tournon*, II, Paris, 1930.

MÜLLER, JOHANN H. *Das regulierte Oval* (Dissertation), Bremen, 1967.

MUÑOZ, ANTONIO. *G. L. Bernini, Architetto e Decoratore*, Rome, 1925.

————. *Roma Barocca*, Milan and Rome, 1919 (also 1928).

MURATORIUS, L. *Rerum Italicarum Scriptores*, Milan, 1734.

NAGLER, A. M. *Theater Festivals of the Medici, 1539–1637,* New Haven, Conn., 1964.

NAPLES, SOCIETÀ TIPOGRAFICA. *Vocabolario universale della lingua italiana,* Naples, 1834.

NICOLL, ALLARDYCE. *The Development of the Theatre,* London, 1927 (also 1958).

NÖRREGAARD, MOGENS KAI. "Ancora della piazza di San Pietro e dell'effetto frontale della Basilica," *Illustrazione Vaticana,* III, 1932, 241–42.

NORTON, RICHARD. *Bernini and Other Studies in the History of Art,* New York and London, 1914.

ORANO, PAOLO. *L'Urbe Massima: L'architettura e la decorazione di A. Brasini,* Rome, n.d.

OZZOLA, LEANDRO. *L'arte nell' corte d'Alessandro VII,* Rome, 1908.

*PALLADIO, ANDREA. *Quattro libri dell'architettura,* Venice, 1570.

PALLAVICINO, S. *Della vita di Alessandro VII,* 2 vols., Prato, 1839–40.

PANE, ROBERTO. *Bernini architetto,* Venice, 1953.

PANOFSKY, ERWIN. *Albrecht Dürer,* Princeton, N.J., 1945.

*———. *Galileo as a Critic of the Arts,* The Hague, 1954.

*———. " 'Die Scala Regia im Vatican' und die Kunstanschauungen Berninis," *Jahrbuch der preussischen Kunstsammlungen,* XL, 1919, 241–78.

*PASTOR, LUDWIG VON. *The History of the Popes,* 40 vols., London, 1923–55.

———. *Geschichte der Päpste,* Freiburg im Breisgau, 1899–1933.

———. *Sisto V: il creatore della Nuova Roma,* Rome, 1922.

———. *Die Stadt Rom zu Ende der Renaissance,* Freiburg im Breisgau, 1916.

*PIACENTINI, MARCELLO and ATTILIO SPACCARELLI. *Memoria sugli studi e sui lavori per l'accesso a San Pietro,* Rome, 1944.

———. *Le vicende edilizie di Roma dal 1870 ad oggi,* Rome, 1952.

POLAZZO, T. A. *Da Castel S. Angelo alla Basilica di San Pietro,* Rome, 1948.

POLLAK, FRIEDRICH. *Lorenzo Bernini,* Stuttgart, 1909.

POLLAK, OSKAR. *Die Kunsttätigkeit unter Urban VIII,* 2 vols., Vienna, 1928–31.

*PORTOGHESI, PAOLO. "S. Maria della Pace di Pietro da Cortona," *Architettura,* VII, 1962, 830–51.

———. *Borromini nella cultura europea,* Rome, 1964.

———. *Roma barocca: storia di una civiltà architettonica,* Rome, 1966.

POZZO, ANDREA. *Perspectiva Pictorum et Architectorum,* 2 vols., Rome, 1693 and 1700 (also Augsburg, 1706).

QUARONI, LUDOVICO. *Immagine di Roma,* Bari, 1969.

QUATREMÈRE DE QUINCY, A. C. *Dictionnaire historique d'architecture,* Paris, 1832.

RASMUSSEN, STEEN E. *Towns and Buildings,* Cambridge, Mass., 1949 (also 1969).

*REYMOND, MARCEL. *Le Bernin,* Paris, n.d. [1911].

*RIEGL, ALOIS, ed. *Vita des Gio. Lorenzo Bernini mit Übersetzung und Kommentar von Alois Riegl,* Vienna, 1912.

ROBB, DAVID M., and J. J. GARRISON. *Art in the Western World,* New York, 1935 (also 1953).

ROBERTSON, D. S. *A Handbook of Greek and Roman Architecture,* Cambridge, England, 1929 (also 1954).

RUBINSTEIN, RUTH O. "Pius II's Piazza S. Pietro and St. Andrew's Head," *Essays in the History of Architecture Presented to Rudolf Wittkower*, London, 1967, 22–33.

*S., O. "La sistemazione dei Borghi per l'accesso a S. Pietro," *Architettura: rivista del sindacato nazionale fascista architetti* (diretta da M. Piacentini), fascicolo speciale, 1936, 21–53.

SABBATTINI, NICOLA. *Practica di fabricar Scene* (1st ed. Pesaro, 1638), Weimar, 1926.

———. *Pratique pour Fabriquer Scène et Machines de Théâtre*, Ravenna, 1638, and Neuchatêl, 1942.

SAVIOTTI, A. "Feste e Spettacoli nel Seicento," *Giornale storico della letteratura italiana*. XLI, 1903, 42–77.

*SCARPA, PIETRO. "L'allineamento degli edifici: verso Piazza Rusticucci e la prova dell' interrompimento," *Il Messaggero,* June 17, 1937.

SCHIAVO, ARMANDO. "Il viaggio del Bernini in Francia nei documenti dell Archivio Segreto Vaticano," *Bollettino del Centro di Studi per la Storia dell'Architettura*, X, 1956, 23–80.

*———. "Piazza San Pietro nel pensiero e nell'opera del Bernini," *Emporium*, XLVI, 1940, 291–300.

SCHMARSOW, AUGUST. *Barock und Rokoko,* in *Beiträge zur Aesthetik der bildenden Künste*, II, Leipzig, 1897.

SCHÖNE, G. *Entwicklung der Perspektivebühne von Serlio bis Galli-Bibiena nach den Perspektivbüchern, in* Theatergeschichtliche Forschungen, XLIII, Leipzig, 1933.

SCHOOTEN, FRANCISCUS VAN. Eerste Bouck der *Mathematische Oeffeningen*, Amsterdam, 1659.

SCHUDT, LUDWIG. *Italienreisen im 17. und 18. Jahrhundert,* Römische Forschungen der Bibliotheca Hertziana, XV, Vienna, n.d. [1959].

*SEDLMAYR, HANS. "Divegenz der Wände am Petersplatz in Rom," *Belvedere,* Forum V, Heft 23 (May 1924), 133–35.

SEGUI, GABRIELE, C. THOENES, and L. MORTARI. *SS. Celso e Giuliano* (Le Chiese di Roma Illustrate, 88), Rome, 1966.

*SERLIO, SEBASTIANO. *Il primo libro d'architettura,* Paris, 1545.

———. *Tvtte l'opera d'architettvra et prrospettiva* (*sic*), Venice, 1600.

SIEBENHÜNER, HERBERT. *Das Kapitol in Rom: Idee und Gestalt,* Munich, 1954.

SIRIGATTI, LORENZO. *Pratica di prospettiva,* Venice, 1596 (also 1625).

*STRONG, EUGÉNIE. "The Approach to St. Peter's, Rome," *Town Planning Review,* VII, 1918, 196–208.

TARDINI, GIULIO. "Basilica Vaticana e Borghi," *Illustrazione Vaticana,* VII, Rome, 1936. 39–65.

———. *Basilica Vaticano e Borghi: Dati storici raccolti dal Dott. Ing. Giulio Tardini,* Rome. 1936.

T.C.I. (Touring Club Italiano). *Guida d'Italia: Roma,* Milan, 1925 and 1962.

———. *L'Italia in automobile: Lazio,* Milan, 1953.

*THOENES, CHRISTOF. "Studien zur Geschichte des Petersplatzes," *Zeitschrift für Kunstgeschichte,* XXVI, 1963, 97–145.

TINTELNOT, HANS. *Barocktheater und Barocke Kunst,* Berlin, 1939.

TOMBOLINI BARZOTTI, LUIGI. *La Basilica di S. Pietro in Vaticano nei simboli e negli elementi architettonici di Gianlorenzo Bernini,* Rome, 1937.

TOURNON, CAMILLE DE. *Etudes statistiques sur Rome,* Paris, 1831.

TOYNBEE, J., and J. WARD-PERKINS. *The Shrine of St. Peter and the Vatican Excavations,* London, 1956.

TROILI (TROGLI), DA SPINLAMBERTO, GIULIO (*detto* Paradosso). *Paradossi per praticare la prospettiva senza saperla* (written in 1672), Bologna, 1683.

TRUFFAUT, FRANÇOIS. *Hitchcock,* New York, 1969.

UNDERWOOD, PAUL A. "Drawings of Saint Peter's on a Pilgrim's Staff in the Museo Sacro," *Journal of the Warburg and Courtauld Institutes,* III, 1939–40, 147–53.

———. "Notes on Bernini's Towers for St. Peter's in Rome," *Art Bulletin,* XXI, 1939, 283–87.

UNIVERSITY OF ST. THOMAS, Houston, Texas. *Builders and Humanists: Exhibition Catalogue,* Houston, Texas, 1966.

VIGNOLA, JACOPO BAROZZI DA. *Le dve regole della prospettiva prattica di M. Iacomo Barozzi da Vignola, con i commentari del Reuerendo Padre Maestro Egnatio Danti,* Rome, 1583.

———. *Regola delli Cinque Ordini,* Venice, 1562.

VITRUVIUS, POLLIO. *De architectura libri decem,* tr. F. Granger (Loeb ed.), London and New York, 1931–34.

———. *The Ten Books on Architecture,* tr. Morris Hicky Morgan, Cambridge, Mass., 1914.

*VOSS, HERMANN. "Bernini als Architekt an der Scala Regia und an den Kolonnaden von S. Pietro," *Jahrbuch der preussischen Kunstsammlungen,* XLIII, 1922, 2–30.

WALCHER-CASOTTI, MARIA. *Il Vignola,* Trieste, 1960.

*WITTKOWER, RUDOLF. "A Counter-project to Bernini's 'Piazza di San Pietro,'" *Journal of the Warburg and Courtauld Institutes,* III, 1939–40, 88–106.

———. *Architectural Principles in the Age of Humanism,* London, 1952.

*———. *Art and Architecture in Italy, 1600–1750.* Harmondsworth and Baltimore, 1958 (also 1965).

*———. *Bernini's Bust of Louis XIV,* Oxford, 1951.

*———. "Carlo Rainaldi and the Roman Architecture of the Full Baroque," *Art Bulletin,* XIX, 1937, 242–313.

———. *Gian Lorenzo Bernini: The Sculptor of the Roman Baroque,* London, 1955 (also 1966).

*———. "Il Terzo Braccio del Bernini in Piazza S. Pietro," *Bolletino d'arte,* XXXIV, 1949, 129–34.

*———. "Palladio e Bernini," *Bollettino d'arte internazionale di studi d'architettura A. Palladio,* VIII, 1966, 13–25.

*———. "Pietro da Cortonas Ergänzungsprojekt des Tempels in Palestrina," *Das siebente Jahrzehnt: Festschrift für Adolph Goldschmidt,* Berlin, 1935, 137f.

*————. "Santa Maria della Salute," *Saggi e memorie di storia dell'arte,* III, Venice, 1963, 33–54.

————. "S. Maria della Salute: Scenographic Architecture and the Venetian Baroque," *Journal of the Society of Architectural Historians,* XVI, 1957, 3–10.

*WOELFFLIN, HEINRICH. *Renaissance und Barock,* 1888 and Munich, 1926; Basel and Stuttgart, 1961.

*ZOCCA, MARIO. *La cupola di San Giacomo in Augusta e la cupole ellittiche in Roma,* Rome, 1945.

*————. "Roma capitale d'Italia," *Topografia e urbanistica di Roma,* in *Storia di Roma,* XXII, Bologna, 1958, 698–700.

ZORZI, GIANGIORGIO. *Le ville e i teatri di Andrea Palladio,* Venice, 1969.

ZUCKER, PAUL. "Space and Movement in High Baroque City Planning," *Journal of the Society of Architectural Historians,* XIV, 1955, 8–13.

————. *Town and Square,* New York, 1959.

ZUNICA, O. *La Piazza di San Pietro e i Borghi,* Tivoli, 1937.

Analytical Index

Roman numerals refer to pages, italics to notes. Location is Rome, unless specified otherwise.

Illustrations

Fig. 1. Rome, Piazza Obliqua, general view from the antepiazza (photo: author)

Fig. 2. Rome, Piazza Obliqua, aerial view (photo: Alinari)

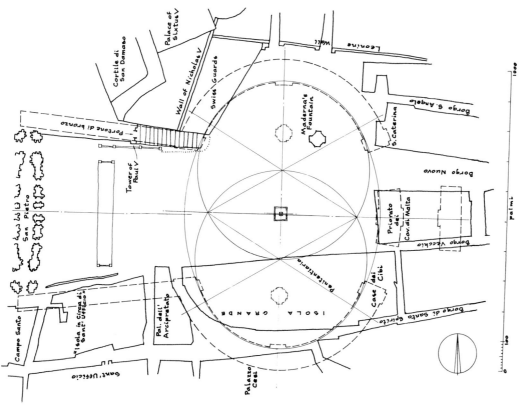

Fig. 5. The Square of Saint Peter's: site plan before construction of Bernini's colonnades (drawing: author)

Fig. 3. Rome, Piazza Obliqua, southern colonnade (photo: Alinari)

Fig. 4. Rome, Piazza Obliqua, northern colonnade seen from the center of its arc (photo: author)

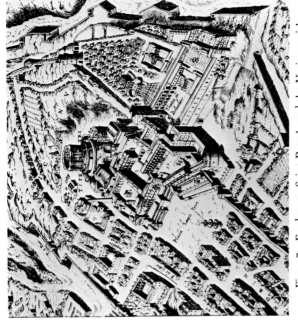

Fig. 7. Ferabosco, Saint Peter's and the Vatican with the Tower of Paul V (from Egger and Ehrle, *Piante e Vedute*)

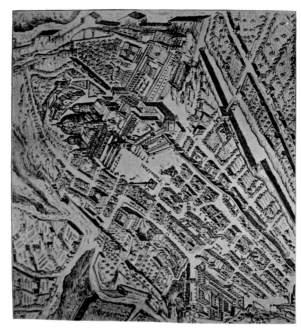

Fig. 8. Du Pérac and Laféri, Map of Rome, 1640 (revision of 1577 edition from Ehrle, "Virgilio Spada")

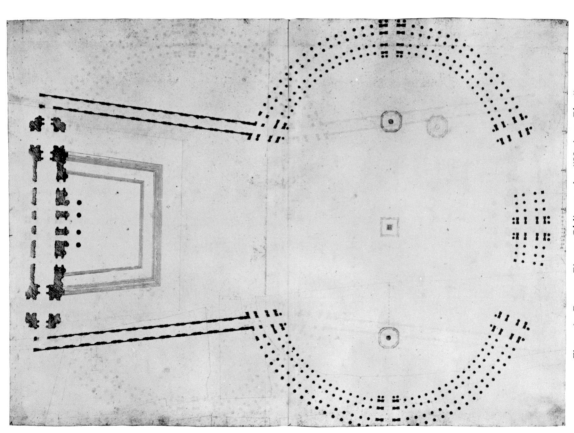

Fig. 6. Rome, Piazza Obliqua, the "Vatican Plan" (courtesy Biblioteca Vaticana)

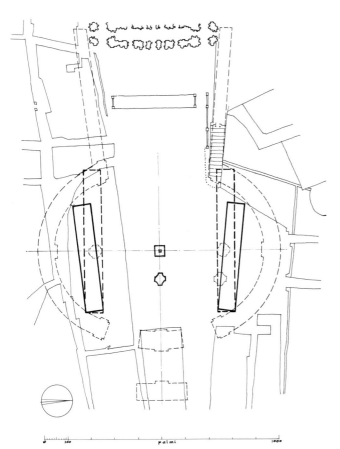

Fig. 9. Bernini's Trapezoid Plan and proposed revision: reconstruction (drawing: author)

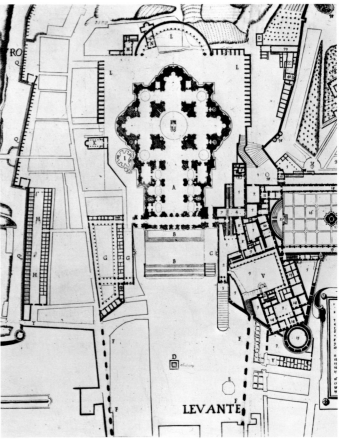

Fig. 10. Ferabosco and Vasanzio, project for the Square of Saint Peter's (from *Libro dell'Architettura*)

Fig. 11. Carlo Rainaldi, project for the Square of Saint Peter's (courtesy Biblioteca Vaticana)

Fig. 12. Du Pérac, the Campidoglio, view

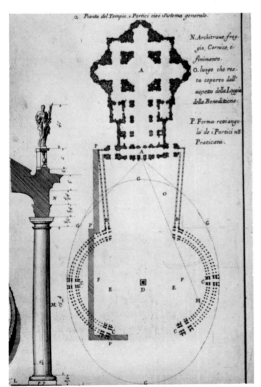

Fig. 13. Rome, Piazza Obliqua, plans and details (from
C. Fontana, *Templum Vaticanum)*

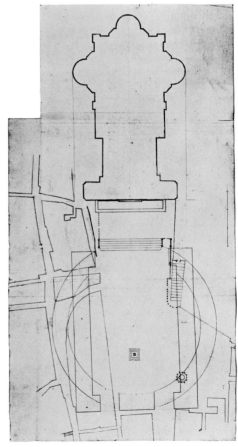

Fig. 14. Rectangular and circular plans for the Square
of Saint Peter's by a "False Bernini" (courtesy
Biblioteca Vaticana)

Fig. 15. Bernini, sketch of semicircular porticoes for the Piazza Obliqua (courtesy Biblioteca Vaticana)

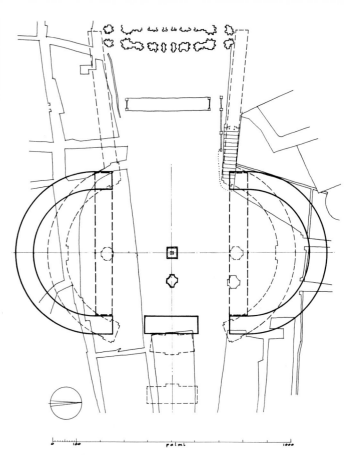

Fig. 16. Bernini's First Oval Plan: reconstruction (drawing: author)

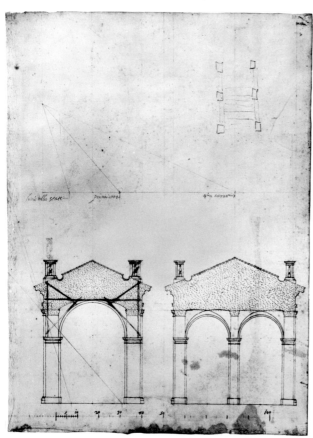

Fig. 17. Bernini Workshop, arcade for the Piazza Obliqua, cross-sections (courtesy Biblioteca Vaticana)

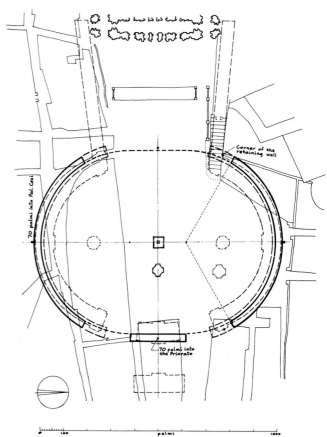

Fig. 18. Bernini's Revised Oval Plan (arcades): key points and reconstruction (drawing: author)

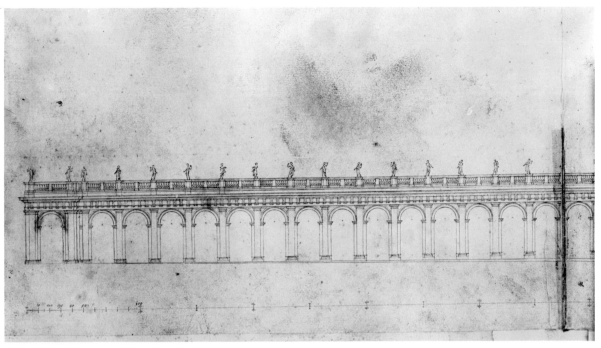

Fig. 19. Bernini Workshop, arcade for the Piazza Obliqua, elevation (courtesy Biblioteca Vaticana)

Fig. 20. Rome, Piazza Obliqua, Foundation Medal I (photo: Fototeca Unione)

Fig. 21. Rome, Piazza Obliqua, Foundation Medal II (photo: Fototeca Unione)

Fig. 22. Rome, Piazza Obliqua, Foundation Medal III (photo: Fototeca Unione)

Fig. 23. Rome, Piazza Obliqua, Foundation Medal IV (photo: Fototeca Unione)

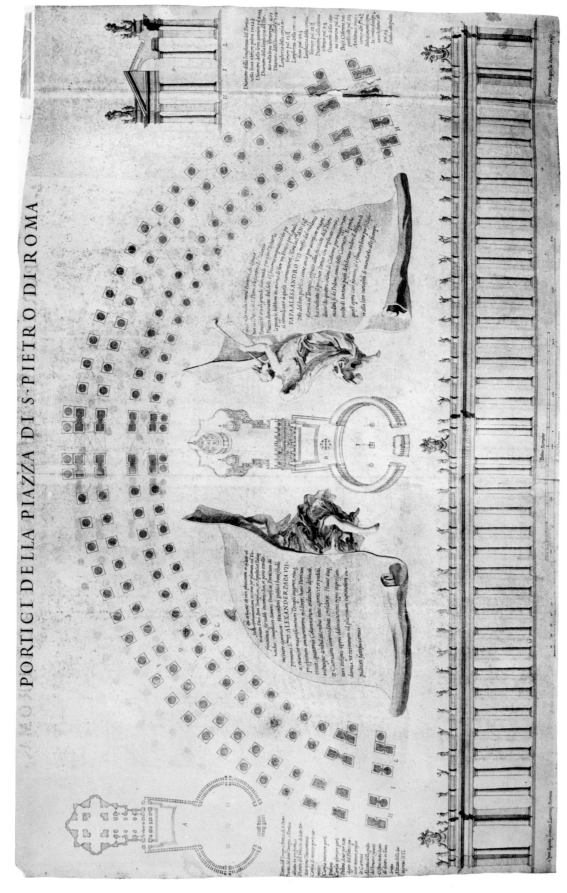

Fig. 24. Rome, Piazza Obliqua, G. B. Bonacina's engraving (courtesy Biblioteca Vaticana)

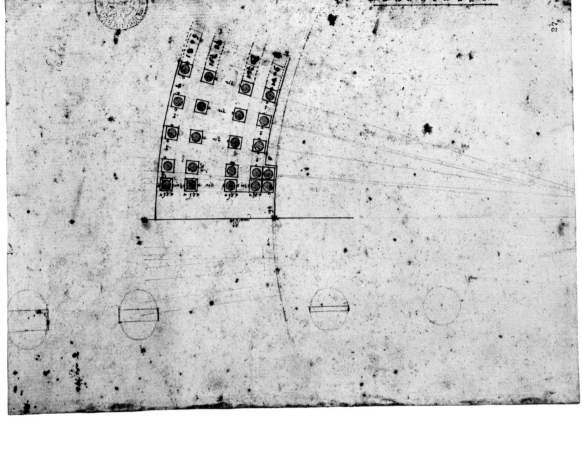

Fig. 26. Bernini Workshop, study for the layout of graded columns (courtesy Biblioteca Vaticana)

Fig. 25. Bernini, sketch plan of the Piazza Obliqua indicating the colonnade-corridor junction (courtesy Biblioteca Vaticana)

Fig. 27. Rome, Piazza Obliqua, Easter benediction, lithograph, Philippe Benoist, 1870

Fig. 29. Rome, Colosseum, detail (photo: author)

Fig. 30. Rome, Palazzo Massimo alle Colonne, detail (photo: author)

Fig. 28. Rome, Piazza Obliqua, colonnade, detail (photo: author)

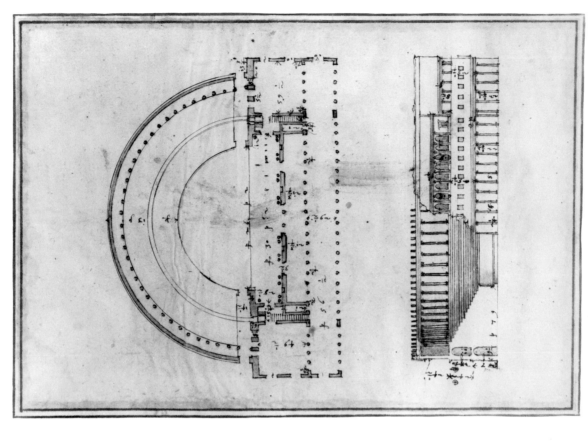

Fig. 33. Palladio, reconstruction of the ancient theater at Pola (courtesy R.I.B.A.)

Fig. 31. Raphael, *Disputa* (photo: Alinari)

TERZO INTERMEDIO DOVE SI VIDE VENIRE AMORE CON TVTTA LA SVA CORTE A DIFIDER LA BATTAGLIA

Fig. 32. Callot, Giulio Parigi's set for an *Intermezzo*, 1617 (courtesy Gabinetto Nazionale delle Stampe)

Fig. 34. Bernini, sketch plan of the Piazza Obliqua with a tetrastyle frame at the colonnade-corridor junction (courtesy Biblioteca Vaticana)

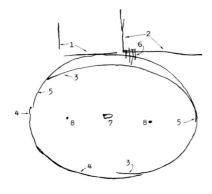

Fig. 36. Square of Saint Peter's, Falda's engraving (from *Il Nuovo Teatro*)

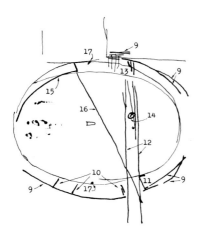

Fig. 35. Analysis of Bernini's sketch plan, Fig. 34

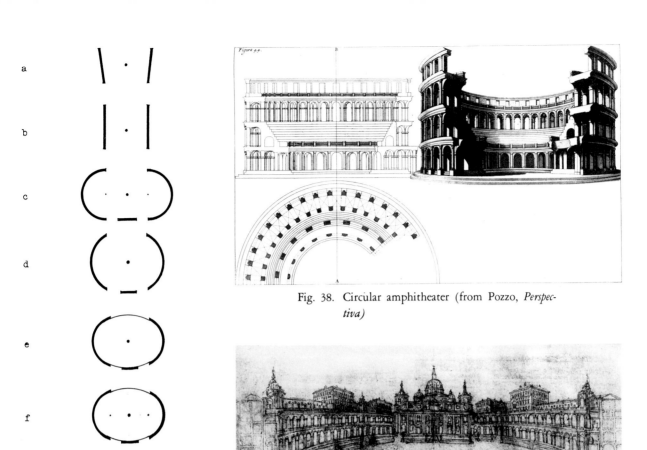

Fig. 38. Circular amphitheater (from Pozzo, *Perspectiva*)

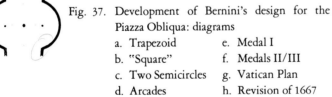

Fig. 39. Counterproject of 1659 (from Busiri-Vici, *La Piazza di San Pietro*)

Fig. 37. Development of Bernini's design for the Piazza Obliqua: diagrams

a. Trapezoid	e. Medal I
b. "Square"	f. Medals II/III
c. Two Semicircles	g. Vatican Plan
d. Arcades	h. Revision of 1667

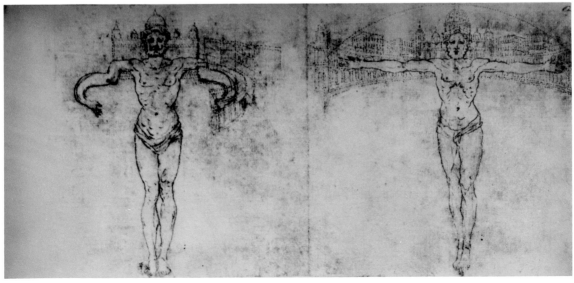

Fig. 40. Counterproject of 1659: argument for a circular plan (from Busiri-Vici, *La Piazza di San Pietro*)

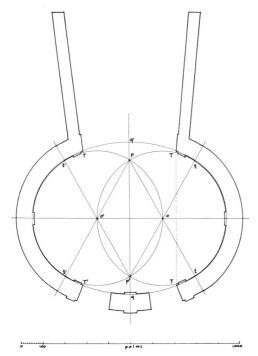

Fig. 41. Oval of the Piazza Obliqua: *Ovato Tondo* (drawing: author)

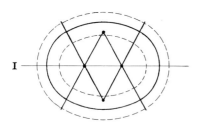

I

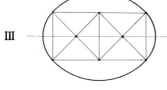

II

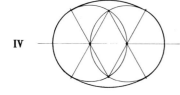

III

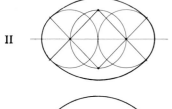

IV

Fig. 42. Serlio's oval constructions (drawing after Serlio: author)

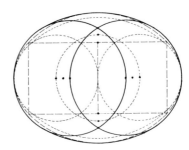

Fig. 43. Serlio's three fixed ovals: comparison (drawing: author)

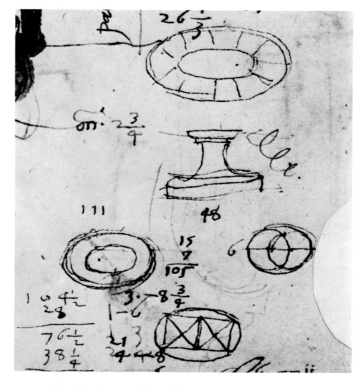

Fig. 44. Peruzzi, sketch for oval constructions (courtesy Gabinetto Disegni e Stampe degli Uffizi)

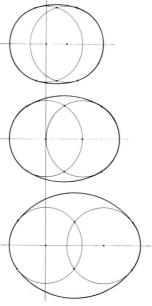

Fig. 45. The oval from two circles: variants (drawing: author)

Fig. 46. Serlio's string method for a flat arch (drawing: author)

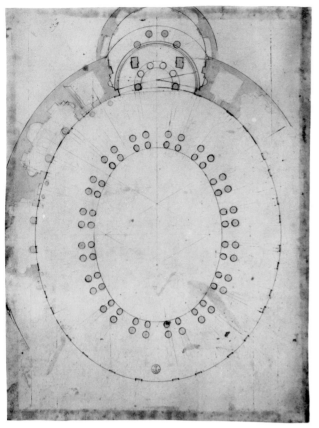

Fig. 47. Peruzzi, project for an oval church (courtesy Gabinetto Disegni e Stampe degli Uffizi)

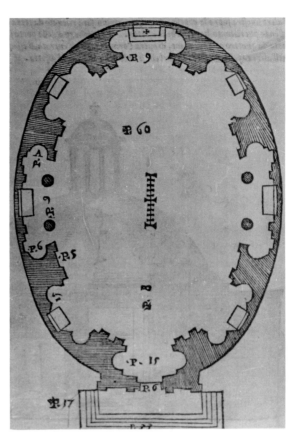

Fig. 48. Serlio, project for an oval church (from *Libro V)*

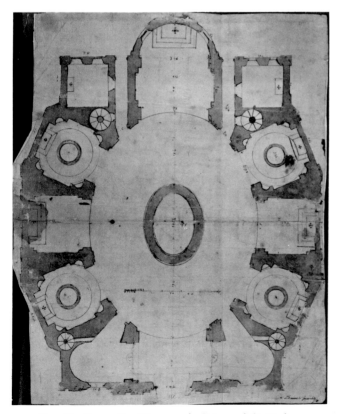

Fig. 49. Rome, San Giacomo degli Incurabili, Maderno's plan (courtesy Albertina)

Fig. 50. Carlo Rainaldi, project for an oval church (courtesy Biblioteca Vaticana)

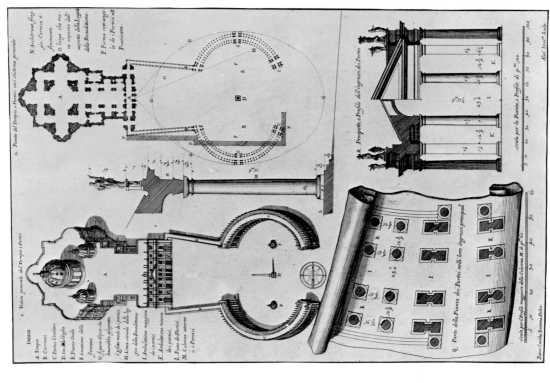

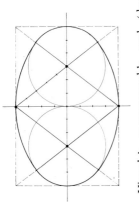

Fig. 51. Vignola's commensurable oval (drawing:
author)

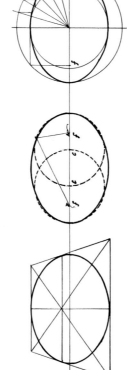

Fig. 52. Ellipse constructions (drawing: author)
right: coordinate method
center: string method
left: foreshortened circle

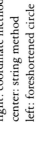

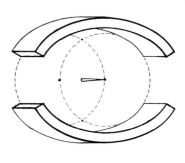

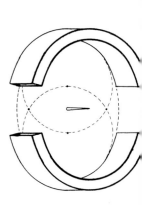

Fig. 53. Transverse and longitudinal oval space
(drawing: author)

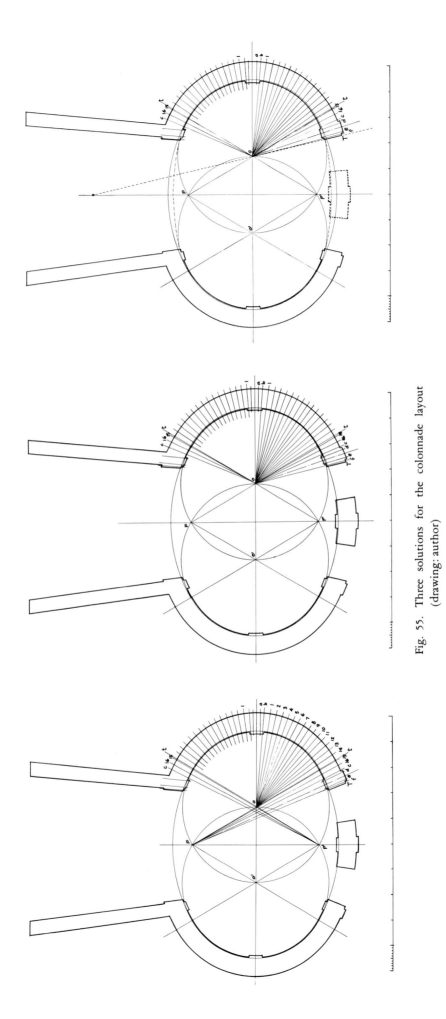

Fig. 55. Three solutions for the colonnade layout
(drawing: author)

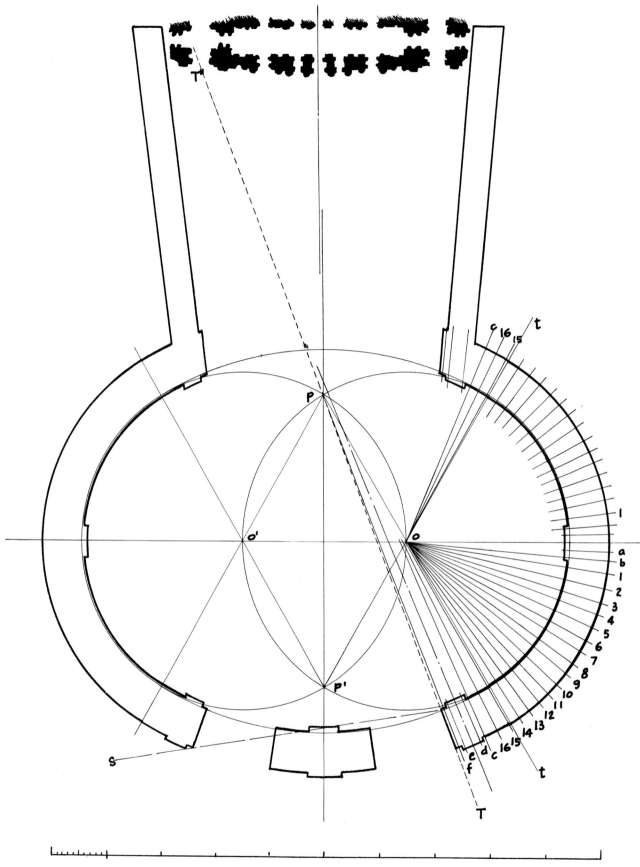

Fig. 56. Rome, Piazza Obliqua, Colonnade layout:
Bernini's solution (drawing: author)

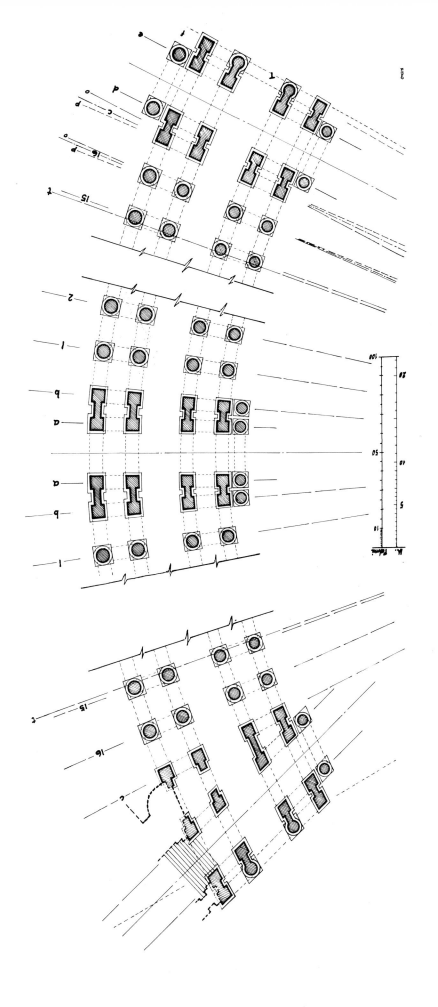

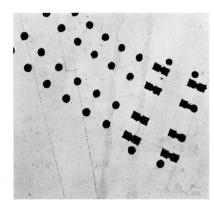

Fig. 57. Rome, Piazza Obliqua, "Vatican Plan," detail of Fig. 6.

Fig. 58. Rome, Piazza Obliqua, radial alignment of columns, west (photo: author)

Fig. 59. Rome, Piazza Obliqua, radial alignment of columns, east (photo: author)

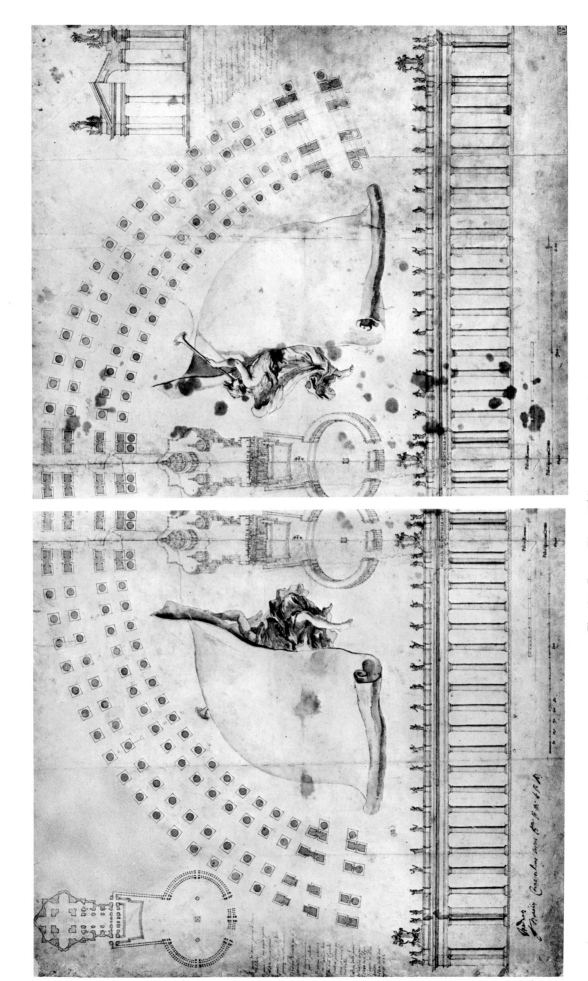

Fig. 60. Rome, Piazza Obliqua, preparatory drawing for the Bonacina Engraving (courtesy British Museum)

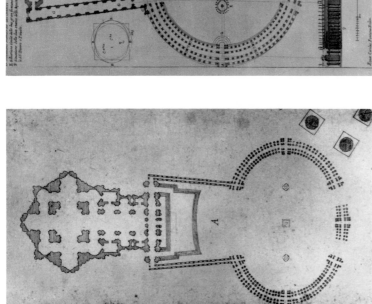

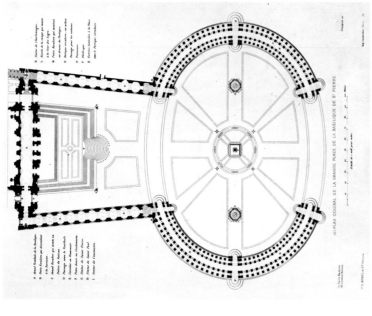

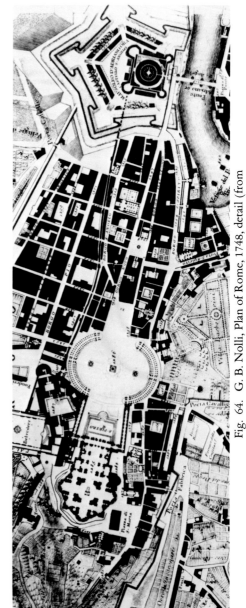

Fig. 61. Rome, Piazza Obliqua, G. B. Bonacina's engraving, detail of Fig. 24.

Fig. 62. Rome, Piazza Obliqua, C. Fontana's plan (from *Templum Vaticanum*)

Fig. 63. Piazza Obliqua, Letarouilly's plan (from *Le Vatican*)

Fig. 64. G. B. Nolli, Plan of Rome, 1748, detail (from Frutaz, *Le Piante di Roma*)

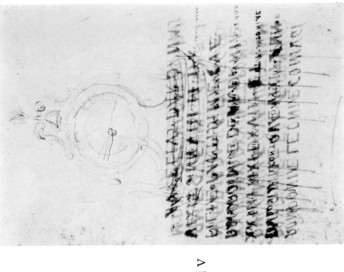

Fig. 67. Bernini, sketch for a clock tower (courtesy Biblioteca Vaticana)

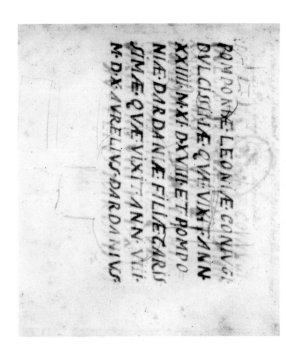

Fig. 69. Bernini, sketch plans for an antepiazza (courtesy Biblioteca Vaticana)

Fig. 66. Rome, Piazza Obliqua, Foundation Medal V (courtesy Fototeca Unione)

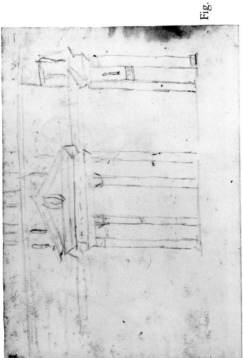

Fig. 65. Bernini, tetrastyle portico for the Basilica facade (courtesy Biblioteca Vaticana)

Fig. 68. Bernini, sketch for a propylaeum (courtesy Biblioteca Vaticana)

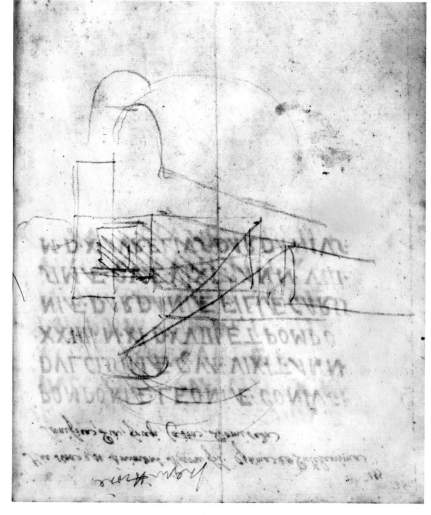

Fig. 71. Bernini, sketch plan for developing the antepiazza (courtesy Biblioteca Vaticana)

Fig. 70. Rome, Piazza Obliqua, Easter benediction, aerial view (from Bruhns, *Die Kunst der Stadt Rom*)

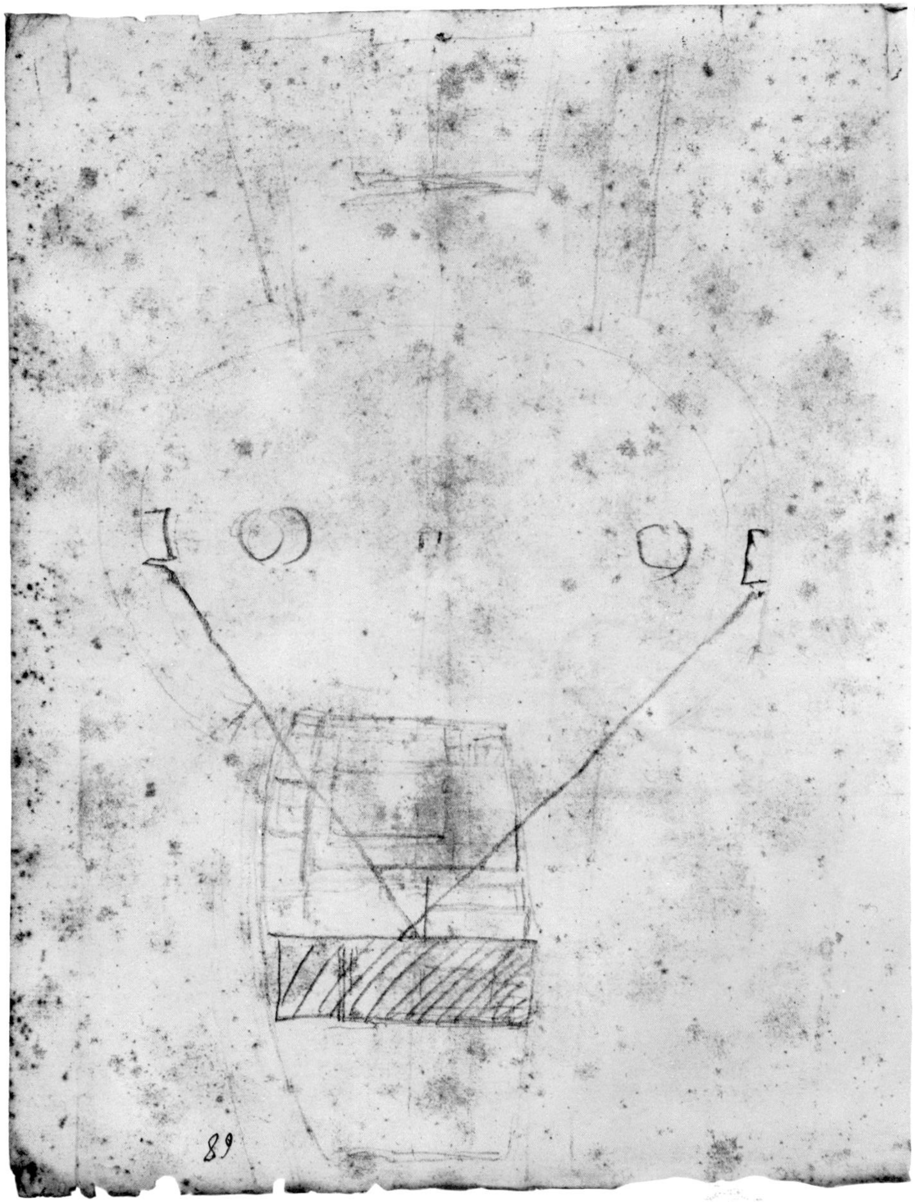

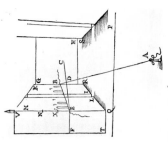

Fig. 75. Danti, scenography with *Visuali* of strings (from Vignola, *Le due regole della prospettiva*)

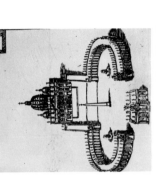

Fig. 74. Rome, Piazza Obliqua, "Conclave Design" of 1667 (courtesy Biblioteca Vaticana)

Fig. 73. Bernini Workshop, Pavement Study I with the propylaeum (courtesy Biblioteca Vaticana)

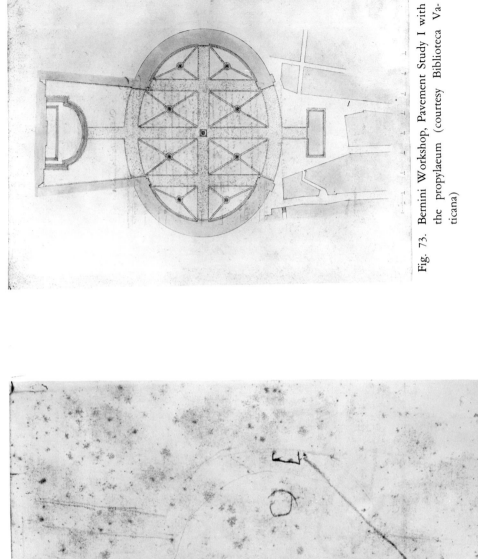

Fig. 72. Bernini, sketch plan with *Visuali* for positioning the propylaeum (courtesy Biblioteca Vaticana)

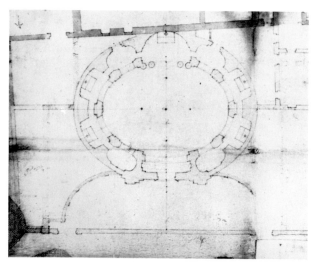

Fig. 76. Rome, Sant'Andrea al Quirinale, "Archives plan," detail (courtesy Archivio di Stato di Roma)

Fig. 77. Meledo, Villa Trissino (from Palladio, *Quattro Libri*)

Fig. 78. Rome, Piazza Obliqua, aerial view 1929 (photo: Alinari)

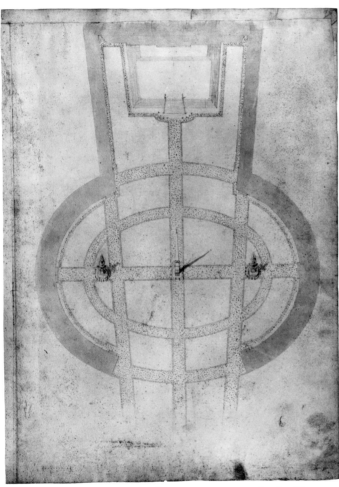

Fig. 79. Bernini Workshop, Pavement Study II
(courtesy Biblioteca Vaticana)

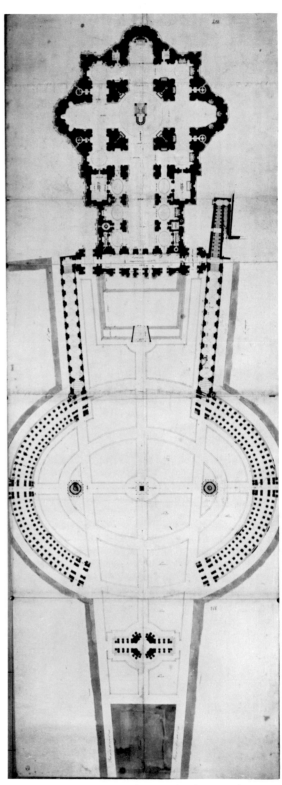

Fig. 80. Rome, Piazza Obliqua, plan by an unknown
Frenchman (courtesy Gabinetto Disegni e
Stampe degli Uffizi)

Fig. 81. Rome, Via della Conciliazione (photo: Alinari)

Fig. 82. Rome, Via della Conciliazione with Bernini's propylaeum (photo: Alinari; drawing by author)

Fig. 83. Silvestre, view of the Borgo (courtesy Fogg
Art Museum, Harvard University)

Fig. 84. Rome, the Campidoglio (photo: Alinari)

Fig. 85. Rome, the Campidoglio, aerial view (photo:
Alinari)

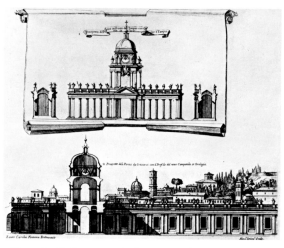

Fig. 86. C. Fontana, clock tower and propylaeum for the Square of Saint Peter's (from *Templum Vaticanum*)

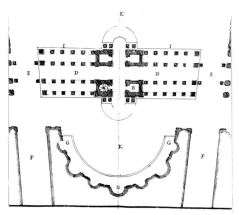

Fig. 88. C. Fontana, hemicycle outside the propylaeum (from *Templum Vaticanum*)

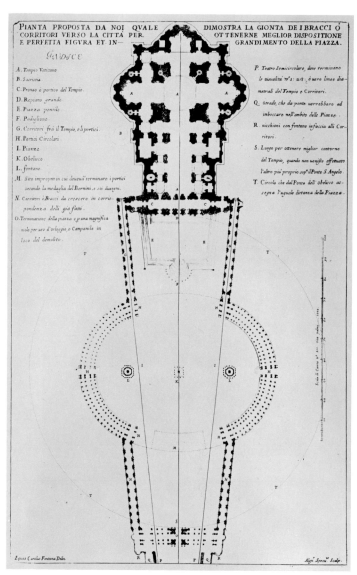

Fig. 87. C. Fontana, proposal for enlargement of the antepiazza (from *Templum Vaticanum*)

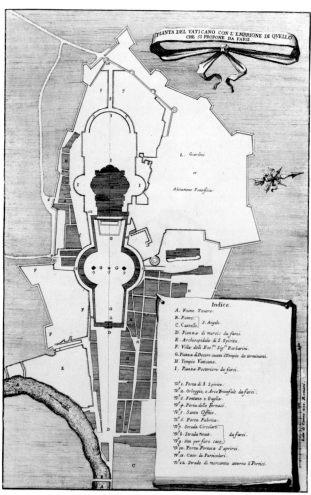

Fig. 89. C. Fontana, proposal for Piazza di Mercato outside the propylaeum (from *Templum Vaticanum*)

Fig. 91. Cosimo Morelli, Borgo project, 1776 (courtesy Biblioteca Vaticana)

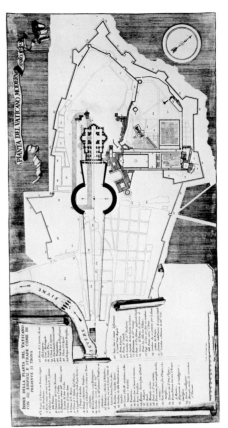

Fig. 90. C. Fontana, open-*spina* proposal (from *Templum Vaticanum*)

Fig. 92. Cosimo Morelli, Borgo project, 1776 (courtesy Biblioteca Vaticana)

Fig. 93. Piacentini and Spaccarelli, project with a "nobile interrompimento" (from *Arte cristiana*)

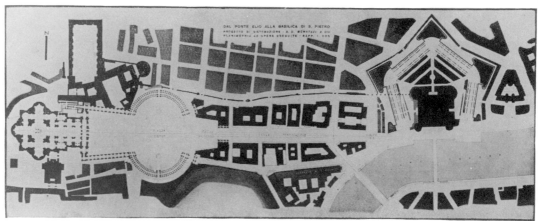

Fig. 94. Piacentini and Spaccarelli, project with a parallel avenue and without "interrompimento" (from *Arte cristiana*)

Fig. 95. Rome, Via della Conciliazione, view from the dome of Saint Peter's (photo: Alinari)